THE CARIBBEAN

JACOB GELT DEKKER

CONTENTS

PREFACE

The book you are holding in your hand is extraordinary for a variety of reasons. First of all, because of its structure: twenty-four chapters each ending with a delightful recipe for Caribbean food or drink. Secondly because of the characters you will meet. Anansi the Spider sitting on the ropes of the author's ship, offering his comments in short and awkward but very effective sentences; Captain Van der Decken, whose ship, *The Flying Dutchman*, is still sailing the seven seas even when the courteous captain himself appears on board the author's ship explaining his motives and adding a bit of historical background now and then. And thirdly, the sailor himself: a young man who decides to take a solo boat trip to reboot, sailing the warm waters of the Caribbean. A fourth reason why this is an extraordinary book is the wealth of information the author provides on the history of the islands. You will learn a lot about slavery, privateering, politics, geography, sea battles and colonialism, and every now and then get a refreshing lesson in economics. It is not so difficult to understand that a young man who is fighting the elements on his own will enjoy the company of Anansi the Spider and Captain Van der Decken, but you as the reader will be easily enticed into doing the same.

It is not a book one reads quickly – it should rather be savored slowly, just like a good meal. Each chapter makes one reflect on the story, the facts offered and the views of the author, who does not shy away from giving his opinion. When he talks about slavery, he does not treat this as an economic or social phenomenon confined to a particular era, something that does not exist any longer. 'How carelessly people deal with history,' he writes, 'not only in the West but also in Africa. Often they prefer fiction to fact.'

And dealing with history is precisely what the author does – carefully, completely and with a deep understanding of how past and present are connected.

Let me also take this opportunity to thank the author, Jacob Gelt Dekker, for his kindness. Together with his friend John Padget, he gave the incentive and the money to the Fulbright Center in Amsterdam to start a grant program for Dutch students to finance an internship period in the United States. Once this program was running, he told me he'd like to contribute to the Center's programs even more by donating his royalties of the current book for grants within the Dutch2USA Dekker-Padget Internship program.

On behalf of all the future recipients of the grants he will sponsor, I thank him profoundly. His support will hopefully lead to more fact finding and a more careful treatment of our common history.

Marcel Oomen, Former Executive Director of the Fulbright Center

INTRODUCTION

Dreams, memories, the sacred, they are all alike in that they are beyond our grasp. - Yukio Mishima

In my twenties, after a devastating cancer diagnosis drastically changed the course of my life, I had to reboot. Losing myself for a while in the Caribbean, an idyllic setting with hundreds of islands, was appealing. At the time, I did not know that I would have to go through similar diagnoses and treatments another six times. New cancers and metastasis called for more surgery, more radiation, chemotherapy, and more time in hospitals. Forty years later, I am still alive and look back on a voyage that lasted years, and entailed discovering countless identities of the Caribbean and its people. Sailing single-handedly from Key West, Florida to Curaçao into a fantasy world of surprises became my forte.

Yukio Mishima, January 1953, from Showa Literature Series: Vol. 23 (October 1953) Kadokawa Shoten

By sheer coincidence, while visiting UCLA in Los Angeles in the 1970s, I became familiar with the works of Yukio Mishima and Tennessee Williams, celebrated authors of Japan and the United States. Mishima, an author, poet, playwright, actor, film director, and fervent nationalist, committed ritual suicide, *seppuku*, on November 25, 1970. But the legacy of his work still made me spend a lot of time in Asia, particularly Japan and China.

Tennessee Williams, 1965, 20th anniversary of "The Glass Menagerie" (detail)

Williams, a Pulitzer Prize-winning playwright, devastated by a witch-hunt led by District Attorney Jim Garrison against Clay Shaw following the assassination of John F. Kennedy, had exchanged his beloved New Orleans, Louisiana for Key West, Florida.

By the time I met Williams in Key West, he had gathered a large group of friends around him, a group that shaped Key West into a literary mecca.

In 1997, when Hong Kong reverted back to China, I lost my Hong Kong citizenship, and re-established permanent residence in Curaçao, at that time still part of the Netherlands Antilles. I became devoted to spending time in Key West and Curaçao, and unfortunately in hospitals in the US and the Netherlands. Studying history and literature could be done anywhere, even from a hospital bed.

The Kura Hulanda Museum founded by Jacob Gelt Dekker in Willemstad. JvL - Wikimedia

Curating exhibitions at Kura Hulanda Museum on Curaçao on West African empires and kingdoms, the Dogon, and the transatlantic slave trade, I became a self-styled expert. As a member of the Board of the US National Slavery Museum, I gained even more insight and knowledge. Years of travel in Africa followed, from east to west, north to south, from heavenly delights to bloody battlefields, and mass starvation; it hardened me and gave me new perspectives.

This book about my Caribbean voyage is not meant to be a history textbook though I have taken great care to research every historical detail. Daily realities do not come in cleanly dissected chapters and paragraphs but rather in complex bits and pieces, often with corollaries beyond our wildest imagination. Reality is often so bizarre that it could never be imagined. At times, I jotted down my experiences as events developed, and incidents occurred. At other times, I had to revert to archetypal fantasy settings; politicians in the Caribbean are easily offended, and brutal attacks often occur, sometimes without explanation. One politician, whom I never met and never had any dealings with, even swore in a radio interview that he would send me back to Europe in a body bag. Unfortunately for him, he got assassinated shortly after, and I am still around.

It was a great pleasure and privilege writing these Caribbean accounts and I hope the reader will enjoy them as much as I did.

Jacob Gelt Dekker

January 1, 2018 - Key West, Florida.

1 KEY WEST, FLORIDA

Changes in latitude. Changes in attitude. - Jimmy Buffet

A King comes to visit

King Abdullah II of Jordan and his entourage drove down US 1, a parade of twenty heavy motorbikes, or sleds, as they are called in bikers' jargon. All riders were clad in colorful leather, heavy boots, and black helmets. It was impossible to make out who was the king. Secret Service agents rode on the sissy bars, the passenger's backrest. Someone pointed out that the king rode his sled alone. It was March 1, 2008, when the odd bikers' parade rolled into Key West, followed by a lengthy motorcade of limousines, ambulances, police cars with bomb-sniffing dogs and Navy SEALs.

The motorcade produced a deep roar that carried for miles, like Flagler's cargo and Havana Express trains once thundered over 150 miles of tracks, overpasses and bridges. The thunder carried over the blue Atlantic Ocean to the south and the murky Gulf on the north side of the highway.

Bob and Martha Sauer, a local attorney and his watercolorist wife, both well into their eighties when I met them, remembered how the Flagler Express could be heard nearly an hour before it arrived at Key West. Upon arrival, the whole town would be at the station peddling anything from bed & breakfast rooms, cigars and sponges to prostitutes to half-intoxicated tourists from New York on their way to a week of gambling in Havana.

King Abdullah II of Jordan

In the king's entourage there was no rippin' up of the asphalt, no loud explosions from double-barreled shotgun exhaust pipes, or back-wheel riding acrobatics of any kind. The king had promised an old school friend who lived in Key West to come down for a hamburger and a Coke, and so he did.

We all watched him in awe in the backyard of the friend's house, as we, the lucky ones who had also been invited, chewed on our own burgers. We were all standing, and there was no pretense. I had met the king before, in Wadi Rum with the Seven Pillars mountain formation in the south of Jordan, from where the legendary Lawrence of Arabia launched his attack on Aqaba. The king had been clowning around with one of his prized possessions on the five-star motorcycle trek, where bikers tell me they have the best ride of their lives. But King Abdullah was not the only biker who rode to Key West with a large following.

For 40 years, the annual Key West Poker Run charity had brought 10,000 bikers to the southernmost town of the United States. Every year, traversing the Florida Keys Overseas Highway, a giant army of bikers takes over the 126-mile road that connects the Keys to the South Florida mainland. The road has 42 bridges, spanning the waters of the Atlantic Ocean, Florida Bay and the Gulf of Mexico.

Sloppy Joe's bar, once Ernest Hemingway's alcoholic hangout, is full from breakfast till way after midnight. Since the 1940s, Ernest's watering hole has become the midpoint of the Duval Street bar crawl. A huge crowd of bikers, mixed with gay bears and leather men, parade up and down between the Gulf Coast and the Atlantic shores, partying all night. Rows of shining bikes on each side of the street stretch from coast to coast.

A similar Mardi Gras atmosphere builds around the annual Hemingway look-alike contest. Thousands of contestants and their supporters congregate in bars and pubs to cheer on their champions. Every year, a perfect look-alike, white-haired and with a beer-bellied body, is elected. The tipsy local audience, supported by millions around the world who watch the event on CNN, witnesses a parade of look-alike Hemingways walk up and down the runways like high-fashion models; in Sloppy Joe's Ernest Hemingway is alive and well.

Ernest Hemingway with sailfish, Key West, Florida, 1940s

Bourbon Street Mardi Gras partying has become the main industry in Cayo Hueso, as Spanish settlers called the island, referring to the bones of the Calusa graves. Once the Calusa tribe inhabited the Florida Keys, but the very last key in the south, Cayo Hueso, was a sanctuary for the dead only, to be treated with the utmost respect. Entering without the prescribed rituals was punishable by death.

Today Cayo Hueso is a barrio in Havana, Cuba, for Key West migrants. Carousing tourists are far from the sanctity of the Calusa burial grounds, and the sophisticated literary tradition that Hemingway brought to the island.

Hemingway

When Ernest Hemingway arrived at Key West aboard a steamship from Cuba in April 1928, the remote coral isle had no literary community. Key West was no more than a shabby Florida outpost of fishermen, rum runners, and square grouper-fishermen-drug-smugglers. Not yet connected by a continuous highway to the mainland, Hemingway and his pregnant wife, Pauline, came to Key West from Paris. Pauline's uncle Gus had ordered a Ford Model A for them to drive north. The Ford had not arrived.

The *Trev-Mor* people - short for Trevor and Morris - put up Hemingway and Pauline at the Trev-Mor Hotel. Two weeks later, when the Ford finally got there, Hemingway was sold on Key West and would not leave till years later. For two years, the small second-floor apartment in the Casa Antigua, then known as the Trev-Mor Hotel and Ford dealership, became their home.

Hemingway house - Andreas Lamecker, Wikimedia

In April 1931, Ernest bought his famous home on 907 Whitehead Street, in Bahama Village - with segregation still at its peak, a no-go area for whites. Hemingway could not care less. The property was cheap and his budget limited. Broad covered galleries, deep Caribbean-style porches, wrought-iron balusters, and green shutters became the enchanting place for the Hemingways to entertain locals, visitors, friends and family. Ernest built a brick wall around the property to keep out the roaming chickens; Pauline bred cats, a special race with an extra toe.

Polidactyl cat at Hemingway House in Key West, Florida - Abujoy
Wikimedia, 2013

This was the birthplace of the new, literary Key West. Ernest remained there till 1939 when he moved to Cuba with a new wife. Pauline and her children remained in the two-story house till her death in 1951. Ernest committed suicide in 1961.

Many followed in Hemingway's wake, including Tennessee Williams, John Hersey, Philip and Richard Burton, and Jean Carper. "In Key West, we have Pulitzer Prize winners tripping over one another," joked Ross Claiborne, a retired New York City publisher. "There's a writer behind every bush."

Key West has become the mecca of the American literary world, with a constant stream of visiting Nobel and Pulitzer Prize winners, as well as at least one hundred resident writers. The old town with its white clapboard, Bahamas-style, American Neo-Gothic and Cuban cigar makers' houses has become a tourist destination for millions every year. This stage, filled with extremes, was Key West and my home.

Bahama Village sisters

Two Bahama Village ladies, Geeah and her younger sister Julie, drew my interest. For years, the two sisters ran a little coffee and breakfast stand on Petronia Street in the middle of the village. The food was formidable, the coffee strong, and the ladies attentive, present and consistent. I never found out what language they spoke beyond some basic English to serve their regulars. Bahamian Creole of sorts, I guess, with some Seminole words and a dialect spoken on Turks and Caicos. It hardly mattered since we had a perfect understanding. Their caring was unmatched; I returned as often as I could and they gradually became part of my daily support system.

Bahama Village on Duval Street and Petronia in Key West - Marc Averette 2007

One time, when I got seriously ill, their actions were extraordinary. Geeah found me one of her relatives, Janeisha - whom I soon called Jane - a wonderful live-in nurse who also cooked. She was as stout as Geeah, with greying hair over a pitch-black face. Jane also spoke the mysterious Bahamian Creole. The sound of her voice was sonorous, and for me, most of the time on large doses of morphine, it became a solid anchor in the ocean of delusional tribulations.

One day, when I asked her to cook my favorite dish of devilled lamb's kidneys, she did not blink an eye. I do not know where she found the kidneys since supermarkets had long stopped carrying offal in the US, but for Nurse Jane that was hardly a challenge; the house smelled of kidney stew for days.

How did these women and their families make it to Key West at a time when segregation was still in full force? The island was a most unfriendly environment for all blacks. Nance Frank, a local gallery owner, born and raised on the island and considered a true Conch, told me that they were descendants of loyalists of King George III. In 1783, when England recognized the new Republic of the United States, not everyone was happy, and many loyal to the British, or afraid of the colonial rebels, fled.

King George III in coronation robes by Allan Ramsay, oil on canvas,
circa 1761-1762 © Royal Collection Trust

Frank was right. A British expedition under the command of Admiral George Van Keppel, 3rd Earl of Albemarle, had conquered Havana in 1762, and swapped it a few years later for East Florida with St. Augustine as capital in the peace agreement of Versailles. The British managed to hold on to St. Augustine and the eastern, coastal sliver till 1783, when King George III finally recognized the new American republic of the former Virginia colonies. As a consequence, in 1783, East Florida reverted back to Spain, who ruled it at first from their capital of Louisiana, New Orleans.

The king was more than a bit tricky. He recognized the new republic but also tried to lure Floridian inhabitants away from the colonial rebels; his loyal underlings were enticed to move to the Bahamas where they were rewarded with homesteads. So, before the British let the Spanish back in, many royalists amongst the Floridians took King George's offer and moved to the Bahamas. They quickly built antebellum-style houses with sugarcane plantations with the help of the British-African slaves, black Seminoles, and others, often run-away slaves from the southern territories and colonies of the American mainland. In addition, thousands of captive Africans, who were liberated from foreign slave ships by the British navy after the abolition of slavery in 1807, were resettled as free persons in the Bahamas. In the early 1820s, hundreds of African slaves and Black Seminoles escaped from Florida, with most settling on Andros Island; three hundred escaped in a mass flight in 1823.

By the time Florida was again given up by the Spanish and became US territory, the world markets had changed dramatically. In August 1834, traditional plantation life ended in the Bahamas with the British emancipation of slaves. Some freedmen chose to work on their own small plots of land where they could. For a while, chaos and confusion ruled.

For most, and especially for resettled black slaves, there was not a lot of work beyond the plantations that were in decline and, consequently, many suffered. A large portion of blacks were eager to try their luck in the new American republic and shipped out to Florida.

Cuban cigar makers had also made the crossing from Cuba to Key West and Tampa, where tobacco was easy to obtain from the North Carolina tobacco plantations set up by Sir Walter Raleigh. In Key West, a thriving business of cigar makers sprung up next to the existing sponge fisheries. Simple cigar makers' houses were put up almost overnight. A cottage industry with five to ten laborers per workshop blossomed.

Eduardo H. Gato House, Key West, Florida - Ebyabe, 2011

Soon, Eduardo Gato built a large cigar factory where he employed hundreds of workers who rolled cigars in an industrialized setup. Bahamas migrants were eager to respond to the call for labor.

In the first half of the 19th century, sponge fishing on a commercial basis grew popular. Following the new British fashion for bathing and bathtubs, accessories like all kinds of sponges became big business.

Grunt Bone Alley, with its fishermen's cottages, was transformed into sponge workshops and small factories. By the end of the last century, sponge fishing was well established in Florida, Cuba, and other Caribbean islands.

Regular steamship services made it easy for traders and their cargo as well as for travelers and migrants to move from the Bahamas to Florida, thus a stream of Bahamian workers and luck-seekers started to trickle onto the island of Key West.

Bahama Village came into existence, with its abundance of migrant workers, predominantly former slaves, African blacks, and some black Seminole Indians.

My research had unraveled a local mystery and there was no stopping now. I had to make it to Cuba, find Admiral George Van Keppel, and much more in the Caribbean.

My journey had commenced.

I geared up my sailboat, a 54-foot ketch, ready to discover the Caribbean.

The night before my departure, Jane prepared a special evening for a group of friends; some were a bit shocked to be served offal cooked by a Bahamian lady.

Devilled lamb's kidneys

Ingredients
6 lamb's kidneys, about 375g/13oz, skinned
2 tbsp. plain flour
25g/1oz butter
1 medium onion, finely sliced
1 tbsp. tomato purée
1 tbsp. English mustard
1-2 tbsp. Worcestershire sauce
4 thick slices of crusty bread
Butter, for spreading
Small bunch of fresh parsley, chopped (optional)
Sea salt and freshly ground pepper

Instructions

Rinse the kidneys under cold running water and pat them dry with kitchen paper.

Using scissors, carefully cut the white cores out of the kidneys and discard them.

Then chop the kidneys into chunky pieces.

Tip the flour into a freezer bag and season well with salt and pepper.

Add the kidneys and toss them until well coated with the flour.

Melt the butter in a large non-stick frying pan.

Add the onion and fry gently for 3-4 minutes, or until soft and slightly golden, stirring regularly.

Shake off any excess flour from the kidneys.

And add them to the pan.

Cook them with the onion over a medium-high heat for 2-3 minutes, turning every now and then.

Add the tomato purée and mustard to the pan.

Then gradually add 300ml/10fl oz. of water while stirring.

Bring to a boil.

Add a tablespoon of the Worcestershire sauce to the pan, and season with salt and freshly ground black pepper.

Reduce the heat and simmer gently for 15 minutes, or until the kidneys are tender and the sauce has thickened, stirring occasionally.

Add a little more Worcestershire sauce to taste.

While the kidneys are cooking, toast the bread on both sides, then spread with butter and put on four small plates.

Spoon the kidneys and sauce over the buttered slices of toast.

Scatter with freshly chopped parsley.

Serve immediately while piping hot.

2 CUBA

We reached solid ground, lost, stumbling along like so many shadows or ghosts marching in response to some obscure psychic impulse. We had been through seven days of constant hunger and sickness during the sea crossing, topped by three still more terrible days on land. Exactly 10 days after our departure from Mexico, during the early morning hours of December 5, following a nightlong march interrupted by fainting and frequent rest periods, we reached a spot paradoxically known as Alegría de Pío (Rejoicing of the Pious). – Che Guevara

---

Granma

The days of the Fulgencio Batista regime were numbered when the *Granma*, a 60-foot, diesel-powered cabin cruiser, landed on Cuban shores. The ramshackle, leaking boat transported about eighty guerilla fighters and an enormous amount of weapons and ammunition from Mexico to Cuba. Fidel Castro, his brother, Raúl Castro, and Che Guevara set foot on Playa Las Coloradas on December 2, 1958. The intended surprise attack was a disaster. The crash landing of the

Granma gave an advantage to Batista's soldiers. The eighty-man invasion force was reduced to only a dozen who managed to escape.

The specific location was chosen to mirror the voyage of the national hero José Martí, who had landed in the same region sixty-three years earlier, during the wars of independence from Spanish colonial rule. José Marti was killed by Spanish troops on May 19, 1895, and independence for Cuba did not arrive until 1909, when the US occupation ended and Jose Miguel Gomez became the first president of the sovereign republic of Cuba. The Castros might not have won the battle, but they certainly prevailed in the legend that quickly spun out of the failure; the revolution suddenly had martyrs.

Fidel and Raúl Castro were born in Birán, Oriente, as sons of a wealthy Spanish farmer. Fidel adopted anti-imperialist politics and a Marxist-Leninist ideology while studying law at the University of Havana. Raúl became a hardline Stalinist. As rich kids, they were no exception in participating in some kind of ideological adventure-revolution tourism. Flower-power and romanticized, utopic socialistic fantasies ruled the 1950s and 60s. In the same tradition, Ernesto 'Che' Guevara, an Argentinian medical student, became the legendary Marxist revolutionary of South America. Deng Xiaoping of China, a few decades earlier, was another example; a rich student who had worked as an intern in the car factories in France, where he picked up Marxist ideology. Even in 2002, when political adventurism amongst students was returning, Tanja Nijmeijer, alias Alexandra Nariño, a Dutch English-language teacher, became a fighter in the Colombian guerrilla group Revolutionary Armed Forces of Colombia. Ironically, it was Raúl, the hardline Stalinist, who presided over Cuba's embrace of the free market in the 21st century.

Fidel, acting out as a nonconformist student, joined rebellions against right-wing governments in the Dominican Republic and Colombia, and soon the young idealist also tried to overthrow the Cuban president Fulgencio Batista. On January 1, 1959, fifty years after the US occupation of Cuba had ended, President Batista resigned and escaped to the island of Hispaniola, to the Dominican Republic, leaving his island country for Castro. Castro became prime minister of Cuba on February 16, 1959.

In a panicked rescue operation, ships from the US were sent to Havana to evacuate stranded American tourists and bring them to safety in Key West.

Just like during the exodus in 1909, the towns of Key West and Ybor City, Tampa, Florida, were flooded with Cuban refugees. Soon the towns turned into tobacco-scented business capitals; they became the new Cuban enclaves in the US.

Castro, as the great leader of communist rebels, eagerly absorbed obstinate adolescents nurtured in those rich colonies. The Cuban-American colonies became hotbeds of both vengeful Batista loyalists and Castro idealists with revolutionary thoughts. Cheered on by the flower-power world of the 60s, Castro led his revolutionary army into Havana, and thus ushered in a new era of Cuban life.

Centre of Havana, Cuba - Eva Blue

I wonder whether this was a new chapter in Cuba's history, or a mere repetition of the past? Was it coincidence that amongst the eighty-odd guerilla fighters who were shipped over on the *Granma* from Mexico, there was also a warrior with the Dutch-British name George Keppel? George Keppel became one of the first martyrs of Castro's revolution on Playa Las Coloradas. In 1762, another George Van Keppel had chased the Spanish out of Havana, on behalf of the British.

Marina Hemingway

Arriving at Marina Hemingway, Havana, Cuba, from Key West, Florida, after the treacherous crossing of the Florida Strait, I was keen to meet a government-assigned guide. The young man was called Adrian, and was a fair-haired and blue-eyed Cuban in a spotless white Navy uniform that eagerly awaited my arrival at the docks.

I had made the trip from Key West to Cuba in the reverse direction of about one million Cuban refugees, who fled north across the choppy straits to a new life in the US under the wet foot dry foot policy. The wet foot dry foot rule gave Cuban nationals rights as new citizens in the US from the moment they set foot ashore. This policy was only revised in 2016. The opposite route, Key West to Cuba, was taken in 1961 with bad intentions when 1,400 Cuban exiles launched a botched invasion at the Bay of Pigs.

The million Cubans in the US have done well, very well. A second-generation Cuban immigrant, Senator Marco Rubio, ran for president in 2016. Congressman Carlos Curbelo, another success story, tried to convince me that Obama's ending of the embargo was a serious mistake. I disagreed with him and welcomed normalized relations, eagerly making excursions to the forbidden evil island.

But what were the capitalist remains, the aristocratic genes, bred in the bones of Castro Cubans? Was there an inherent capitalist metabolism in communist Cuba?

Reconquista

The marriage of Ferdinand and Isabella, on October 18, 1469, resulted in the unification of their kingdoms, Aragon and Castile, leading to the beginnings of modern Spain. The Reconquista, with the fall of Granada in 1492 and Columbus' New World discoveries, was the onset of greatness and wealth; the world had not witnessed such power since the Roman Empire.

I was in search of the turning point that ended the mighty Spanish kingdom with its four colonies in the New World: the viceroyalties of New Spain, Peru, Rio de la Plata, and New Granada. The British invasion of Havana in 1761 marked the beginning of the end for Spanish power overseas, especially in the New World.

The Cuban Foreign Service had informed me that Adrian Keppel was a distant descendant of the British-Dutch Admiral George Van Keppel who took the island of Cuba by brutal force in 1761. Adrian's grandfather, George Keppel, had been one of the original guerillas with Castro on the *Granma*. Adrian was a Castro-regime child; a model student at the Cuban Naval Academy, no more than maybe eighteen or nineteen years old, and a little nervous. Cuban Foreign Service officials, responding to my request, had traced him and his ancestry. He was instructed to guide and assist me in my historical explorations.

The attitude of the Castro regime towards foreigners and the association of foreigners with locals was rather ambivalent; you could never tell exactly what was going on, but so far, the organization and preparation had been excellent. Over the years I have met many very qualified, extremely experienced Cuban underwater archeologists and historians.

Adrian was tense at first, stumbled over his words and the lines he had probably practiced days in advance. "Senõr, welcome to my island, welcome to Cuba. You have a nice trip from Florida?"

Adrian stood to attention and saluted.

For a second, I thought that he was going to recite a revolutionary devotional or a Pledge of Allegiance, exhorting me, the foreign visitor, to be a loyalist and join the Cuban struggle against American imperialism.

"Dear boy, call me Jacob, or Tió, uncle, if you wish, and you do not have to salute me. I am not in the navy, and no more than a silly, nearly lost, solo sailor in the Caribbean, on a long voyage from north to south, from Florida to Venezuela, in search of history. And to answer your question, the seas between Florida and Cuba are always rough, and I had a hard time cutting through the strong currents, motoring most of the way. The winds were not favorable. It is easy to overshoot one's target and finish up too far east, well beyond the safe harbor of Havana. I understand that was once a tactic of pirates who chased richly-laden merchant ships on their way to Havana harbor. Pirates used little chasers and burners that forced their prey way out from the protective coast, where they could catch wind, and speed, to escape. But the currents would take them well beyond safe harbors and they would run aground, mostly in the shallow Matanza Bay, and thus become easy prey for any of those vultures."

Adrian Keppel proudly told me that he was the grandson of a Castro martyr who sacrificed his life on the beach during the unsuccessful landing of the *Granma*. He was also a scion of an old Dutch-British family that left its marks and offspring on the Spanish island of Cuba, once the jewel of the viceroyalty of New Spain, more than two hundred years ago. A Dutch-British aristocratic heritage acting out on communist Castro Cuba was so very unlikely, but the very embodiment welcomed me at the docks; reality is often beyond our imagination.

"My family is a little bit Dutch and British, especially my family name, but I am really Cuban, heart and soul," Adrian said with a big smile when I quizzed him.

I am sure he had studied and carefully rehearsed his testimony with an official. He seemed somewhat insecure and confused, as confused as most of us are about ourselves, and our heritage.

As a guide, Adrian was to lead me through the intricacies of Dutch-British-Spanish history, but far more, also through his most intriguing family history, his 1760 ancestor and his grandfather. How could another scion of the Van Keppel aristocratic family have been amongst Che's *Granma* fighters? Was that person simply following in the footsteps of other revolutionary students out to change the world in the 60s? Was grandfather Keppel just another fraternity boy who joined in? Was his sacrifice true or merely a concocted family legend? As a rule, revolutionaries always seemed to come from well-to-do, elite students, never from the suffering poor.

Subconsciously, I had pictured a descendent of a Dutch-British privateer with an eye patch and a peg-leg, clad in pirate rags; or in a more modern version, as a Che Guevara fighter, in battle gear with ammunition belts across his chest. Adrian Keppel was a crisp and clean naval officer in a white, starched uniform; he could not have been more of a contrast to my distorted concoctions.

Adrian was noted by his peers for being an exemplary scholar, a volunteer diver in the navy, and an aspiring student of underwater archeology. All this I had gleaned in advance from his resume.

"Yes Adrian, I understand. Over the ages, so many boats from England and the Low Lands skirted the Cuba coast, mostly privateers and pirates in search of riches. And so many ran onto the reefs or aground and sank. I bet that there is a countless number of wrecks out there, all the way along the south coast, from the year 1,500 and onwards."

As I watched Adrian handling the mooring lines at the dock, my eye searched for something I could recognize, something familiar, a Dutch or British look. His blond hair was not really blond and his eyes mysteriously olive green; his facial features bony with a square chin and high cheekbones. Maybe, maybe, there was something. Or maybe I was just staring at a glimpse of Cuban, Cordoba masculine beauty, mixed with some Nordic genes. I almost loathed myself for a moment as I was searching for heritage rather than the real person in front of me.

Adrian was something of a would-be Dutchman, and not like most Cubans. He liked biking and proudly showed me one of his latest, racing bike models. Was that endeavor a Dutch-Calvinist attribute that somehow had come with his genes? He was special, no doubt, but I could not put my finger on what exactly it was that made him so.

"You see, Adrian, Spanish soldiers were in Holland for a very long time. In the Low Countries by the North Sea, an independence war erupted in 1568 and lasted for eighty years. You can only imagine how many children the Spanish left behind, and many of them look exactly like you. Masculine, Spanish beauty must have been irresistible for the blond, Nordic women, and vice versa. Even today, four hundred years later, you can easily trace the presence of Spanish troops in the countryside just by looking at the people and their genetic make-up. Somehow, they are different, or maybe I should say more indifferent. The Spanish-Dutch can be rather arrogant and lazy, according to some."

It was too much, too overwhelming for the young man. To ease the nervous tension, we sipped a beer together, as we stood around on the dock, giggled, talked about nothing, and whistled at a few teenage girls on a Canadian sailing yacht a few boat slips down.

"One day, maybe you take me to Florida, to St. Augustine," Adrian suddenly exclaimed. "My grandma told me that, once, my family moved from here to St. Augustine, a long time ago, but they came back again to Cuba, and a few went to Jamaica. In Florida, I have uncles. Their names are Kurt Marshall Keppel and cousin Curtis George Keppel. They are very rich and important in their community, grandma told me."

Fascinating, I thought, here was a kid who was the very embodiment of hundreds of years of colonial history in the Caribbean and he still lives with the ghosts of his ancestry, past and present.

"That St. Augustine migration must have been in 1763 or so. You see, Adrian, the British conquered Cuba, and then exchanged it with Spain again for the eastern part of Florida, with St. Augustine as its capital. Spain got Cuba back and also Louisiana and made New Orleans its capital. The western part of Florida, with Pensacola, ended up under the control of the Mexican viceroyalty and later became the

Independent Republic of West Florida. Already in 1693, the Mexican Viceroy Gaspar de Sandoval Silva y Mendoza, the Conde de Galve, used Pensacola as a base to explore the Mississippi and other territories.

The other elongated sliver of Florida was towards the east. The capital, St. Augustine, was just an outpost with Seminole Indians and some Spanish settlers with their Ciboney slaves. Going there, for the British conquerors, was a great opportunity to make large profits.

The Spanish viceroyalties controlled the Caribbean, Middle, and South America from 1500 onwards. They formed a major, powerful kingdom. The British, French and Dutch started to nibble at its edges in the 17th and 18th centuries, conquering some islands as trading posts and for colonial settlers, but never establishing a nation of equal power. After one conquest or another by the Europeans, there was usually not much left for the locals but warring communities, mostly stripped of their sovereignty, infrastructure and natural resources."

Admiral George Van Keppel, 3rd Earl of Albemarle

"The Van Keppels belong to a lineage of old Gelderland nobility whose members have been described in the knighthood of Zutphen since the 16th century. A member of an older branch was elevated in the 17th century to the English nobility that produced the Earls of Albemarle."

"You mean, my family, the Van Keppels, arrived in Cuba in 1760 and left again in 1763?" asked Adrian, somewhat doubtful.

"Yes, I think so. The deciding years of strange migrations in Cuba were 1762 and 1763, and then 1783, 1803, and 1823. The final mass departures were in 1909, and after 1959."

In the late 16th century, Sir Francis Drake, a slave trader, privateer and the darling of Queen Elizabeth I, had eagerly snooped around the coastline of Cuba but never risked an expedition to conquer the riches in the heavily fortified harbors and towns. England, in the 16th century, did not have large battleships yet; they were invented and constructed about a hundred years later.

Nearly two hundred years after Drake, in March 1762, a British fleet of 4,000 troops and five man-of-war battleships sailed from Portsmouth and, on June 6, laid siege to Havana.

Later, when I toured the harbor with Adrian, I pointed out to him where the British had entered, and how their offenses had developed. "After a brief blockade, the commander, Admiral George Van Keppel, the 3rd Earl of Albemarle, entered the city as the supreme conqueror. Admiral Van Keppel was close to the Princes of Orange who had moved to England in the 17th century. His father was Willem Van Keppel, 2nd Earl of Albemarle.

Adrian Keppel and Arnold Joost van Keppel, 1st Earl of Albemarle
by Sir Godfrey Kneller

George Van Keppel started his military career in the Netherlands, fighting against the French and, in 1745, participated in the battle of Fontenoy as an aide to Prince William, Duke of Cumberland; the battle decided the Austrian succession.

After the siege of Havana, almost instantly, Cuba became British. Traffic and trade with the Virginia colonies and the rest of the Caribbean began immediately. Although the British occupation only lasted one year, the changes were enormous. Merchants of Liverpool placed their slaves in Havana and the occupied territories, directly from the slave warehouses in Jamaica. Jamaican know-how and sugarcane processing equipment arrived within weeks. Soon, sugar plantations were set up all around Havana. An estimated 11,000 migrants, settlers, servants, and slaves of British distinction were on the move, changing the ethnic mixture of the region once again; the Mediterranean mix got a bit of Dutch-British flavor. Thereafter, Cuba imported some 800,000 African slaves into a total population that was hardly a quarter million by 1800.

Adrian, a child of that British conquest generations back, still cherished its fruits, the privileges, ethnically and culturally. His martyred grandfather on the *Granma* and his ancestry probably had a lot to do with his privileged upbringing. Adrian personified the permanent marks of history that even Castro could not erase, and therefore rather cherished and shaped it to his communist straightjacket.

At the time of the British conquest of Havana, thousands of Spanish settlers, their slaves, and domestic servants fled from the invading troops to Veracruz.

The Cuban conquest by the British marked the major turning point that changed the Caribbean from the backyard of the Viceroyalty of New Spain that it had become in the 18th century to a playground of pirates, privateers, and buccaneers. A new episode of traffic and trade emerged, with Great Britain, France, Denmark, Sweden, and the Republic of the Low Countries as the new players, soon to be joined by the new nation of the United States of America.

Less than a year after Havana was seized, the Peace of Paris was signed. The Seven Years' War between France, Spain, and Britain was over. Britain's maneuvering resulted in an exchange of Florida for Cuba with the Spanish and, at the time, was considered a poor deal.

The irony is that today Florida is infinitely wealthier than Cuba, and the safe harbor to about one million Cubans who have fled the poverty and horrors of Castro's communism. Countless were ready to risk their lives and floated across on inflated truck tires and makeshift rafts. Nobody can say how many drowned."

On bicycles, Adrian and I made a *tour de ville* but the cobblestone *calles* in the old town were not very bike-friendly. Fortunately, the swarms of hustlers, usually as annoying as black flies, who hawk everything from pork to peanuts, stayed away from me as soon as they spotted Adrian.

Today, the central piazza of Havana does not quite look like the market square it did in 1762, with a fountain and public well, and lined with modest two-story arcaded buildings. Van Keppel's boastful entry may not have been more than driving into muddy military exercise grounds.

One year earlier, in anticipation of an invasion, Commander-in-chief Juan de Prado had hastily fortified the city and upgraded its defenses with the little money he had scraped together from the coffers of King Charles III of Spain. Re-enforcements arrived with Admiral Gutierre de Hevia, with seven ships-of-the-line and 1,000 troops, but yellow fever killed thousands almost immediately, reducing the defending forces dramatically.

Morro Castle

Adrian crossed himself as we entered Morro Castle, named after the three biblical Magi, or the three Wise Men, Balthazar, Melchior, and Gaspar. Generations of Castro's communism had not erased the power of religion, of magical thinking.

Especially amongst the blacks in the plantation regions Cuba has Santeria, a mix of Christianity and African religions. Santeria on Cuba is the 'worship of saints' and is a concoction of Roman Catholicism and Yoruba rituals; the rites and ceremonies are full of magic formulae, and are muttered in a secret Lucumí language. Usually, the darker the skin of a Cuban, the poorer they are, and the more devoted to the magic of Santeria.

Adrian was embarrassed when I asked him about it, almost a little insulted. No, it was not his thing to be bothered with religions. That was something for the mulattos and the Negroes. Making jokes about their hocus pocus was more his tune.

I don't practice Santeria, I ain't got no crystal ball. I hummed the tune and whispered lines of a popular song, in encouragement, maybe a little provocatively, but I only caught a somewhat annoyed glance from the young man.

Morro Castle was haunted by the souls of thousands who had died in futile battle or from yellow fever during the days of the Havana Siege. Not surprisingly, it was also Adrian's favorite location in Havana; the heroism of war and revolution appealed to him.

The mighty Morro Castle looked like it was suspended on the cliffs on the opposite side of the harbor from Old Havana; an epiphany in brick and mortar that dominated the port entrance.

Morro Castle was the key to the military success of any assault, and the British knew it. But before they could take it, it became a slaughterhouse.

"Adrian, you might like to know this. I will give you a short account of what happened in a little over eight weeks during the siege back in 1762.

June 11: The British stormed Cavannos Heights. The Morro was too strong, surrounded by dense brushwood and protected by a large ditch.

July 20: Siegeworks were advanced enough for the British to begin mining the right bastion of the Morro.

July 24: The British Commander Albemarle offered Velasco the opportunity to surrender, allowing him to write his own terms of capitulation. Velasco decided to fight on.

July 31: At 9 a.m., Velasco died of his wounds. The British now occupied a position commanding the city as well as the bay.

August 11: After Prado had rejected the demand for surrender sent to him by Albemarle, the British opened fire on Havana. A total of 47 guns, 10 mortars and 5 howitzers, pounded the city from a distance of 500-800 meters.

August 12 and 13: Negotiations regarding the terms of capitulation continued, and Prado and his army obtained the honors of war."

My rattling off the Morro's siege events of 1762 had made Adrian uncomfortable and he ogled me somewhat suspiciously.

"You British?" he asked, astonished.

"Not all Europeans are British, Adrian! Don't worry. I am not a spy. I just like history and study it wherever I go. Battles are the rapids of history. So much happens in such a short time that it often takes decennia or even centuries to digest the events."

"I always go diving for shipwrecks," said Adrian.

Maybe we had something in common, archeology in search of history, albeit underwater.

"There are so many shipwrecks along the Cuban coastline, maybe as many as one or two thousand. In Cuba, we have the best underwater archeologists in the world. Many times, they have found the mother lode of sunken silver and gold. I take you to the museum. When Admiral Van Keppel was in Cuba, he also lost some very large man-of-war battleships."

Adrian took me through the streets of Calle Aquila, Calle Inquisidor, Avenida Reina, Calle San Antonio, Calle America, Calle Infanta and Calle Santiago, all named in memory of the ships the British captured from the Spanish during the Battle of Havana.

"The high honor of a martyr's cemetery," I mumbled, not sure if Adrian understood. "How exciting, Adrian, your diving and underwater archeology in these waters must be like being a kid in a candy store. I knew Mel Fisher in Key West, Florida. He found the wreck of the *Nuestra Señora de Atocha*. I was a little bit involved in his museum and the reconstruction of hundreds of artifacts. After a few hundred years, the encrustations on objects by coral, sand, and shells are like hollow molds. We developed a method to fill them with resin and get a positive. It is amazing to learn what kind of things were on board a ship in those days.

The *Atocha* was a galleon bound for Spain that was heavily laden with copper, silver, gold, tobacco, gems, and indigo from Spanish colonial ports at Cartagena and Porto Bello in New Granada, currently Colombia and Panama.

The ship had been delayed in Veracruz before she could rendezvous in Havana with the other vessels of the Tierra Firme fleet. The story goes that the treasure, arriving by mule in Panama City, was so immense that it took two months to record and load it onto the *Atocha*.

After even more delays in Havana, the *Atocha* did not depart until September 4, 1622, six weeks late. Every sailor knew that one should not sail after August, in the hurricane season, but warnings were ignored and advance warning systems like we have today did not yet exist.

In a horrible hurricane that seemed to have come out of nowhere, the *Atocha* lost all of her crew and passengers except for three sailors and two slaves who survived by clinging to the mizzen mast. It happened just 35 miles south of Key West.

Mel Fisher and his family salvaged all the silver, gold, and emeralds in July 1985, but at the expense of Mel's son and daughter-in-law, who drowned when their boat capsized. The very rare and precious Muzo emeralds that were supposed to be on board are still missing. The mother lode was forty tons of gold and silver, and seventy pounds (32 kilos) of emeralds, but that could never make up for the loss of the lives of Mel's son and daughter-in-law."

Adrian took in the story with excitement but fell silent when he realized the price paid in human lives. Youth expects to live eternally; death is never an option. They are so very convinced that they are untouchable, immortal supermen, much like I was at that age.

"After a bottle of wine, Mel Fisher, salvager par excellence, often told me about the treacherous grounds and shipwrecks that have cost so many archeologists' lives."

Adrian suggested that I visit Cuba's most exciting diving sites, and, full of expectations, I followed him for a few days to the Queen's Gardens, or *Jardines de la Reina*, named after Columbus' Queen Isabella, the Galapagos of the Caribbean. It was the graveyard of hundreds of years of shipwrecks; encrusted monsters with tranquil schools of colorful fishes swimming in and out.

Jardines de la Reina is located 60 miles off the southern coast of Cuba. It is a virtually unexplored natural environment without any inhabitants or commercial activity. Its 250 small islands of corals and mangroves bathe in a crystal-clear turquoise sea. Encrusted wrecks litter the ocean floor. You can find an abundance of cannons, anchors, and sunken treasures of 17th- and 18th-century galleons that once sailed these seas. Mackerel, shad, grunts, schoolmasters, and yellowtail snapper spadefish swim in and out like it is their natural home environment. Walls of Elkhorn, leaf and star corals, with giant sea fans, set a décor of unmatched drama and beauty.

One evening, I got back to the question that had been on my mind since I arrived. "I am still curious to find out how your family managed to move from Cuba to St. Augustine and then back again, and maybe onto Jamaica."

Adrian was hesitant but after a while, and a beer, he proudly retold the stories he had heard from his grandma. "In 1763, my family went to St. Augustine, Florida, as most British serving under Admiral George Van Keppel did. And in 1784, when Spanish rule returned to Florida, some of them came back to Cuba. Only in 1821 was Florida transferred to the United States, and from then on, there was a Cuban and an American branch of the family."

"Well, Adrian, did you know that shortly after England was awarded the Floridas, commerce started with the Indian villages on a barter base? Trains of pack horses carried supplies like razors, knives, gun parts, glass beads, silver combs, earrings, and buckles to the Indians and returned laden with beaver skins, dried venison, beeswax, honey, and other commodities. Yes, Van Keppel was eager to make his fortune too with lucrative barters, and set up shop in St. Augustine, where slavery capitalism was at its peak in those days.

St. Augustine had been a hub in the slave trade in Spanish colonial Florida, but under British rule it became more of a plantation. It did, however, maintain its dominant position in the slave trade. In the twenty-year occupation of St. Augustine by the British, slave ships arrived regularly, either after stopping in the colonies or coming directly from Africa. Ships carried about one hundred Africans at the time, including West Indian natives.

In 1784, Spanish rule over Florida returned, but this time not by conquest. Florida was taken from British control and became Spanish again, as some kind of reward for Spanish assistance during the American Revolution. The Treaties of Versailles, part of the Peace of Paris, assigned sovereignty over Florida back to Spain.

Just like when the whole Spanish population of Florida moved to Cuba when the British took control in 1763, this time most of the British settlers in Florida departed for British colonies in the Caribbean, like Jamaica, in spite of the new Spanish governor's promise of equal treatment.

What little was left, and found by the Spanish when they returned to Florida, was reflected in a report to the governor. St. Augustine recorded 574 blacks, free blacks and slaves, and only 1,418 white residents. Slaves or indentured labor in Florida were West Indians and Africans, as well as Europeans like the Menorcans.

Menorcans were especially happy with the Spanish return to power. Menorcans were a group of forced labor migrants from the island of Menorca and other Mediterranean islands. Turnbull, an English businessman, transported them forcibly to Florida as indentured servants, to work on his indigo plantation at New Smyrna, south of St. Augustine. At that time, Menorcans were also the most recent carriers of pure Spanish culture, far more than the Spanish settlers in Cuba who had become acclimatized to the Caribbean and had mixed with many other races and cultures.

By 1802, St. Augustine had been back under Spanish rule for almost twenty years. The slave trade was changing worldwide, as European countries and the American colonies started banning the importation of African slaves. Spain did not.

Just imagine those days, how the changed attitude towards the slave trade changed business. Slave trading was a long-term investment in labor and people. It took years before profits were made and investments recouped. Take Liverpool, a center for the slave trade, and all these ships from Africa there, and suddenly there was a ban on trading. Traders there simply packed up and headed for ports in Fernandina, a harbor city in Nassau County, Florida, and St. Augustine.

The second Spanish occupation continued until 1821 when Spain transferred Florida to the United States. Historians established that the slave culture in St. Augustine expanded because it not only included the slaves who returned with Spanish owners in 1784, but also those from the British period, African and American born.

During this second Spanish period, slaves were also holding down paid jobs when they were not working for their owners. This was an attempt towards buying their freedom. They worked as butchers, seamstresses, or rowers. They also held parties and markets to sell produce. Whatever they did, it took a long time to amass the required sum. Most were paid only 1 and ½ to 2 pesos a day and the minimum to buy their freedom would have been about 400 pesos.

The sugarcane plantations of Cuba, where most of the African slaves were employed, gave life to an exuberant rum industry. Even today, every tourist seems to be familiar with Daiquiris, the traditional drink in Hemingway's Floridita bar in Havana. There are several variations on these cocktails, such as the Daiquiri Floridita, Hemingway Daiquiri, Banana Daiquiri, and Strawberry Daiquiri.

Competing is the Mojito, a drink made with rum, sparkling water, sugar, lemon juice, ice, and mint. This was also a favorite drink of Hemingway's.

The Cuba Libre, a blend of rum and cola, is third and most popular amongst the youth. In Spain, it has been named *Cubata*. Both are very refreshing drinks which incorporate a squeeze of lemon and some ice cubes.

Saoco, a drink made with coconut milk and sugarcane brandy or rum, is gaining in popularity. Cuban Ginger, apple liquor, and alcoholic ginger ale are recommended. The rum that is used in its production is the Havana Club Añejo, seven years old. Then there is Havana Loco, a fantastic cocktail made with Havana Club rum and tropical fruit. Canchanchara, Cult of Life, or Havanisima, can also be found in any region of the country."

Once we returned to Havana, I hosted Adrian on my boat for a grand meal. At my request, Adrian invited his brothers, sisters, nieces, nephews, and friends, who helped me prepare a sumptuous family-style goodbye dinner. The kids drank beer and Cuba Libre, most puffed cigarettes and played loud disco music. They all looked like very happy, normal boys and girls, products of Castro's Unión de Jóvenes Comunistas, the Young Communist League.

Castroism

For the young, Fidel Castro was a historical figure and not a human, more fable than flesh. The brothers Castro were old men; the walking dead. They all heard the stories of how different and difficult it had been in the 1960s and 70s. Even the enthusiasm and rally for the return of the refugee child Elián González in 2000, who had made the crossing to Florida on a raft with his mother who drowned, was no more than a local legend.

The social-economic system Castro put in place was to be respected and even disobeyed, and then left behind. For many, it was no more than a constraint on further development.

My visit to Castro's workers' paradise had been delightful, full of surprises and discovery, and a great springboard to the rest of the Caribbean.

That evening, as I stated earlier, I prepared a little onboard feast for Adrian Keppel, his brothers, sisters, and cousins. Here it is.

Cuban roasted pig

Appetizer
The girls prepared croquetas, made with pollo; these crispy fried potato dumplings make for mouth-watering appetizers before the main course.

Main course
Roasted pig: The roasted pig is a huge part of Cuban holidays and special occasions. It's traditional to purchase a whole pig from the butcher to roast in the backyard in a Caja China roasting box.
Alternatively, a smaller suckling pig is the perfect size to feed a smaller family. I got a much smaller suckling that fit on the outboard grill of my boat.

Side dishes
Black beans and rice, also called Moros y Cristianos.
No Cuban meal is complete without a generous helping of this staple of black beans and rice.

Tostones are savory fried plantains that can be dipped in various sauces for an absolutely scrumptious side dish.

Yuca con Mojo. Yuca is a root vegetable and a staple in the Cuban diet. They're delicious sautéed with lots of garlic.

3 HENDRICK VAN DER DECKEN

The Flying Dutchman is a legendary ghost ship that can never make port and is doomed to sail the oceans forever. - *Travels in various part of Europe, Asia and Africa during a series of thirty years and upward* (1790) by John MacDonald

---

Saint-Saëns' Opus 40, Dance Macabre

"Death appears at midnight," I shouted into the tempest. "Death calls forth all the dead to rise from their sea graves. You must dance for me with the fiddle playing a Triton, a Diabolus in Musica."

To my initial disbelief and utter surprise, on the front deck, just below the jib and the flying jib, something extraordinary happened, mostly at midnight, and only in rough weather. It could not be true, and yet it was.

During those nights, howling winds rattled the sheets against the main and mizzenmasts, in a constant rattling staccato. Pattering rain splashing down on the decks sounded an ear-deafening noise. Lightning flashes set ablaze a grand theatrical drama on my little front-deck stage. When giant sparks struck across the heavenly expanse, pitch-dark shadows in overexposed, white light dwarfed my yacht on the waves into a tiny dinghy.

Sleeping was no option on those wild nights. I played Saint-Saëns' Opus 40, *Dance Macabre*, and blasted Halloween's orchestral tone poem at maximum volume from the ship's speakers. It became my favorite - not that it ever occurred to me that I was playing a funeral march.

After a few of these storm séances, I became convinced that more was happening than I could observe from my sheltered cockpit. These happenings were not hallucinations, induced by any chemical stimuli. They were very real. As a rational person, I admit that it does not sound like it, so I surrender to your judgment. It did not take long before imagination turned into living beings.

So, one night when gales were playing havoc again, awakening even the dead from their graves, I mustered the storm, sheets of rain, blistering thunder and lightning.

In slickers and boots, I worked my way to the front-deck stage; riding a bucking bull at a rodeo would have been easier. Saint-Saëns' thin, ting-tingling xylophone was the rattling of dancing bones, while the fiddle sang a wiling dada, dada, dada throughout the night. Folded drums unnerved in the background.

Then, as in a closing act in a grand drama, drum roll after drum roll accompanied the dead who rose from the ocean floor. And their skeletons danced and danced. They danced throughout the night on my front deck, the disco dance of eternity. Carcasses dressed in navy uniform rags and pirate garb whirled and pirouetted until the Sea Rooster crowed at dawn, and all returned to their sea graves.

Just before the party was over, from behind a grand stage curtain of thick sheets of rain, a distinguished gentleman, dressed in a 17th-century captain's uniform, stepped forward.

"May I introduce myself," the gentleman spoke politely, with a somewhat bellowing voice. "I am Captain Hendrick van der Decken of Amsterdam, explorer in the services of the VOC, the Dutch East Indies Company. As most would know, sir, I have been challenging the devil for long, for very long."

The dark and rain obscured a full view of the captain on the small stage.

But that it was Captain van der Decken was unmistakable. He was the one and only legendary Flying Dutchman, as the world got to know him.

"Sir," the captain continued, "you may have heard of my ship. My ship was distinguishing itself from all other vessels in the world by bearing a full press of sails in the wildest storms and especially when other ships were unable from the stress of weather to show an inch of canvas. My Port of Registry became the Bottom of the Ocean."

"Captain!" I hollered into the wind, "you are blown off course and quite a bit. You were to round the Cape of Good Hope in Africa on your way to Batavia, or vice versa, to Amsterdam. But you are in the Caribbean now."

I was thrilled to meet my childhood hero.

"Also, captain, your timing is off. You lived in 1641, and today is more than 350 years later."

When I said it, I sensed the silliness of my remarks. After all, the image I saw must be a ghost; I was talking to a phantom.

"Captain, why do you come haunting a single-handed sailor on a hurricane night in the emptiness of the black ocean?"

The Flying Dutchman by Charles Temple Dix, oil on canvas, 1860s

Civility in every way dominated Captain van der Decken's behavior. Once known as a ruthless privateer, the infamous Flying Dutchman who cared more about accomplishments than life itself, behaved like a gentleman.

The captain set out to explain his actions. "Let me explain my motives, Sir. I heard that my eighth descendant, Hendrick van der Decken IX, once a Japanese bullhead shark fisherman, is now the captain of the Flying Pirates of the Caribbean. My crew and I have messages to deliver to our loved ones, and we will not cease our efforts to do so till our death day and hell freezes over. You may understand that messages are much like wine; they get better as they mature over time. Yes, what we have to say gets better all the time. Hendrick IX is my flesh and blood, and he may be ready to pass on our last messages."

Portent of doom

Waves crashed over the deck. My boat became a roller coaster car as we dove down from the crest of a groundswell into a deep valley.

Undisturbed, Van der Decken continued his roaring speech. "Yes, sir, as I already said, you may have heard of my ship. Whenever hailed by another ship, my crew tried to send messages to land, or to people, now long dead."

His words got lost in the howling wind, but I could make out the message: "In ocean lore, the sight of my ship became a portent of doom."

Portent of doom? Was I about to go under? The weather was bad but was it really that bad? Feeling sorry for my forlorn ghost standing out in the pouring rain, I was about to invite him in for a tot of rum, or even a pint of beer, but as the first rays of daylight peeked over the horizon, the sheet of rain shattered into atoms and the captain was gone.

The Flying Dutchman is the popular name for Hendrick van der Decken. He aimed to round the Cape of Good Hope, but did not succeed; the currents were too strong. But he pledged to keep trying till Judgment Day. He and his ship became ghosts of the sea and the idols of perseverance. *Never give up, even if you have to keep trying till doomsday.* That may not have been the full story. Sooner or later the captain would yield all the relevant details.

In 1881, the future British King George V was a midshipman aboard the H.M.S. *Bacchante*. He reported that the Flying Dutchman had crossed their bow. Thirteen men on the *Bacchante* and two other ships saw it, and it remains in the Admiralty's official publication, *The Cruise of H.M.S. Bacchante*. The records do not report on the number of tots of rum consumed by the prince and his crew.

A strange red light as of a phantom ship all-aglow, in the midst of which light the masts, spars, and sails of a brig 200 yards distant stood out in strong relief as she came up on the port bow. Nothing of any material ship was to be seen either near or right away to the horizon, the night being clear and the sea calm. Thirteen persons altogether saw her.

And another account reads:

Van der Decken was a staunch seaman and would have his way in spite of the devil. For all that, never a sailor under him had reason to complain; though how it is on board with him nobody knows. In doubling the Cape they were a long day trying to weather the Table Bay. Just after sunset, a voice spoke to the Captain, asking him if he did not mean to go into the bay that night. Van der Decken replied: "May I be eternally damned if I do, though I should beat about here till the Day of Judgment."

The Flying Dutchman became the mascot of Dutch entrepreneurship in the 16th until 18th centuries, and Captain Van der Decken, the man who never gave up trying, became its superhero role model.

Ships off the Cape of Good Hope by Jan Luycken, etching, 1693, Rijksmuseum Amsterdam

Ghosts

The Caribbean people and their customs, prejudices and preoccupations are fascinating in every aspect and way; their history is bloody and cruel and their survival remarkable. The Caribbean is the melting pot of people from around the world: of refugees, slaves, bandits, pirates, colonizers, luck seekers, and ideologists.

Surviving alone on board a boat for any length of time meant creating a family, even an imaginary one. The mind spins stories and stories look for sounding boards.

Thus, I got to talking into the wind, talking to Thor, the weather god, and the mast and sails.

Richard Bach's *Jonathan Livingston Seagull* may have had a good ear but the seagulls nose-diving across my boat never did talk back. These birds only came with deadly shrieks and destructive ammonia-rich poop - lots of it.

After I left Marina Hemingway in Cuba with a promise to Adrian that I would search for his family members in Jamaica, sheets of rain, gusts, and roller coasters of waves wreaked havoc with my boat and me, week after week. Heading down for the Lesser Caribbean and the Leeward Antilles of Curaçao took months. From a sailing point of view, it was the wrong course. The brutal exercise diverted my mind and a new mindset emerged as I went along.

A novice to sea life for any extended time, how was I to know that soon I would have a stowaway crew?

The weather did not leave me any choice. I had no time to contemplate my solitude, study the climate, or its changes, or complain about the way things should have been.

Mother Nature put me in an incredibly subservient role. I was her slave, and acted and reacted appropriately - there were no second chances on the ocean. The elements became my company, friend and enemy and my boat my closest family.

Only half joking, a friend told me that I was in my own floating casket, getting used to the idea. Another, an amateur psychiatrist, told me that by sailing on the ocean I was crawling back into the uterus and enjoying the pacifying babbling of amniotic fluids.

In the end, whatever they said or thought, I could not find anyone to join me.

The main hurricane tracks are all parallel to the equator, with a tilt. The safest, though not the most comfortable, way to sail in a hurricane is to allow the storm to blow you into the wide-open sea of the Gulf of Mexico, and that is what I had done.

Cayman Islands

After days in rough weather at sea, the storm exhausted itself and I managed to maneuver into a safe harbor. Reaching the yacht harbor of George Town on the Cayman Islands alive and well was my first real triumph.

"Hi, kid, please catch my docking line, will you?" I called out to a teenager sheltering under a dripping awning, while I was standing alone on the front deck bow in the pouring rain, with strong winds blowing me away from the dock.

Tying up at a pier in a Caribbean yacht harbor cannot be taken for granted. As docking lines are fastened to cleats, extensive hand waving and discussions between the skipper and the person on the dock are part of the arrival ritual. Catching a docking line is what life is all about.

Languages spoken on the dock could be Spanish, English, French, Dutch, Creole, Papiamento, or some gibberish you will never be able to understand. Body language was by far the best communication. Curiosity had to win over reluctance and deep-seated suspicion; the Caribbean had a long history to justify both.

Since the kid was not about to come out from under his shelter, I jumped on the dock with the line and all and pulled the boat in. Such maneuvers are not recommendable; you could easily miss the dock and drown, or break a leg in the process. "Break a leg" used to be what understudies said when the prima ballerina went on stage, since that would mean good luck for them; they would finally get to perform. "Break a leg" is now an expression for actors, not athletes.

Sailing from island to island in the Caribbean, some inhabited but most uninhabited, with hurricanes brewing on the horizon, finding shelter in hurricane holes and harbors, became my survival mode. It took days in George Town harbor to fix the damage on the boat. It was more extensive than I had anticipated, and since parts were not available in this remote port, I had to make do with some improvisations. Soon I was off again, heading eastward.

The ghosts of the ocean floor who had come to haunt me on stormy nights seemed forgotten, but were they? I struggled to anchor my sailboat and at times winds were so strong that I needed extra securing lines. On a few occasions, I preferred to be out on the open, drifting with the bow in the wind, pulling along a few floating anchors.

Danger lured everywhere, like dragging anchors in hurricane holes. Huge swells could easily land boat-with-captain on the beach, or shatter all against the coral reefs. I had studied sailing guides, listened to every sailor's story in the ports, but soon enough received some on-the-job training. The Caribbean, with all its natural beauty, looks at times like a theme park, but you better be ready when it turns into a roller coaster. It is not for the fainthearted.

A Ship on the high seas caught by a Squall by Willem van de Velde the Younger, oil on canvas, circa 1680, Rijksmuseum Amsterdam

17th-century sailors in the Caribbean

In those days, from the 16th till the 19th century, the western world was ruled by mercantilism, an economic system dominated by the major European trading nations. The medieval feudal organization in western Europe, especially in the Netherlands, France, Spain, the Austrian Empire, and England, had created a small elite of aristocracy and a large pool of indentured labor and serfs.

The emergence of towns created a new class of citizens, self-employed workers in trade and shipping. Unpaid apprenticeships were the way by which one entered a trade. It would take a few hundred more years before labor laws, as we know them today, were invented and the conditions of workers were protected by regulations.

To become a sailor, a boy started as an apprentice no later than at age fourteen. The boy's parents, if they had the means, paid a ship's master or first mate a hefty sum to train the boy for up to nine years as an unpaid apprentice. Gradually, some kind of wage system was introduced, especially when countries set up formal navies. Sailors, often drafted against their will, sometimes enjoyed a share of the booty, but nobody could be sure that treasure was waiting for them - for most death was the only thing that awaited them. Sailors did not enjoy formal wages of any kind and conditions below deck for the common crew have often been described as being similar to those in a concentration camp.

Exporting goods in exchange for precious metals, like gold or silver, became the new mercantile gospel. During the Age of Exploration, the 16th through 17th century, large parts of the globe became trading destinations for western Europe.

The forerunner was the kingdom of Spain, the mighty realm that shipped massive amounts of gold and silver back home from the South American colonies. The rest of Europe followed. In the vacuum left by law and order, greed ruled. The Caribbean became a playground for the adventurous, the get-rich-quick, the desperadoes, and, last but not least, the opportunists. Ongoing wars in Europe legitimized piracy, plunder, theft, and ruthless killings.

The seas were full of roving gangs, wandering businessmen, itinerant naval officers, ruthless pirates, buccaneers, and privateers. Local indigenous Caribbean populations were taken by surprise, and soon, most of them lost their lives to disease and European cruelty. With the emergence of industrialized agriculture, African populations replaced the diminishing number of locals as slave labor in a work pool of millions.

I was sailing through the Madame Tussauds wax museum display of the Caribbean Sea, filled with stilted images of history, now surrendering to the imagination of the sightseeing visitors.

After the Caymans, the weather was mostly fair again, with the thermometer reading a tropical eighty-five to ninety degrees. But doldrums followed the storms. I floated for days without the least bit of wind. A mirror flat, steel-grey ocean loomed, with Fata Morganas just over the horizon, beckoning those at sea but always beyond the reach of mortals.

Picture by Tony Alter

4 HOW I MET ANANSI

Anansi is an African folktale character. He often takes the shape of a spider and is considered to be the spirit of all knowledge of stories. - From Wikipedia, the free encyclopedia

---

There was not a puff of wind. The air was hazy and balmy. For days, I had not spotted land or even a seagull. North of the equator, between the north and south trade winds, is a notorious belt of calms and squalls. To keep me company, a few small sharks circled the boat eager for refuse; swimming was not to be recommended.

When it comes to doldrums, poetic words bubbled up in memory. The strings of an *oud* began their chords while the heel of a hand beat a rhythm on the dull. An *oud* is a short-neck type of lute, a pear-shaped stringed Byzantine instrument, still popular in the Middle East.

Caught up in the inevitable, I languished in the unsolicited leisure of nothingness, staring out over the water without a ripple. Every once in a while, I got my hopes up when baffling light winds pushed the boat one way or another.

Making more repairs helped pass the days. The nights were oppressive down below, so I slept out in the open in the cockpit, under the starry skies, and gazed for hours at the glittering diamonds speckled over the huge expanse.

Prince Kwaku

Then, one night, a tiny voice, like a boy's countertenor, squealed over the water, "Ship ahoy, anybody aboard? I am Captain Hendrick van der Decken. My vessel is *Huis de Kreuningen*."

If that squeak was not my imagination, then it had to be another sea ghost, an imposter who claimed to be Captain Hendrick van der Decken's descendant.

"No, you are not," I replied immediately. "Only a few nights ago, your so-called great grandfather told me that his descendant, Hendrick IX, was captain of the vessel *Pirate of the Caribbean*, and not *Huis de Kreuningen*."

Whoever the rascal was with his tiny voice out at sea, he must have overheard my conversation in the gale winds with the Dutch captain and was making a mockery of it all.

"And what is more," I continued, "you are at least two hundred years too late. The vessel *De Kreuningen* got lost in a bloody fight with French colonists, by the coast of Tobago, in Rockley Bay. The entire fleet of fourteen ships sank there, and two thousand sailors perished. The date was March 3, 1677."

"Applause, applause! Photographic memory," squeaked the tiny voice. "You right, sir, not Captain van der Decken's great, great, great, great grandson. I, just poor castaway, drifting on endless ocean. Please rescue me."

Towing from the stern of my boat, I spotted a tiny, torn banana leaf, rigged with cobwebs and manned by a fat, lazy spider in a makeshift cockpit, lounging in a silk-thread hammock. The spider was talking in his tiny voice, trying to draw my attention and solicit my compassion.

"You, Spiderman, you are more likely a stowaway, and not a castaway, coming along on my journey. The sharks are hungry, and will soon come and eat you. I bet you, you are no more than a scoundrel and an imposter."

"Mercy, sir!" the spider pleaded, "All alone, no winds. Me, good company for discussions. You great scholar. Hungry, very hungry. Please give me little food."

"To me, Spiderman," I said, "you look like an imposter castaway."

I remembered Kwaku, the son of Nyame, from my time in West Africa. Nyame was the most benevolent sky god of the Akan in Ashanti land, the land they call Ghana nowadays.

"Spiderman, isn't it Nyame, the sky god, who knows and sees everything and is omniscient and omnipotent? Nyame, I was told, became so annoyed with your mischief, little man, that he turned you into a spider. You are now, Kwaku Anansi, the Spider of Wednesday! Haha!"

I was maybe a bit cruel to condemn the creature, but then he was infamous and best kept away. My attack caused a slight shiver to run along the Spiderman's web.

"You, sir," squeaked the little spider again. "You, so very cruel. Mentioned horrid family drama, and so many strange words I never heard. You right, I was Prince Kwaku, son of King-God Nyame. Life is full with cards of misfortune. Such is my ordeal. Making the best. I go across Atlantic, back and forth. Home country of my family, no visit since long time. Not since end of slave trade, two hundred years ago. Now, I hide in dark, in suitcases. Fly in airplanes over the ocean. Old days better; then a trip was weeks, months. Yes, last week, I hear your conversation with Dutch ghost captain. Amsterdam, Van der Decken's city is also my hometown. Family members live in Bijlmermeer and Almere. My wife name Shi Maria."

Then the Spiderman fell silent.

"Oh, please, Spiderman," I said. "Move on. You know what, I will be generous and give you a good push in the direction of Africa."

As I propelled Spiderman Anansi eastward with my longest docking hook, I felt some regret. Melancholy gripped me.

Stowaway, castaway

The next morning, ready for a bacon-and-eggs breakfast in my cockpit, I spotted Anansi luxuriating in a cobweb hammock way up on the mainsail mast, well beyond my reach. He must have spun a rope, tied it to my docking hook, and come aboard.

"You scoundrel, steal away before I squash you," I roared.

"Steal away, steal away," sang Anansi from his hammock, still in his boy-soprano pitch. "Steal away to Jesus! Steal away, steal away home. I ain't got long to stay here."

And after a while of silence, he whispered, "Yes, they sang in shackles and chains. In the gallows, many ruthless watchmen. In songs many messages for runaways, much like myself. I tell you all secrets!"

Anansi's proposal to divulge true secrets of the transatlantic passage tempted me. In many ways, Anansi, as the ghost of this fateful journey, was first-hand material. You could view him as the immortal spirit of millions of Afro-Caribbeans who came across the Atlantic. He could be a treasure trove of stories, of undiscovered testimony. Maybe I had had my lucky strike and was about to hear an unusual account of events, of history.

"You scoundrel, that song comes from the Underground Railroad in the US and has nothing to do with your Middle Passage experience. Escaped slaves in the US fled north, making use of secret passageways. If you, Anansi, do not stop cheating, you leave me no choice but to crush you, and feed your tiny skinny legs to the fishes!"

After that little encounter, Anansi continued to sing all day long with his squeaky voice. This time real slave songs from the islands.

Papa Siwe,
At'é negru tribí ku a lanta ku blanku
Papa Siwe,
At'é negru tribí ku a lanta ku blanku
Mat'é Hork'é.

Papa Siwe,
Look at this cheeky slave
challenging his white masters.
Kill him. Hang him.

"Anansi, your singing is out of tune! Please, turn off that broken record.

42

By the way, there are no coded messages in that song. Slave owners, afraid of revolt, forced their house slaves to sing this little refrain of *Mat'é Hork'é* (kill him, hang him) all day long, to underline what happened to disloyal slaves."

I knew the song well. After the Tula slave revolt on the island of Curaçao in 1795, that song was a warning to slaves from their masters. The masters forced their slaves to sing it all the time.

With the sailors and traders, stories had arrived at the ports about the French Revolution and how freedom was imminent for all people, including slaves.

Freedom and what freedom meant were hard to imagine, since hardly any other form of employment than in industrial agriculture existed. Free slaves often lobbied for years with plantation owners to be re-absorbed into the slavery system, where they would receive a little house, a small plot of land, food, clothing, and medical care. None of these fringe benefits were available to the freemen.

Freedom and being a freed slave meant poverty, and having to take care of basic needs by becoming a day laborer. The colonial government paid the same for a day's work to freed slaves as they did to company slaves, but the status of a free slave was low.

Many slaves were dreaming about the liberty of this faraway French Revolution and the abolition of slavery, but had no idea how to handle their freedom. Freedom was a dream of being in heaven, never having to work again, with unlimited supplies of food, drink and sex. After the abolition of slavery, hardly any economic base existed to provide for the freed slaves. The lucky ones who had a trade were able to set up as cabinetmakers or skilled carpenters.

Creoles

By the end of the 18th century, most slave masters were Creoles, the offspring of Portuguese fathers and African mothers, and mostly dark-skinned. The color of the skin became very important as a class distinction. A *quadroon* was a mixed-race person with one-quarter African and three-quarters European ancestry. Similar classifications were *octoroon*, for one-eighth black, *terceron, mustee, mustefino*, all the way down to *hexadecaroon*, for one-sixteenth black.

Thomas-Alexandre Dumas, a mulatto, Alexandre Dumas, père, a quadroon, Alexandre Dumas, fils, an octoroon

Governments incorporated the terms in laws defining rights and restrictions. Children's place in the society was determined according to their color. After facilitating the European transatlantic slave trade in the 17th and 18th century, Creoles settled mostly on the Caribbean islands, often as slave traders, overseers, and plantation owners.

In 1863, the year of the abolition of slavery under the Dutch colonial system, extensive damage payments were made to slave owners. The extent of slavery in the island societies is reflected in the lists of names of the recipients. Most slave owners had four to six slaves.

West Indian Creole woman with her black servant, by Agostino Brunias, oil on canvas, circa 1780 © Yale Center for British Art, Paul Mellon Collection, New Haven

Entrepreneurial free slaves often started a business of selling and buying slaves. Many slaves already owned other slaves, often offspring from other women. Only twenty to thirty percent of the slave owners were Europeans, not counting the government-owned trading companies, like the WIC, the Dutch West India Company. Most slave owners were themselves former slaves or Creoles.

Let me tell you, you may have wondered why so many blacks preferred to stay in the US, Caribbean, and Europe after abolition, instead of going back to Africa.

Well now you know, Anansi, blacks of the West Indies were mostly Creoles, and were not very welcome in Africa. They were seen as profiteers, as collaborators who had made local chiefs and kings super rich by rounding up local slaves for sale."

"Yes," cried Anansi, drunk with sarcasm, after listening to my story intensively. "Europeans in Africa, only on goodwill mission, teach stupid Africans how to work. Rescue souls from the devil. Bring Jesus gospel. All slavery trips, only love-and-peace missions, foreign development aid. Hehehe."

Anansi's sharp tongue, spitting ridicule, threaded my arguments to pieces. Nevertheless, I resumed, knowing that my sermon probably already sounded like that of a drunken preacher teacher. But then, so what?

I was in my boat's cockpit, lecturing a spider in a hammock on the main mast. It did not matter, and with fire and brimstone, I spoke like a great orator. "The mixed black, colored, and white population of the Caribbean was a real concern to the Europeans, ever since they set foot ashore. It was not so much the racial difference, but rather the cultural and social divide. After the abolition of the slave trade and slavery, slaves would become full citizens, but Europeans did not look forward to living amongst free slaves, thus the return-to-Africa movement was born.

Many Europeans and American southerners believed that going back to West Africa would have been the preference for most black islanders. With big funding in the UK and US, free states like Liberia and Sierra Leone were founded in West Africa to welcome those who returned.

A counter movement came from the Creoles, who wanted to stay and were afraid to go back. Many with mahogany skin claimed to have ancestors amongst the local Indians, *Taino*. Matriarchs desperately tried through arranged marriages to make their offspring lighter. Even today, the darkest receive the least social recognition. For a shopkeeper to promote a dark sales girl over a lighter one can set off riots and strikes.

For many years after the abolition, Creoles continued with clandestine slave markets, especially for domestics. They had no interest in returning and fought every such effort, even resorting to kidnapping candidates.

How wrong the Europeans and Americans were is demonstrated by the low numbers of people returning to Africa over the years. Less than a trickle of Caribbean black colonists made the return voyage. Even in Liberia and Sierra Leone, sovereign countries set up for this very purpose; the locals hated Creoles. To make things worse, those who did go back quickly built a plantation economy in Liberia and Sierra Leone, in every aspect identical to the one in the American south. They enslaved locals as they had been enslaved themselves. I will tell you a lot more about it later on.

So, now you know, Spiderman Anansi, that you are also a reflection of opportunism and all the bad characteristics of the Creoles. Sorry, the truth always hurts."

My ship's speakers blasted The Wailers.

Get up, stand up
Stand up for your rights.
Get up, stand up
Don't give up the fight.
You, preacher man don't tell me
Heaven is under the earth.
You a Duppy and you don't know
What life is really worth.
It's not all that glitters is gold
And half the story has never been told.

"Yes, Anansi, we are going to Jamaica."

And with a puff of wind, we sailed eastward again.

That evening, I prepared a doldrums recipe. My freezer was full, but a little improvisation with ingredients is allowed at sea.

Doldrums recipe

Ingredients
Red pepper flakes
Cumin seeds
½ spring onion, diced
2 cloves of garlic, chopped
½ green pepper, chopped
A small bunch of chard or beet greens, chopped
2 small Japanese eggplants, chopped
2 cups pre-cooked or canned chickpeas
¼ cup chopped mint
2-3 tbsp. tahini
A squeeze of lemon juice
Lots of olive oil

Instructions
Toast the cumin seeds.
Add a few tablespoons of olive oil, along with the red pepper flakes and onion.
When the onion is soft, add the garlic and pepper.
Cook a few minutes till the garlic begins to turn golden and the onions brown.
Add the greens, cover and cook for a few minutes.
Add water if necessary.
Once the greens begin to cook down, add the eggplant.
Drizzle with lots of oil, as it soaks up the liquid.
When the eggplant has softened, add the chickpeas and mint.
After a few minutes, turn off the heat.
Drizzle with tahini and lemon juice.
Serve with more fresh mint.
Goes great with couscous or quinoa.

5 DUPPY BOY

Duppy, a malevolent spirit or ghost in Caribbean folklore. - Jamaican folklore

It was a long way to Jamaica, and we passed many little islands where nobody lived. On one of those tiny islands, I anchored in a sheltered bay, carefully avoiding shallow shoals. The shape of the clouds told me that another storm was brewing on the horizon.

At night, I stared at the grand display of the glittery, tropical sky; a never-ending delight that turned me into the soulmate of astronomers of bygone ages. Many generations of sailors sought guidance in the stars during their long voyages, and I witnessed that celestial navigation was so obvious. At every hour of the night, guiding bodies offered their splendid services, making orientation and course-plotting easy.

One early evening just after sunset, I dinghied ashore. My small boat, gently carried by long rolling breakers, landed with a little crash on a white sandy beach. A pale blue moonlight made me feel like I was on a stage. A massive fence of tropical jungle formed a black wall offsetting the white sands. Hundreds of critters and crawlers jumped in and out of sand castles. Sand crabs left elaborate, batik patterns behind on the wet sand, to be washed away seconds later by the waves; if only I could read what they wrote.

Ole Higue

And that is when I ran into a dark Duppy boy. Just so you know, *Duppies* are spirits or demons on abandoned Caribbean islands. They do not like light and only come out when it's dark. At night, they sneak onto islands and invade people's homes. That is why locals burn candles in a house with a dead body lying in state. Otherwise, Duppies could come and steal the remains of the deceased in the dark and carry them off to their secret hiding places to occupy those souls for eternity.

Duppies are enough to scare the living daylights out of many Caribbeans. You better keep Duppies on your side, but as far away as possible. Some people call them *Jumbees*, but for me, that means something else.

Jumbees are all the malevolent ghosts of the world. Duppies can be quite benevolent if they want to. So, I rather limit myself to this kind of Caribbean spooks, Duppies. And today a Duppy boy, my Duppy boy that night, was clearly out of haunting practice.

"Is there nobody for you to haunt?" I asked him politely.

"Boohoo, pooh! I am the Ole Higue, the Three-Footed Horse, the Rolling Calf, all in one. And you are supposed to be very scared of me," Duppy said, a bit surprised by my polite kindness.

"Come on, man, Ole Higue was an old wife and you look like a mere boy. She comes out at night and sucks all blood from sleeping babies. Where are your blood-dripping lips and tongue, my friend?"

Duppy boy was taken aback by my critical remarks.

"And my dear Duppy boy, the Three-Footed Horse, the one you try to imitate, is a real big-time Duppy, a creature whose breath is poisonous, like that of a dragon."

This scared my Duppy boy and he was about to run away, but somehow his curiosity won out over his fear.

"And now look at yourself, Duppy boy. Do you have two hind legs and one front, like the Three-Footed Horse of Jamaica? No, you have just two legs and two arms, just like me. Haha! You better be careful, I could be Ole Higue in disguise. Pooh! Boo, I am thirsty for fresh baby blood. Boohoo, pooh!"

And I clowned around as a spook. I could see that Duppy boy knew that he had lost, but I had to give him the *coup-de-grace*. "And a Rolling Calf with a chain coiled around your body, you are not either. That is a punishment for wicked pirates. I know an evil person when I see one, dead or alive, and you are not one of them. Only dead and evil characters turn into Rolling Calves, you know."

Now that the ice was broken between us, we knew that, in the tropical heat, we had nothing more to fear from each other. We laughed and exchanged some more ghost stories.

"Times are bad," muttered my Duppy boy. "I do not even manage to haunt the only visitor who has set foot on this island for years."

I saw deep disappointment growing in his ghostly face, but could not stop myself from giving him some solid advice.

Unions

"Mm," I said, feeling sorry for him. "Why don't you file a complaint with the Union for Duppies, Jumbees, and Mendoes? Unions were founded to protect your livelihood, guarantee your continued employment, and give you meaningful existence. Haha! By the way, do not ask me what a *Mendo* is. I do not know, but it happened to be part of the official name of the union. Maybe at one time there were also Mendoes in this area. You, as a Duppy boy - no matter how young you are - you have rights! And when you are at it, you should also demand better education and training for all Duppy boys. Please, take some haunting lessons as well. You are far too clumsy and need shaping up. I am so sorry to say, but you are like so many people on Caribbean islands who work in hospitality; poorly trained and out of shape. How can you support a growing tourist business without well-trained hospitality staff?"

I noticed that my words made a great impact on my young friend, the Duppy boy of Starry Island. He was digesting my advice, word for word. Maybe it was all a bit too much for him; after all, he said that he had not seen a visitor for years.

"Yes, sir," he mumbled. "Once upon a time, my mother told me, people would enter their houses at night, walking in backwards, just to make sure no Duppies sneaked in with them. Those were the heydays for us. That was when we as a Duppy community still carried prestige. And in those times, people would do everything to ward off diseases for which they blamed us Duppies, though we had nothing to do with them.

Did you know that on the islands, men would wear around their neck a few hard red seeds to prevent a sudden rush of blood to the head? And women would wear anything scarlet. No matter how small the slip, it would keep away whooping cough.

They say that on most islands Duppies are disposed to evil, but that is not true. Duppies are also the guardians of folk medicine and health. You can always tell their customers. They wear Jumby beads, little red seeds, very bright, and with a black spot. They are called 'crab eyes' on Barbados.

In Aruba, people believe in the magic forces of the *djuku*. Djuku is a brown, flat seed, with a black rim or a dark pit with a brown stripe. You can find it by the shore after certain winds. It brings health and wealth. The djuku came from the rainforest of the South American mainland. In Aruba, this tree no longer exists, so its fruit is very rare. Locals make necklaces from just one djuku seed on a string. People often give such a necklace as a welcome in their house, but it only brings luck when you find it yourself."

Jumby seeds

"So my foreign friend," said my Duppy boy, in a voice that seemed to say that a divine ceremony was to follow. "Now that I cannot scare you, I will give you a present. Here, I give you a Jumby bead necklace, and I put original scarlet strips on either end. It will protect you from my competition, from Jumbees and Mendoes."

"Thank you, my friend. One more suggestion, as we now both wear Jumby bead necklaces. You have heard of a table of pure gold that lies at the bottom of the riverhead, there where the source of the river comes out of the rocks. In the pond that is immediately at the source, a golden table will rise briefly to the surface from time to time, particularly at midday, affording onlookers a glimpse of its golden beauty. Whoever sees it becomes obsessed. We have witnessed very important Spanish and British men, captains, admirals, and princes, get mesmerized at first glance. But many drown as they try to remove the table of gold from the water, and it was never even possible to dredge their dead bodies from the waters. The golden table, Duppy boy, is the most dangerous. So, my dear friend, let this be a warning. There is never only gold in a pot at the end of the rainbow, or at the source of a river. With gold comes risk, great risk. And, what can you do with gold? You cannot even eat it for breakfast."

I went back to my boat. My Duppy boy and I embraced, wishing each other luck. Either as a malevolent or benevolent spirit, I did not hold high hopes for the boy's future career. But I did wear his magic beads for a very long time until they fell apart, and I never had whooping cough.

Back on board, it was time for my share of Duppy rum. Caribbean legend has it that between the islands, Duppy spirits steal the best rum, their so-called *Duppy share*.

Just like Anansi the spider, Duppies came with slave transports from Africa, from the Bantu folklore and, according to others, from the Ashanti people, which is more likely. Duppies can be a person, an animal or just a ghost of a dead person. Nothing could take the ghosts away from the Africans.

On one of the islands, I asked a lady who came to the boat with her 11-year-old boy to do my laundry why the child was not in school. She told me that a Duppy had attacked her son for no reason whatsoever. Immediately after the incident, while the kid still had blood on his face, she took the boy to church, but even there the Duppy followed them, and the poor child had to run for his life. Then she called the police, who told her that they had caught the Duppy. But she never saw him, and the Duppy never had to appear in court in front of a judge. She was convinced that the Duppy had taken the body of the policeman. Now, her boy did not dare to go to school any longer, afraid that the Duppy would break loose from the policeman's body and attack him again. Many children on Caribbean islands do not go to school, and many will tell you that Duppy attacks are the reason why.

The Jamaican reggae musician Bob Marley complained about the many hangers-on in his life and, once he acquired fame, he called them Duppies. One day he wrote the song *Duppy Conqueror*. I hummed the lyrics while Marley's reggae echoed over the water of the sheltered cove.

Duppy share rum

Duppy share rum is marketed as a big, bold, 3-year-old, 100-percent-pot, still-Jamaican rum, followed by smooth, 5-year-old Barbadian rum, giving it a warm, buttery finish. It comes distilled by the fourth generation of rum masters. The spirits are aged in American bourbon oak barrels, blended in Amsterdam, and bottled in London.

6 PORT ROYAL

Both opponents and advocates of so-called 'forced trade' declared the town's fortune had the dubious distinction of being founded entirely on the servicing of the privateers' needs and highly lucrative trade in prize commodities. - Nuala Zahedieh, lecture at the University of Edinburgh on Port Royal

In 1661, pirate governor Henry Morgan granted forty new licenses for taverns, to cater to every need of Blackbeard's men. They came to Port Royal, Jamaica, the Sodom and Gomorra of the Caribbean, to spend their stolen riches. The wickedest city in the New World, as the Jamaican tourist board now calls it, was hardly discernible from the ocean as I approached the end of the Palisadoes, at the mouth of Kingston Harbor, in southeastern Jamaica.

Earthquake

With the light winds, it took a few days before I, accompanied by my ghosts, reached the sunken port. Most of the town was built on a narrow peninsula, a sliver of land stretching from Kingston into the ocean, and had disappeared into the sea during a devastating earthquake on June 7, 1692. The story goes that at 11:43 in the morning, about two-thirds of the peninsula broke off and slid into the ocean.

Port Royal, Jamaica, before the earthquake of 1692, artist unknown, print, project Gutenberg 2010

The fracture marked the boundary between two tectonic plates, the Caribbean plate and the Gonâve micro-plate, but to many it was the dividing line between what evil God could possibly condone, and what had to be punished and destroyed.

Wild whirlpools of the ensuing tsunami swallowed up the rest of the town and at least 2,000 people. Another 3,000 were lost from injuries and disease in the days that followed.

This most wicked and sinful city of the Caribbean was famous the world over for its rum, the total blackout Kill Devil Rum. Its residents were pirates, cutthroats, and prostitutes. Not only was it a free harbor for loot and treasure, but also a playground for vile companions, full of debauchery.

Nearly 6,500 people lived in Port Royal in the 17th century. In addition to prostitutes and buccaneers, there were four goldsmiths, forty-four tavern keepers, and a variety of artisans and merchants who lived in 2,000 buildings, crammed into fifty-one acres (21 ha) of real estate. More than 200 ships visited Port Royal every year.

A local custom for visiting pirates was to put a pipe-of-rum in the middle of the street. Every passer-by would be obliged to drink from it. A pipe was half a ton, or 1,008 pints. Patrons of Port Royal were mostly big spenders. They were known to sometimes spend 2,000 or 3,000 *pieces-*

of-eight in one night. A *piece-of-eight* was a Spanish silver dollar, equivalent to eight reals, and used throughout the Caribbean as currency. In today's market, a piece-of-eight coin is worth much more than a dollar. The price of silver has increased considerably since the days when pieces-of-eight were used as currency.

One story goes that a pirate gave a strumpet, a harlot, 500 Spanish dollars just to see her naked. Another legend has it that animals were partaking in debauchery. Even the most respectable Jan van Riebeeck, a Dutch VOC explorer and founder of Cape Town in the mid-17th century, was so impressed by the *Dance d'Animaux* in the taverns that he mentioned it in his ship's log. He wrote:

The parrots of Port Royal gather to drink from the large stocks of ale with just as much alacrity as the drunks that frequent the bars that serve it.

Another story tells how Edward Thatch, alias Blackbeard, met a howler monkey while drinking in a Port Royal alehouse. He named the animal 'Jefferson'. The animal became his mascot for life, and even today, Blackbeard's movie alternates carry a monkey on their shoulder.

The taverns of Port Royal poured rum like water, powerful stuff prepared at the local sugarcane plantations by thousands of slaves. At times, the town boasted of having one drinking house for every ten residents.

Wine and women could drain pirates' deep pockets for all its gold and silver overnight; some of them, once thrown out of the tavern into the gutter, were instantly reduced to beggary. Staggering drunks and slaphappy drifters, eager to pull a cutlass and stab the next man in the street, became the image of Port Royal.

In 1687, Jamaica passed anti-piracy laws, and the city's reputation changed. Selling slaves instead of being a center of libidinous corruption became the new business of Port Royal, still a human hellhole.

The city became noted for its Gallows' Point. Dead bodies of pirates dangled on the rack, with new ones being added every day. Only the famous female pirate Mary Read seems to have escaped the gallows by dying prematurely in the Jamaican prison of Port Royal.

With the earthquake one of the busiest and wealthiest ports in the West Indies had vanished forever. Efforts to rebuild it and to rescue its treasures from the seafloor failed. Sodom and Gomorra were never rebuilt and neither was Port Royal, and so things will remain according to the faithful who believe that the earthquake was an act of God, an act of divine retribution.

Earthquake at Port Royal in Jamaica, artist unknown, print, 17th century

Hearse tour around Port Royal

A local Port Royal Duppy boy showed me around the cemetery and the fort at midnight. My ghostly visitor was invited to come along. I stuck Anansi in a corner.

When the bell rang midnight, the call of a Duppy boy echoed over the bay: "Avast there, shipmate, welcome to the wickedest city on earth, you will never find a more wretched hive of scum and villainy anywhere else in the Caribee, what say you drop anchor and explore? I will be your guide. You need a pair of wheels to get around. I got you a hearse and a donkey, a solid rig that gave many old-timers their last ride. Hop on, and we are off."

Van der Decken, the experienced corpse he was, nestled comfortably in the padded coffin of the donkey-drawn hearse. The hearse was elaborate, with canons as pillars at all four corners, six open windows with crossed muskets and different military coats-of-arms, rather a catafalque, once used to carry off powerful generals and politicians to their last resting places.

I sat on the box alone, balancing my feet on the dashboard. The coach driver's seat remained empty. The donkey knew his route around the cemetery and the remains of the city fort.

Our royal Duppy boy, always carefully hiding in the dark, phased in and out at every stop. As already stated, most of Port Royal had slid into the ocean with the earthquake of 1692. What was left was the good part, but it was not much more than the remnants of the old fort and a few streets with barracks.

"The earthquake, sir, was divine retribution. God's wrath for the town's wicked ways," mumbled our Duppy boy in the dark.

Duppy boy's tour was full of ghost stories about treacherous buccaneers, rape, opportunistic prostitutes, and ruthless, bloodthirsty pirates.

Many schools in Florida feature a buccaneer or pirate as their mascot, something hard to believe in a country where morality is held in such high esteem. Buccaneers were the living sin of those days; murderous rapists and plunderers, immoral villains with a vile lifestyle. The ignorance and stupidity of school administrators is often overwhelming.

Van der Decken got excited for a moment when he heard about Blackbeard. The mentality of VOC commanders excluded opportunism for private gain. Cuts of any loot were received by contract, and that was sufficient. Blackbeard's greediness was not in accordance with Van der Decken's VOC ethics.

Van der Decken sat straight up in his coffin as he started his exposé. With a booming voice, he narrated his own VOC history, "Even after the VOC moved their headquarters to Jakarta, in 1613, many servants of the VOC continued to be a moral embarrassment. Maybe only incompetent people were sent to the Indies, who by their carelessness, drunkenness, and life of debauchery spoiled the best opportunities. A contract was written, first and foremost a moral one, to keep in check VOC drunkards, prone to street fighting and adultery. The company ordered that every trading station was to have one or more *dominees*, pastors. Attending Sunday services became compulsory."

"You are right, Captain," I said. "No matter on what side of the world you were in those days, settlers and adventurers had no manners, and morals were foreign to them. Sodom and Gomorra were everywhere. Human rights were only formulated by the United Nations in 1948. For many respect did not exist; others were not considered human beings, let alone given any rights."

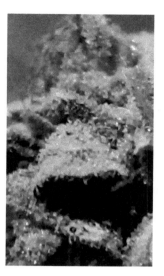

Ganja, Jamaica weed - Cannabis pictures Wikimedia, 2015

Ganja

"Tell me, Duppy boy, with all that money stolen by pirates, have they not established anything of lasting value? Was their pleasure only super consumption in the filthiest thinkable fashion? Where are the pirates' achievements of a philosophy of freedom and culture?"

"Did you say 'philosophy', sir?"

Our Duppy boy chuckled and was clearly affronted by my mentioning that word. He bit back with mockery, "Yes, sir, the philosophy of situational ethics and instant gratification were invented here! Haha!"

Suddenly, his voice cracked and became that of an ancient and wise Duppy. His message sounded like a eulogy and tore through the night, "You see, sir, nobody wanted to think about tomorrow; you could be dead. Even today, most descendants living on the Caribbean islands have a hard time thinking about tomorrow. Their motto is drink, party, get stoned, and enjoy the night. Tomorrow does not exist."

Duppy boy fell silent for a while and a thick midnight air saturated with night jasmine inebriated us. Then Duppy boy spoke thoughtfully as if he were talking to himself, "When worries about life become too much, we also have *ganja*, sir, the divine weed. This wonder wildflower was named after the city Gyandzha, founded by an Arab governor who had an apparition. A *Jinni*, a Muslim Duppy, told the governor where to find a treasure, and thus, he built a city in Azerbaijan. Its divine produce became the Mecca of our rescue. Ganja, the heavenly blessing, lifts us out of our sorrows and worries.

Yes, sir, ganja became our rescue. Ganja inspiration will build our lasting treasure and the Kingdom of Jah for eternity. That is why we are now in the birthplace of a new religion. That is the legacy of the pirates. They created fertile grounds for what you call philosophy."

Sarcastically, I responded, "It must be a strange coincidence to have the *Kingdom of Eternity* founded on the moral scrapheap of Port Royal, the definitive center of gross opportunism and sin."

"No, sir, there are no coincidences in this life. It was all written before. Yes, redemption, redemption! This Port Royal will be Babylon, but first, we have to go back to Ethiopia, to the promised land of Zion. An incarnation of Jah on earth arrived there in 1930, the Second Coming of Jesus of Nazareth. His name is Haile Selassie, our living God. The crowning of Haile Selassie as Emperor of Ethiopia fulfilled a biblical prophecy. Before his coronation, Emperor Haile Selassie was Ras Tafari, King Tafari of Harar, Ethiopia, and that is why many call themselves Ras Tafarians."

Our donkey-drawn wagon had come to a standstill. Before Duppy boy disappeared into the dark, he said, "Tomorrow night, I make sure you go and attend our Groundation, sir, with music, chanting, discussions, and the divine smoking of ganja as a sacrament."

Diving Port Royal

The sunken city of Port Royal lies just off the coast from the little village that remained after the earthquake. A dive required special permits which local authorities happily issued. Joined by a few underwater archeologists, I explored the remains.

The vastness was overwhelming. Many structures were still together, like assembled buildings, even after being underwater for 400 years. Others were strewn all over the ocean floor as the ravaged toys of a child after a tantrum. Layers of encrustation by shells, coral, and baked salt made droopy plasterwork, a macabre *mise-en-scene*.

Sharks floated stately along the highways in search of prey. Thousands of colorful fish, schooling in one direction or another or just hanging around in shoals, completed an unmatched spectacle, a true *tableau vivant*. There were no human remains of any kind, but it did not take much imagination to picture the legendary citizens of the British kingdom's cesspool.

Under water pictures of Port Royal

7 GROUNDATION

Groundation Day (April 21), is an important Rastafari holy day and second after Coronation Day (November 2). It is being celebrated to honor Haile Selassie's visit to Jamaica in 1966.

On that very Thursday, hysterical crowds greeted Haile Selassie at the airport in the capital of Kingston. Jamaica's Rastafari population was in a trance, as touched by divine fervor. Some 100,000 Rastafari from all over Jamaica had gathered in ecstasy to see their God descend from his plane. Many mumbled prayers; other smoked ganja, beat calabash drums, lit firecrackers, and sounded *Maroon anbeng* horns.

When Haile Selassie's Ethiopian Airlines flight finally landed at the airport at 1:30 p.m., the crowd broke through the security cordon, stormed out onto the tarmac and surrounded the plane. After about half an hour, the door swung open and the emperor appeared at the top of the steps. A deafening roar from the crowd drowned out the sound of the jet engines.

For a few minutes Selassie waved to the crowd and then stepped back into the plane. Later I learned that the emperor rejected the notion that he was a divine person and the second coming of Jesus Christ. When the emperor did not reappear, Jamaican authorities entered the plane and negotiated the emperor's descent. After about an hour, he came out again.

His Imperial Majesty Emperor Haile Selassie I

Evangelicals

Groundation. The word puzzled me, and ganja as a holy sacrament even more. The drug-of-oblivion always seemed to be a sacrament to the user, Rastafarian or not, at least in regard to the pleasant effects of total forgetfulness. So, in the early morning, I reached out to my African spider friend who'd already smoked a joint. Van der Decken I left alone in his happy memories after his VOC sermon on morality.

"Anansi, please tell me, is your Akan family Christian now Catholic or Protestant? Here in Jamaica, there are almost no Catholics; all have become Protestants, Protestants of the second reformation, Evangelicals."

"How, sir? I Kwaku Anansi, son of Nyame. Sky-God of the Akan in Ashanti land. Sky-God knows, sees everything. That is my father, so, no other God."

"Yes, that makes a lot of sense, but most Africans in the Caribbean have become fanatic Evangelicals. They also practice Voodoo, and here in Jamaica they gave birth to a new religion, Rastafarianism. They made their interpretation of the truth their homemade gospel. Protestantism nowadays means individualism, you and your relation to your god. It is also the basis for individualism, equal representation through democracy in island governments, and a level playing field for entrepreneurs."

"Nyame, sir, Sky-God of Akan. No discussion. He is what he is. Everything he said is the truth. We all his slaves."

"Anansi, the western world sank over one trillion dollars in foreign aid into Africa over the last few decennia and it appears to have been a waste. Poverty is prevalent wherever you go and disease is everywhere. A small super-rich elite takes advantage. Corruption rules. In Africa, the feudal system is still firmly in place. Most people, especially in the agricultural regions, are still slaves. That means that Africans have central hierarchical societies, much like the Catholics. And these systems tend to be highly corrupted. People have no rights, and options are to be purchased with lavish donations. Corruption in Africa is so widespread that it threatens the continued existence of many economies. Protestants reject bribery and corruption, dismiss any hierarchies of power, and respect every man's rights. That part must appeal to Africans. Here in Jamaica, there is a Protestant church at every corner of every street."

"What difference, sir? Yes, for sure people adopt Gods of masters, especially slaves in new world. Slaves looked for an escape, new Gods. You call this chance of religion Stockholm syndrome - in modern lingo? Haha!"

"But Anansi, the continent of Africa has become the largest Christian community in the world. Most of Africa's faithful today are disciples of that second reformation, Evangelicals. Evangelicals, in a way, are mystics rather than dogmatic fanatics. They experience the truth by intuition but are unable to argue the theological details."

"You got it, sir. Evangelicals very practical, do whatever needs to be done. Meantime, always loyal to Nyame."

"So, you claim that African Caribbeans avoid the debate. They are not interested in the correct exegesis of Scripture, like the Protestants of the first reformation were. Not so much for religious reasons but to have enough space for their ancestral deities. Reborn Christians and Akan Nyame followers can all proselytize together and say, *God is love, and we are his flower-power.*"

Downpressor

The next night, a Johnny Depp look-alike with a dreadlock-framed face appeared at the docks and yelled, "Hey you, you need Downpressor to take you to Groundations?"

"Anansi, who is this? What does this guy want?"

Anansi was hanging in his hammock, puffing a fat joint. Not a sensible word would come out of his mouth for a while. What can you expect from a spider, even a metaphorical spider, when it comes to being the conscience of millions?

It's a humpy, dumpy, bumpy, rocky road, sang the Downpressor.

> *Rain, or sunshine on life's rocky road,*
> *It's a humpy Groundation.*
> *Lord them say, all they know.*
> *Love and see, as they row.*
> *A living God is 'just'*
> *In this one Black Downpressor,*
> *A man from the Land called Zion,*
> *With an Amharic-Christian name,*
> *The name of the Holy Trinity.*
> *Haile Selassie is His name.*
> *The Black, Black Reggae music*
> *Is a message from This Man.*

Rastafarianism

At dusk, I sped through the lands, clinging to Downpressor for safety on the back seat of his ramshackle motorcycle, spitting thunder and fire like a rocket. We were off to my first Groundation ceremony. We stopped at a little snack bar along the road so I could catch my breath.

"I am Naphtali," explained the young man. "My root is Akan. Ours is the story of Scripture, the twelve tribes of Israel. We together are the

65

Rastafarian religious group and make up the *Mansions*. In the book of John 14:2 we read, *In my Father's house are many mansions.* Mansions of Rastafarian are of the Bobo Ashanti, the Niyabinghi, the twelve tribes of Israel, and several smaller groups like African Unity, Covenant Rastafari, Messianic Dreads, and the Selassie Church.

Like in Protestantism, we have a deep distrust of institutionalism shared by many. Haile Selassie taught that faith is private and a direct relationship with the deity. It requires no intermediary. How much dreadlocks, vegetarian diet, and ganja smoking a Rasta follower puts into his life is entirely up to that person. This is in keeping with the principle of freedom of conscience.

Each member belongs to one of the twelve tribes, determined by the Gregorian birth month, represented by a color, a part of the body, and a character trait often called 'the faculty'. We all descend from the migrations of Hebrew Israelites throughout the continent of Africa, with West Africa being the starting place for the transatlantic slave trade."

Assyrians of the 8th century BCE exiled ten out of the original twelve Hebrew tribes, according to the biblical text. Exiling conquered tribes is what the Assyrian Empire did to maintain control and exercise power, not only with the Hebrew Israelites but with all tribes.

The belief that American tribes and Afro-Americans descended from the Hebrews, or the ten lost tribes, has grown ever since the 1930 elevation of Ras Tafari to emperor. Mormons also claim such roots. It must be that the desire to belong to a selected group of divinely chosen ones, a holy family, overcomes all reason and historical facts.

Groundation celebration

Groundation Day is a grand feast commemorating and celebrating Haile Selassie's first visit.

In Addis Ababa, on November 1, 2000, I had attended the re-interment of Ethiopia's last emperor, Haile Selassie. The grand ceremony had taken place twenty-five years after the death of the emperor under mysterious circumstances, despite objections from Rastafarians who claimed that he was not dead, but living in suspension. For them, he was the living reincarnation of Jesus. Selassie's family maintained that he was smothered with a pillow by military dictator Mengistu himself.

The story goes that for years Selassie's bones had remained somewhere in the old imperial palace of Addis in a box marked 'Do not open'. Finally, they were discovered and re-buried in the family tomb.

Seventy years after the young king, as Ras Tafari, had stood on the podium for the world to see him crowned Emperor of Ethiopia, another grand ceremony saw him to his final resting place, in the imperial tomb next to the empress.

About one million onlookers gazed in silence at the procession as it moved slowly from church to church, to finally finish at the Addis Ababa Holy Trinity Cathedral. Priests in lavish robes, elderly warriors with lions' manes on their heads, and dread-locked Rastafarians joined the funeral procession. I stood next to the tomb when his casket was lowered into the vault by muscled monks. Ethiopia's last emperor, Haile Selassie, had finally been laid to rest.

The Groundation I attended was hardly a religious ceremony. The party was on a small, bare plot in a sugarcane field. The venue quickly filled up with a ganja-smoking congregation. The heavy, acrid smell of burning hemp filled the air and made me cough. People were out for a celebration.

A touch of religion came with black-veiled priests, wrapped in thick smoldering clouds, who mumbled something unintelligently, probably about fate and the future. One blew smoke onto a pregnant lady's protruding belly as a blessing for the unborn. Another slaughtered a chicken and sprinkled the blood around. A haze made the air even thicker and concealed the moon.

A slow root-reggae wailed through the night; musicians showing off their locks, some as long as they were tall. Percussion instruments purred softly, and bass guitars sang songs of melancholy.

I was the invisible white man, an intruder with Naphtali, my Downpressor. Agitated after an altercation with what looked like an alderman, and fearing for my safety, Naphtali whisked me away after a while. With shock and disbelief, I noticed that he had tucked a gun into his jeans belt. I never found out what was at stake. Being white must have been the wrong thing.

In the pitch-black, we rode Naphtali's motorcycle up an endless winding path, up the mountain slope to a yellow brick road, towards safety in a mountain cabin.

Maroons

The next morning, I woke up to the cool air of the Blue Mountains. A thick carpet of jungle covered the peaks, exuding a blue haze and accompanied by a cacophony of bird cries and monkey calls. Gazing out into the sky of steep mountain slopes, a double rainbow bridged the valley. The cool air made my skin crawl, and I pulled the comforter a bit closer. Someone had lit a wood fire in the stone hearth and put out a can of coffee with biscuits. The aroma filled the air.

Blue and John Crow Mountains National Park, Jamaica

Most Ethiopian Jews, the *Falashas*, lived in an area around Lake Tana in the Gondar region of Ethiopia, among the tribes of Wolqayit, Shire, Tselemt, Dembia, Segelt, Quara, and Belesa.

I had coffee with them, roasted over hot coals. Happy, golden memories filled me, even without ganja. Not a person was in sight. Up in those mountains I was in heaven, quite a change from the paradise down at the beaches.

Cudjoe

Plantation slavery dominated Jamaica's economy for hundreds of years. Many run-aways, Maroons, escaped to these mountains to live in freedom. They built their economy with Blue Mountain coffee some 2,000-5,000 feet above sea level. One little swig would make you sit straight in seconds. After a little walk down some steep stairs, I reached the village of my improvised stay. Preparations for a celebration were in full swing. The festival was to honor their hero, Captain Quao, "The Invisible Hunter".

In 1655, the British conquered much of Jamaica, forcing the Spanish to flee to the northern coast. Vast numbers of Spanish slaves took this opportunity to join the Maroons in the hills. At first, Maroon resistance impeded British efforts to drive the Spaniards from Jamaica, prompting one Spanish commander to conclude that the Maroons were loyal to the Spanish crown.

But that was hardly true. By 1660, the last Spanish rulers had fled for Cuba. Maroon leader Lubolo served the British governor as a colonel, and as a collaborator brought Maroon factions under British rule. A few years later, another Maroon faction, led by Juan de Serras, ambushed and killed Lubolo. That bloodbath marked the beginning of an 80-year guerrilla war with the British. The Maroon mountain fortresses were too well defended for the British to take over. Gradually what had started as a rebellion and a guerrilla war developed into full-fledged fighting, with endless and senseless killing. Captain Quao became the leader of the Windward Maroons, while Cudjoe led the Leeward Maroons. Cudjoe was a Maroon leader at the time of Queen Nanny.

The legendary Queen Nanny was an 18th-century leader of all Maroons. The folktale says that she was born into the Ashanti tribe in what is today Ghana, and escaped from slavery after being transported to Jamaica.

Cudjoe had the reputation of being the greatest of the Maroon leaders, but also the bloodiest; he could never be a man of peace. That part was reserved for Quao.

Thus, it had been Quao, the hero and wise old man, who signed the Windward Peace Treaty, on June 23, 1739, that ended a ten-year war with the British. Quao brought peace and independence to the Maroons. Even today, they seem to care little for the government of Jamaica.

Charles Town on the Buff Bay River and Scotts Hall, both famous Maroon towns, would soon explode with the sound of drums, and the rapid taps of dancing feet, celebrating Quao's victory.

That evening, with my new friends, I gorged on jerk chicken. It is said that jerk chicken stems from the time the Maroons brought African techniques for cooking meat to Jamaica, which were then combined with native island seasoning and ingredients. The word *jerk* may have its roots in *charqui*, a Spanish word for dry meat, or it may derive from *jerking*, or poking holes in the meat to hold spices before cooking.

Jerk chicken

Instructions

Clean, skin, and cut chicken into medium pieces,
then wash with lime or lemon juice.
Rub the chicken with the jerk seasoning
Be sure to rub under the skin and in cavities.
Marinate overnight.
Grill at the lowest possible setting over a low fire until done.
Pimento, allspice, branches - this is what is used in Jamaica, mixed with charcoal.
If not available, try to use an aromatic wood when barbecuing to enhance the flavor.
Chop the meat into pieces.
Serve traditional-style with hard-dough bread.

Only when a barefooted, large lady danced in trance with intensive shivering and shaking, and a priest mumbled a vocation, the spirituality of the séance dawned on me. Meals always have something religious in them.

Here in the Blue Mountains of Jamaica it was something of a Last Supper adapted for the jungle.

8 A KING

"The trial cannot proceed," said the King in a very grave voice,
"until all the jurymen are back in their proper places, all," he
repeated with great emphasis, looking hard at Alice as he said so.
- *Alice in Wonderland*, by Charles Lutwidge Dudgson

All emperors, kings, and queens of the Caribbean are dead, most
brutally murdered or replaced by presidents. There are still ten
constitutional monarchies in the Caribbean. The sovereign inherits his
or her office, usually keeping it until death or abdication, and is bound
by laws and customs in the exercise of power. Ten of these monarchies
are independent states but share Queen Elizabeth II, though she resides
primarily in the United Kingdom.

None of the monarchies in the Americas have a permanent resident
monarch. Queen Elizabeth II is the sovereign queen of the monarchies
of Antigua and Barbuda, Barbados, Belize, Grenada, Jamaica, St. Kitts
and Nevis, St. Lucia, St. Vincent, and the Grenadines.
Anguilla, Bermuda, the British Virgin Islands, the Cayman
Islands, Montserrat, and the Turks and Caicos Islands are British
territories, and also have Queen Elizabeth II as head of state.

Curaçao and St. Maarten are constituent countries of the Kingdom of the Netherlands, and thus have King Willem-Alexander as their sovereign, as well as the remaining islands forming the Caribbean Netherlands, B.E.S., Bonaire, St. Eustatius, and Saba.

Amongst the countless uninhabited islands in the Caribbean archipelago are still islands with castaways; they lived on and on. On one such little island in the Caribbean there was a king. The king lived all alone, so I decided to pay him a visit.

The island was the perfect *Blue Lagoon* fantasy island for young lovers, with white sandy beaches, dense jungle, and a steep volcano beset with thousands of wild orchids and screaming colorful birds. Crystal-clear water surrounded the island, with an abundance of coral at the sea bottom on display. Remarkable were patches of mango trees in the gorges, almost large enough to be called mango groves. The ear-piercing trumpeting of a large number of peacocks filled the air.

There were no beacons of any kind, no port, no landing docks, or dockyards, and not even a bonfire. The shore did not look very welcoming. Someone told me about a protected cove, directly next to a rock formation with big old tree on top. Once I spotted the natural marker, I anchored, sheltered from wind and waves.

Commander of the Order of Two Mangoes

There was not much else on the island but the king's palatial, one-room building, surrounded by the royal gardens. Two thrones stood on a platform, the Seat of the Sovereign Island State for the king, and another for his royal consort. From the wide open doors, once guarded by lackeys, the public could observe the king seated on his throne wearing stately regalia. The public and lackeys have long left the island, but the sight was still majestic.

A scarlet red cloak with an ermine border was artfully draped around the elevated platform. His Highness wore a diamond-studded golden crown on his little head, and held a two-feet-long golden scepter in his right hand. In his other hand, he held the famous Globus Cruciger, a golden orb with a cross and studded with emeralds, sapphires, rubies, diamonds, and lapis lazuli. The king's love for precious stones and gold could not be mistaken.

His Majesty was a man of modest posture but bore all the fine features of nobility. He looked as if he had shrunken somewhat over the years. Whatever he was wearing looked two sizes too large and appeared to demean him.

"I command you to approach and kneel," spoke the king when I entered his grand audience hall.

Sire is the most respectful form of address for reigning kings in Europe, so I directed myself to him with that most honorable title.

"Yes, sire, of course, but I am not your subject," I informed him politely, silently objecting to the king's pompousness.

"All people are my subjects since I am the king. And now I order you to rise again, and rise you will as Commander of the Order of Two Mangoes."

"Oh, Your Majesty, thank you. You are very generous. Are you sure that you want to elevate me to Commander of the Order of Two Mangoes and not just One?"

"I have spoken, and my word is the law. I am a benevolent ruler, beloved by all my subjects. The mango is the most important fruit on my island. To have you as a recipient of the Order of Two Mangoes is a great privilege."

"But sire, you are the only person on this island. Who are your subjects?" I muttered with surprise.

The king stared back as if he had heard something that was totally new to him. "Everybody is my subject since I am the king, and all will obey my command. Herewith, I command that the sun will set today at six o'clock and twelve minutes. And I command you to witness the event so that you can attest and, if necessary, testify to my glory as to the absolute loyalty and obedience of all my subjects, even the sun."

I smiled, noticing that the king had quickly peeked into a big book giving the times for sunrise and sunset. What if he had picked out the wrong time?

"I read your mind," the king said. "If I command evil and wrong things, subjects will not be obedient. I was trained from my very birth never to command wrong things so that I could rule in perpetuity."

With the ceremonial pretentiousness behind us, it was time to come to business.

"Sire, I was told that thieves come to your island in the night and steal precious golden mango fruits from your royal gardens. As a Commander of the Order of Two Mangoes, it is my duty to report this to you."

"That is scandalous!" shouted the king, upsetting the formality of the royal audience. "We should do everything possible to catch the rascals, put them in jail, and then hang them from the highest tree on the island, so all passersby can see how we treat criminals. After all, we are a nation of law and order."

"Very well, sire, but the abundance of mangoes in your royal gardens is so great that you could never eat them all yourself. It does not hurt anyone when you close your eyes a bit and allow hungry kids of neighboring islanders to steal them. Your Majesty, think of the pleasure it would bring to their little children to have a belly full of your golden sweetness! But if Your Majesty insists on prosecution for theft or even persecution for corrupting children's minds, how do you suggest we catch the thieves?"

"Hm, that I do not know, but I order you to form a committee, study the options, and report back to my cabinet. My prime minister will eventually present me with a bill for signature."

"But sire, it could take quite a long time before Your Majesty will be able to form a cabinet since you have no people on the island. May I be allowed to present you directly with just a personal petition?"

"Yes," nodded the king, and he waved his hand as a sign that it was time to depart.

Sticking to protocol, I trod backward, out of the audience hall, and could not help but think that being a king on a little island had to be a very exhausting occupation, especially without subjects and a staff.

Pòpchi di breu, a tar doll

Back on the boat, I consulted with my dear Anansi, whose family were all farmers at one time. Maybe he had some experience in rural matters and could make some suggestions. Also, Anansi should know all about poor free slave families who tried to feed themselves. Isn't it true that the ethics of filling your family's belly go far beyond those of property rights?

After I explained the situation, Anansi giggled and said, "Pòpchi di breu, a tar doll. Everybody knows the story. Me feeding my hungry children. An African king tricked me. Many cinnamon apples and mangoes in king's garden. Fruit for my hungry children. That king, smart cookie, put a fake guard, straw with tar, in fruit gardens. Yes, got caught. Very dark night. Me and soldier, straw tar doll collision. Tar all over. Next morning, police catch me. Court Judge, me hanging. Escape jail. Hole in ground. Shia Maria, my wife, dug tunnel. Runaway! Stowaway on a slave boat. Bad luck!"

"Brilliant, Anansi. I will advise the king to put out a sticky straw watchman, as you suggested. And the king should reward you for your valuable counsel with a very special gift. He should give you a sack full of mangoes, and since I am a most Honorable Commander of the Order of Two Mangoes, I am sure he will listen to me."

The king liked the plan and instructed me to file a petition so he could study the plan and rule on it.

On my way back to the boat, I remembered that it had been Anansi who had told me that thieves were stealing mangoes on the king's island. How could Anansi know about thieves since no one lived on the island and could have told him?

It dawned on me that the smart little Spiderman was taking us all for a ride. Anansi was a trickster. I had to outsmart him, so I dinghied back to the island and had a very private conversation with the Queen of Bees. She agreed to my secret proposal and instructed thousands of her worker bees accordingly.

Trial

The next day Anansi was hiding in his web in my cockpit. He claimed that a swarm of wild bees had tried to kill him.

"But Anansi, bees do not like to eat spiders and why would these hard-working bees try to kill you?"

As I was quizzing Anansi, a fresh swarm of bees flew low across the water, caught my Anansi by all his arms and legs, bundled him up, and took him away.

As fast as I could, I made it ashore and went to the palace just in time to witness the royal court in session, with His Majesty presiding.

Anansi was cuffed in the docket of the accused.

"Anansi, you stand accused of stealing the royal mangoes last night," spoke the king-judge. "The worker bees discovered you this morning since sweet jam was spread over paths and fruit trees, and you were sticky. What do you have to say in your defense?"

"Your Majesty, Honorable merciful judge. You right. Mango so sweet, very sweet. Royal mango best. Before, tar doll night guard, I arrested. Next morning, me full tar. Me, worthless, Sire, glutinous scoundrel. Me liar, imposter. Confess, made up story. No thieves in Royal Gardens. Just tricky me. Please, Sire. Punish hard please. Hang from the highest tree on island. Everybody see me hang in tree. Sire, you benevolent. Sire, you compassionate. Sire, please request."

"Please, speak man," hollered the king-judge. "What is your final wish?"

Anansi, with tears in his eyes, whispered shyly, "Sire, you my hangman. Please, you with me to tree. You hang me. A big honor for me thief."

"Without any hesitation," the king ruled. "Petition granted, execution to be carried out at sundown."

The highest tree was out on the cliffs overlooking the bay where my boat was anchored.

At sunset, a parade approached the natural gallows. The king, dressed in full regalia, led the parade, and the prisoner, encased in a swarm of worker bees, followed.

Escape

The king and Anansi slowly climbed the tree of execution. Each stride was taken with great dignity. Many breaks were necessary because the king was out of shape. He had not climbed a tree since boyhood. After nearly an hour, they reached for the highest branch. Once they arrived at the place of execution, the king solemnly read out the verdict and greeted the prisoner.

Then Anansi crawled to the end of the top branch and without any further notice, jumped down on a long silken thread, like on a bungee cord. He dangled for a while until the wind got hold of him and blew him over to the topmast of my ship.

While the king was crying foul on top of the tree, we sailed into the sunset, away from the island where nobody lived but a king who was too greedy to share his abundance with hungry children.

The king and his attitude were just an example of the kings and emperors we were about to meet in the Empire of Haïti. They never cared for the poor but themselves indulged in super consumption.

"Anansi!" I yelled up the mast. "You are a true scoundrel, but a smart one."

Local Caribbean fish

That evening, I slaved in the galley for hours to prepare a local Caribbean fish with mango salsa, adding in Zatarain's Caribbean Rice®, and ½ red bell pepper and ¼ cup of fresh pineapple.

For additional taste, add:
1 tbsp. paprika
2 tsp. curry powder
2 tsp. ground cumin
1 ½ tsp. ground allspice
1 tsp. ground ginger
1 tsp. ground coriander
3/4 tsp. salt
½ tsp. freshly ground black pepper
¼ tsp. ground fennel seeds (optional)
1/8 tsp. cayenne pepper (optional)

Mango salsa
1 mango, peeled, seeded, and diced
1 cup chopped, fresh pineapple
½ red bell pepper, chopped
½ cup black beans, rinsed and drained (optional)
½ red onion, finely chopped
3 tbsp. chopped fresh cilantro
3 tbsp. fresh lime juice
1 egg
1/3 cup milk
1 cup panko bread crumbs
1 tbsp. dried unsweetened coconut, or to taste (optional)
1 tbsp. olive oil, or as needed
5 (4 oz.) fillets tilapia

Mix together the paprika, curry powder, cumin, allspice, ginger, coriander, salt, black pepper, fennel, and cayenne pepper in a bowl. Set the spice mix aside.
In a bowl, carefully toss the mango, pineapple, red bell pepper, black beans, red onion, and cilantro.
Pour lime juice over the mango mixture and toss again.
Cover the bowl and refrigerate at least 30 minutes.
Whisk together the egg and milk in a bowl.
In a separate, shallow bowl, stir together the panko crumbs and the coconut.
Stir about 1 tbsp. of spice mix into panko crumb mixture.

Heat olive oil in a skillet over medium heat.
Dip tilapia fillets into the egg mixture, press gently into the panko crumb mixture to coat both sides of the fillets.
Brush off any loose crumbs and put fillets into the hot oil.
Pan-fry until the fish is opaque inside and golden brown outside, 3 to 5 minutes per side, or as needed.
Serve with mango salsa.

9 PORT-AU-PRINCE, HAÏTI, AND THE EMPERORS

The Governor-General of Haïti, Jean-Jacques Dessalines, created the Empire of Haïti on September 22, 1804. Proclaiming himself Emperor Jacques I, he held his coronation ceremony on October 6. - Public records

---

Research into Jamaica's public records did not produce any Van Keppel or Keppel descendants on Jamaica. Some shipping accounts suggested that some time after 1783, maybe after a brief stay in Jamaica, then still a British colony, they moved to the United States, to Oklahoma City, OK, Kansas City, KS, and Tulsa, OK. I would have to pursue other rulers and aristocracy on the islands - on Haïti, its infamous empire.

Port-au-Prince

I made Port-au-Prince in about a week, after about 260 nautical miles eastward straight from Kingston, still tacking up the wind. Port Royal and Port-au-Prince are sitting on the same fault line; devastating earthquakes are inevitable in both cities, though they may occur hundreds of years apart. Civilizations of all kinds prefer to build their structures on fault lines in earthquake-prone areas. And, from time to time, nature plows under the weeds and people grow their corn all anew.

Port-au-Prince was not named after a particular prince but rather after a vessel called *Le Prince,* under the command of a French pirate, or filibuster, Captain de Saint-André. Port-au-Prince is the capital of Haïti, and Haïti is the western half of the island Hispaniola; the eastern part is now called the Dominican Republic, not to be confused with Dominica. Dominica is part of the Windward Islands in the Lesser Antilles archipelago in the Caribbean Sea.

In the early 1700s, the French and Dutch competed for the leather trade on the Spanish island of Hispaniola since game was plentiful in that region and hides an easy product of nature. Pirate Captain de Saint-André was always cruising up and down in search of ships laden with fresh loads of leather that he could snatch.

The language of Haïti is still of those French and Dutch settlers and traders. Maybe a bit antiquated like any colonial tongue, but it dances around melodiously, at times with a little foreign sidestep like a *pas-de bourrée,* and then again in the perfect harmony of a *pas-de-deux.*

In 2003, UNESCO included the Tumba Francesa version, brought to Cuba by Haïtian slaves, on the List of Safeguarding Oral and Immaterial Heritage of Mankind.

Just taste a little of the melody of the Wongol Poem by Emmanuel Ejen.

Gendele m'rete
M'gade-ou Ayida.
Loloj-mwen vire.
Tet-ou gridap se vre
Men lannuit genle
Domi nan cheve-ou.

Sometimes I stop
I look at you Ayida.
My head spins.
Your hair may be kinky
But the night rests
In its tangles.

Government

Monarchs in the Caribbean may be limited to Queen Elizabeth II and King Willem Alexander, both absentee constitutional rulers, but once the islands swarmed with aristocracy searching for a domain to rule and exploit. Emperor Napoleon of France became an inspiration for many revolutionaries in the French colonies in the early 1800s, especially after the Haïtian Revolution.

The Haïtian Revolution began on August 22, 1791, and ended in 1804. It was the only successful anti-slavery and anti-colonial insurrection that led to the formation of a sovereign state. Self-liberated slaves fought a bloody guerrilla war for years against French colonial rule in Saint-Domingue. They prevailed but at an enormous expense.

The resulting nation remained divided against itself, as a French colony, as an early independent republic, an empire and a kingdom. Today, Haïti is still in constant turmoil due to competing factions that never managed to form workable, effective coalitions.

A contemporary French philosopher, Paul Fregosi (1922-2001), put it as follows:

Whites, mulattos and blacks loathed each other. The poor whites couldn't stand the rich whites, the rich whites despised the poor whites, the middle-class whites were jealous of the aristocratic whites, the whites born in France looked down upon the locally born whites, mulattoes envied the whites, despised the blacks and were despised by the whites; free Negroes brutalized those who were still slaves, Haïtian born blacks regarded those from Africa as savages. Everyone - quite rightly - lived in terror of everyone else. Haïti was hell, but Haïti was rich.

I agree with Fregosi. Yes, Haïti was very rich because of its sugar - the demand for sugar in Europe was enormous. In spite of the horrible Haïtian climate, and devastating yellow fever and malaria that cost the lives of 50 percent of imported slaves, greed prevailed at all times. The French and British transported at least 100,000 African slaves to Haïti to keep up production.

The Haïtian revolution was inevitable. After the enormous bloodshed it was time to set up new governmental structures. The available administrative models for the new rulers were inspired by feudal Africa, and Europe in its early days of enlightenment. The most popular option was to follow the example of Napoleon's new aristocracy, based on eugenics. A new ruling class in Haïti had to be nurtured and put together from genetic blacks only.

This decision was not that strange, no matter how it might look today. Alternative models, all European inventions, like socialism, communism, fascism, National Socialism, and free-market economies came much later, after World War I and II. The French model appealed to rulers around the world, including African leaders. Let me tell you about my encounters with two emperors.

Jean-Bedel Bokassa, 1970s, Wikimedia

Bokassa

Emperor Jean-Bédel Bokassa I of the Central African Republic (CAR) was unbelievably rich. CAR had diamond mines. For his coronation, Bokassa demanded a very large diamond from Mr. Albert Jolis, the president of Diamond Distributors Inc., one of the country's largest diamond-mining corporations.

The diamond had to rival the private jewel collections of other monarchs around the world. Jolis was made to understand that anything smaller than a golf ball would be considered an insult. He not only stood to lose his company's mining concession in Central Africa but also his life. He had no choice but to deliver the diamond. Fortunately for Jolis, the Central African Republic is one of the two places in the world where exceedingly rare black diamonds, called *carbonado*, can be found. However, finding a large black diamond of high quality was very unlikely.

What was available was an imperfect near-diamond, known as a *boart*, a fake diamond. The emperor was not told and believed that his 70-carat, black diamond ring was worth hundreds of thousands of dollars. He loved it, and joyfully showed it off to a room full of his cabinet members. In reality, a black rock worth a mere $140 made the show. Even with the inclusion of a white diamond on top to give it extra sparkle, the ring's worth barely surpassed $500.

In December 1976, Bokassa, president of the Central African Republic, invested himself emperor. In his coronation speech, he referred to his great inspiration; Napoleon I. CAR became the newly-founded Central African Empire. The coronation ceremony in 1977 cost US $20 million ($80 million today) and practically bankrupted the country. His diamond-encrusted crown alone cost $5 million ($20 million today).

In 1995, on a trip to see forest elephants, I took time out from the expedition and visited the former emperor in Bangui, the capital of the Central African Republic, where he had built an enormous cathedral, the Cathédrale Notre-Dame of Our Lady of the Immaculate Conception.

Cathédrale Notre-Dame, Bangui (Central African Republic)

Foreigners were sparse in those days, and my arrival was known days in advance. I circled over the little airfield three times to announce my imminent landing, and allow him a little time to send some cars, drivers, and a military escort. He was dressed in all his finery when I met him in front of the Cathédale. This time the regalia was that of a bishop, but he was humble and very kind, though he was no Jesus about to wash my feet.

For true or fabricated atrocities, the former emperor had been sentenced to death, but the death sentence was later commuted to life imprisonment and commuted again to public service. In 1993, he was freed and became a priest in his Cathédrale.

When I asked him about the exorbitant expense of the construction of a European brick cathedral in the jungle he said, "Building this church was cheaper than five F16s." At that time, an F-16 cost about US $20 million.

Selassie

Ethiopia's Haile Selassie was even grander than Bokassa, especially on the world stage. He inspired Jamaican Rastafarians in their belief that he was a god.

Emperor Haile Selassie I (center) and members of the royal court, photo taken before 1930

On a more mundane level, it was whispered that in the palace yard the emperor kept lions, living symbols of the Lion of Judah, a unique breed with huge manes. Every morning, in a small ceremony, the emperor would come out to feed his lions huge pieces of meat dripping with blood on golden plates.

But Selassie was not only grand, he also had greatness that distinguished him from others. Bob Marley's song with lyrics almost literally derived from a speech made by the Ethiopian emperor before the United Nations General Assembly on October 4, 1963, eternalized the Selassie, the Lion of Judah, as a Messiah of Peace.

Jacques I

But Haïti's Emperor Jacques I was the most remarkable sovereign of them all, as he took after his great idol, the Sun King, King Louis XIV of France, the oppressor and slave-trader king.

Dessalines holding a severed head of a white woman, artist unknown, print, 1806

In 1804, about one hundred years after Captain de Saint-André established the safe harbor of Port-au-Prince, Jean-Jacques Dessalines, Toussaint Louverture's principal lieutenant, became the new black leader in a country that would eventually occupy most of the island of Hispaniola.

Inspired by the French Revolution, Jean-Jacques ordered the massacre of the entire white French-Haïtian minority, which he equated with the corrupt French aristocracy. Ethnic cleansing was an essential part of Napoleon's strategy.

In cold blood, he slaughtered about 5,000 French colonists and their mulatto servants. With corpses still dangling from the trees, Jean-

Jacques proudly decreed Haïti an all-black nation and prohibited whites from owning property or land.

His symbolic act did not solve the dire economic situation. The island was affluent thanks to its sugar plantations, but the vast former slave population remained penniless. Quickly, a small black nobility formed around the new leaders. They seized all wealth without delay.

Like Bokassa two hundred years later, Jean-Jacques Dessalines was looking to Napoleon I and proclaimed himself Emperor Jacques I of the Haïtian Empire.

He and his newly-created aristocracy of princes, dukes, barons and counts lived a splendid life of leisure and luxury, paid for by the sugar. Hundreds of thousands of slaves toiled daily and more than half of them died. It could not last.

Emperor Jacques I and Empress Marie-Claire Heureuse Félicité of Haïti had but a brief reprieve from violence. In 1806, competing negro rebels assassinated the emperor in an ambush.

Henri I, with the somewhat more humble title of king, succeeded Jean-Jacques and a bit later Emperor Faustin I succeeded Henri.

The social divide remained, as a limerick of those days sarcastically points out:

> *Nèg rich se milat,*
> *milat pov se nèg.*

> *A rich Negro is a mulatto,*
> *a poor mulatto is a Negro.*

The palace

A grand white palace in Port-au-Prince, once the French governor general's residence, remained the symbol of power for generations.

Like a revolving door, emperors, kings, queens, and presidents had moved in and out. The posthumous portrait of Dessalines in the reception hall was the one symbol that made it very clear that the residence was no longer a colonial abode but had become the imperial palace of the sovereign Empire of Haïti.

Presidential Palace of Haïti in Port-au-Prince

Emperor Faustin I and his wife, Empress Adélina, understood their symbolic and ceremonial position more than anyone. They used the palace extensively to impress visiting dignitaries and exalt the person of His Majesty in the style of Louis XIV, pushing honor guards and elaborate court ceremonial.

John Bigelow, an editor at the *New York Evening Post,* visited the palace in 1850, and wrote:

The floor of one waiting room is white marble, the furniture in black hair-cloth and straw. On a richly carved table appeared a beautiful bronze clock, representing the arms of Haïti - namely, a palm-tree surrounded with fascines of pikes and surmounted with the Phrygian cap.

The walls were decorated with two fine portraits... One represents the celebrated French Conventionist, the Abbé Grégoire, and the other the reigning Emperor of Haïti... The latter does honor to the talent of a mulatto artist, the Baron Colbert. An adjoining salon, where grand receptions are given, displayed portraits of all the great men of Haïti.

The hungry and destitute had little time to waste. New revolutions were always brewing on the horizon, ready to spin into devastating hurricanes, destroying everything in their wake. The grand imperial palace was destroyed on December 19, 1869, during another black revolt.

A new national palace in the French Renaissance style by Baussan was built in the early 20th century. No matter how poor the country, a national palace was seen as indispensable.

Kuser, a visiting US dignitary, wrote about the new palace in his diary:

It is more than twice the size of our White House and is shaped like the letter E, with three wings running back from the front. In the main hall, large columns rise to the ceiling and, on each side; a staircase is winding up to the second floor.

The National Palace features a domed entrance pavilion. Four Ionic columns supported a pedimented portico; at either end of the main façade were matching domed buildings, also groined with grand vaulted ceilings. It was all set up for grand receptions with a Louis XIV-grandeur.

The proud National Palace and symbol of Haïti as a sovereign nation was severely damaged by a massive earthquake on January 12, 2010. After the tremors, the collapsed cupola in the center made a deep bow toward Toussaint Louverture Square. The entire front wall, ceremonial stairs, and columns supporting the portico collapsed. Only the back wall was still standing. The media reported that the central pavilion, an area once containing the main hall and royal staircase, had turned into rubble. The second floor of the building collapsed almost entirely, taking the attic floor with it.

Imperial gala benefit

This dramatic display of nature's might would be the ideal setting for a grand feast that would lift the spirit of all Haïtians and raise vast amounts of money for the restoration. I became a part of the drama and proposed the makings of fantastic projections for a *Dance Macabre* and a Grand Charity Imperial Ball and Banquet.

The skeletons would form a magnificent backdrop for His Imperial Majesty Jacques I's Grand Banquet and Ball of Ghosts. Emperors and kings, they would all have to rise from their tombs.

A draft for an imperial invitation, embossed and engraved, landed in my boat cockpit, undated and with a handwritten note by a diplomat friend: *Please advise us about the best mise-en-scene for this gala.*

The invitation read:

His Majesty Emperor Jacques I,

and Her Imperial Highness Empress Marie-Claire Heureuse Félicité of Haïti

request your presence at the Grand Charity Banquet and Ball of Ghosts

Venue: Imperial Palace, starting at midnight

Dress: Grand Gala Ghostly

"Anansi, let us picture a grand gala fundraiser. It must be pro-forma since no date is set yet, but we will go out and check out venues. Nothing brings in more money than celebrating disasters on the very spot where they happen. Haïti is rich in disasters, mostly earthquakes, and they always involved the town. I think the imperial palace sounds like the ideal location. Unfortunately, the imperial palace no longer exists, so we have to settle for second best, the presidential palace.

Anansi, I will introduce you to the black emperors of Haïti, and you tell me if they match up to their West African counterparts. Just imagine. We will make 5,000 French skull Jack-o'-lanterns for the illumination of the surrounding gardens, and build grand candelabras swinging from the exposed beams of the collapsed cupola. A solemn procession of zombies will march around the premises, shuffling feet and waddling without end. Louis XIV flute and harpsichord music, so loved by the emperor and his wife, will sound throughout the night, alongside blasts of resin bands, rappers and folk music. Fine linens and floral damasks set with crystal, silver, and gold will cover the rubble, turning it into elegant banquet tables. Behind each gilded chair will be a lackey standing to attention, outfitted in deep red and navy livery embellished with gold embroidery, catering to all of the celebrity guests' whims.

At midnight, at the height of the *Ball séance*, the emperor, wearing the empire's golden coronation crown studded with jewels and precious stones, will rise from his tomb. Dressed in an elaborately embroidered long ermine coat with a 20-foot train, carrying Haïti's golden scepter and orb set with precious stones, he will greet his most favorite guests.

Louis XIV, Le Roi Soleil, the Sun King of France and his retinue, will be the emperor's guests of honor and sat on display for all to see, under a canopy directly under the kneeling cupola. Individual tables will be set up for present monarchs of the Caribbean: Queen Elizabeth II of England and King William Alexander of the Netherlands. Hendrick van der Decken in his commander's uniform, as The Flying Dutchman, and you, Anansi, as the ambassador for the black migrant population of the Dutch kingdom, in white tie with tails, with all your decorations, will greet His Majesty and Her Imperial Highness with suited respect. The Highnesses will exchange pleasantries for a while and maybe remember some of the bitter, but always glorious, battles that go along with establishing a new regime.

Anansi, I am so excited and can see the entire party in front of me already."

A motorbike taxi from the port delivered me from the yacht harbor to Toussaint Louverture Square. I searched and searched but could not detect either a palace or a pile of rubble. The National Palace was gone and so were its ruins. The poorly maintained lawns looked like a forgotten city park for kids ready to play street football. But there were not even any playing children.

*The Presidential Palace (National Palace) in Port-au-Prince on 13
January 2010, the day after the 2010 earthquake - Logan Abassi*

Poof, gone was my reverie about a Charity Benefit Grand Gala for ghosts. There was not going to be any banquet, no procession of zombies, no worldwide charity fundraiser. The world I had imagined had vanished forever.

With the palace no longer in existence, the spirit of the people and their minds were also gone. Creating new realities on the scrapheap of the old, the way empires were once built on the corpses of bloody revolutions, had become an impossible dream for Haïti. Someone had turned off the lights, once and for all.

Haïti, once a proud empire and the richest of all the islands in the Caribbean, is today the poorest nation in the western hemisphere, filled with desperate people, their hopes extinguished forever.

"If you not lead the living, lead the dead," Anansi whispered.

Was Spiderman becoming the master of my history lessons?

That evening I dined alone with Haïtian stewed chicken, a traditional recipe that is typically served with rice, and *Rhum vieux Labbé*. The famous *rhum* (rum) is aged in oak barrels in the traditional Haïtian-style of Cognac distillation.

Haïtian stewed chicken

1 lb. chicken
½ onion, diced
2 tbsp. minced garlic
1 tbsp. of lime juice
4 sprigs of fresh thyme
4 sprigs of fresh parsley
1 Scotch Bonnet pepper
1 tbsp. black pepper
½ red pepper, julienned
1 Maggi chicken bouillon cube
1 tbsp. of Adobo seasoning
½ cup white vinegar
2 tbsp. tomato paste

Clean the chicken using the Haïtian meat-cleaning method - use lemon or sour orange juice and vinegar. Rinse in hot water.
Create a marinade with the garlic, parsley, thyme, black pepper, chicken cube, and seasoning salt.
Season the chicken with the marinade and let it marinade for at least 15 minutes.

Marinating the chicken overnight in the refrigerator will give the meat more time to take on the flavor.

In a large saucepan, brown the chicken on both sides.

Add half a cup of water to the saucepan along with the tomato paste, onions, and peppers.

Stew the chicken on medium-high heat for 25 minutes.

Reduce heat to low and let simmer until ready to serve.

10 DEAD RECKONING: A SCIENTIFIC SAILOR'S CHALLENGE

Astrolabe, an instrument formerly used to make astronomical measurements, typically of the altitudes of celestial bodies, and in navigation for calculating latitude, before the development of the sextant. In its basic form (known from classical times), it consists of a disk with the edge marked in degrees and a pivoted pointer. - Google Dictionary

---

Tagging along Hispaniola's south coast from Port-au-Prince, Haïti to Santo Domingo, took six days, or was it eight? I hardly remember. It was, as always, treacherous and, especially at night, very tedious; the seas were bumpy. With a GPS compass linked to my rudder, navigation was child's play.

Compass

Being aboard with just my Flying Dutchman ghost and my spider, I had plenty of time for contemplation and monotonous dialogues.

In the 17th and 18th centuries, the intricacies of navigational techniques became the key to success in trade for European nations. Navigational science was in the beginning of the Age of Exploration, a most carefully guarded secret. Bloody wars were fought over it, and sailors were taken hostage and pressed for information.

In those days, these were the most closely guarded secrets of any trading company in the world. Today, just about any textbook will divulge all the secrets to the eager student. How, I wondered, did navigating the globe work in Anansi's cobweb mind?

"Anansi," I asked, "you are a spider of the world, a world nomad, right? With Akan ancestry, exiled in Surinam, Demerara, Berbice, and the Antilles, and re-migrating to Europe, to Holland, England, and France, you have done your globetrotting, and you have become a celebrity, a man of stories and experience. How did you manage to find these places? Coastal navigation is relatively easy when you go from lighthouse to lighthouse and from beacon to beacon. But how could you figure out longitude and latitude, or whatever you call it in a spider's brain, in oceans without any coastline in view?"

"Well, silly white man, navigation was always by slave trader crew. Black man only cargo, in ship hole."

"Did you ever study your cobwebs, the radials, the tangles of silken threads?"

This was a topic that appealed to Anansi. Spiders are stereo-metric artists by nature.

"My webs always perfect, but wind comes and all broken. So web after wind, big mess. In my head perfect web. For navigation, only perfect web."

"Anansi, I will try to explain. Every day, the moon and the stars travel across the night sky in a huge arch. When the celestial bodies move along their route, the angle to the horizon changes. Look at a sundial; the shadow moves with the progression of the day. Yes, of course, the dinner plate of 360 degrees became the astrolabe, or a 90-degree quadrant, as was used in Persia, a 60-degree sextant or a 45-degree octant, still used today in the West.

Modern Astrolabe

Place the dinner plate of 360 degrees or the smaller instrument vertically, and add a few wires, one for the horizon and one for the sun – that way you measure angles. The face on your analog wristwatch is the same; it shows angles and progression from which one determines what time it is.

Bookkeeper-astronomers of all times and locations kept extensive logs of angles measured at specific dates, times, and places of evening and morning stars and of sun and moon. In those logs, you can look up which time goes with which angle at a certain location.

Or do it the other way around: know your time and determine your progression from the zero meridian, which is nowadays in Greenwich. A meridian is an imaginary straight line that runs from the North Pole to the South Pole, and through a home location called *point zero*. Before the Greenwich Prime Meridian (1851), the island El Hierro near Tenerife was used.

In this way it became easy to measure time and place with angulation and tables indicating the times celestial bodies appear in certain constellations.

Zero starting points, like the Greenwich Meridian today, have been in many different locations in the world, especially in holy places, capital cities, palaces, or laboratories. Muslims used Mecca, the Dutch, Amsterdam, the English, London, the Catholics, Rome, and the Portuguese, Lisbon."

"Yes!" shouted Anansi enthusiastically. His web was dancing. "Smart sailors, all with perfect cobweb. Look at sky, astrolabes."

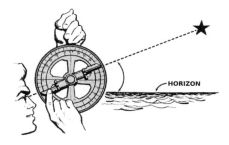

Line art drawing of astrolabe - Pearson Scott Foresman, Wikimedia

"I am beginning to understand a spider's cobweb. They put reference points on cobweb grids for fixed far-away stars. These cobwebs became star maps. Every spider, like many birds, has star maps programmed into their brain.

Indeed, Anansi, by putting several circular cobweb star maps on top of a plate to measure angles of moving celestial bodies, one could determine the time from a known location, or a location at a specific time. The Hellenistic instrument astrolabe was useful to Muslims, who used it to determine the correct hour of prayer. Without imitating spiders and their cobwebs, sailors of the world would still be lost at sea and Muslims would not know when to pray and in which direction."

Getting my midnight ghost to give up his precious VOC secrets on navigation was a bit more challenging.

"Captain, how did you manage to know where you were? Did you know longitude and latitude? Did you have instruments?"

With reluctance and only after a few tries, the captain finally shared some of his classified VOC navigational knowledge. "In Holland," he started his exposé, "modern navigation started with Gemma Frisius (1508) of Dokkum, an instrument maker and a brilliant mathematician, cartographer, physician and philosopher.

My father always told me that he had known the Frisian scholar when his name was still Jemme Reinerszoon. In those days it was fashion for scholars to change their names to something more Latin sounding. Gemma, or Jemme Frisius, became very famous. The shipping and trading communities were all very proud of him as he gathered more and more fame in Brussels, Antwerp, Ghent, and Middelburg, finally ending up as a professor at the University of Leuven.

Gemma Frisius by Maarten van Heemskerck, oil on panel, circa 1540-1545, Museum Boymans van Beuningen, Rotterdam

Many followed in his footsteps, like Plancius, Snellius, Stevin, and Blaeu. Frisius understood that the position east or west from home called longitude could be found by comparing the time of the actual position with the time at home, his zero-point.

The globe rotates around its axis every 24 hours; so one hour is 360 degrees divided by 24, which makes 15 degrees per hour. Each degree divided again by 60 minutes comes out as one minute equaling one nautical mile. Thus, with triangulation, Snellius (1580), or Willebrord Snel van Royen, measured the distance between two provincial towns in Holland, Alkmaar and Bergen op Zoom. He got the exact measure of the length of a minute, from which he then calculated the circumference of the globe.

For latitude, the location north or south of the equator, Frisius used the cross staff, or Jacob's staff. By day, it was necessary to measure the height of the sun above the horizon precisely at noon. To make some money, Frisius's heirs passed on some of his secret methods to the VOC, and later the WIC. Using a clock for longitude was a simple but revolutionary idea since no clocks existed that could be used on a moving boat.

Portrait of Petrus Plancius, by Reinier Vinkeles (I), etching after Jacobus Buys, 1791, Rijksmuseum Amsterdam

Almost unfortunately, around 1600, Plancius, an Amsterdam clergyman and cartographer, devised another system. Eventually, Simon Stevin and Plancius' theory gave birth to mathematical formulae in their book *De Havenvinding*.

For nearly a hundred years thereafter, Dutch sailors were confused by these competing systems of Frisius and Plancius, and often preferred simple coastal routes and navigation on *dead reckoning*. In navigation, dead reckoning is "the process of calculating one's current position by using a previously determined position, or fix, and advancing that position based upon known or estimated speeds over elapsed time and course."

Yet another Dutchman, Christiaan Huygens (1624-1695), was convinced that the solution was to be found in timekeeping. He invented the clock pendulum, which was an improvement but still very sensitive to the movement of the waves. Salomon Coster, a clockmaker, built the first pendulum clock after Huygens's design.

Huygens used Galileo's discovery of isochronism applied to the swinging of pendulums. Galileo may have had the idea of a pendulum clock about twenty years before Huygens, but amongst friends a little borrowing of ideas did not matter. The pendulum clock rapidly gained popularity as the design became more and more sophisticated.

Finding one's correct position at sea became so very important that, in 1714, the English issued the Longitude Act, which promised rich rewards to inventors who could construct a seaworthy clock. Finally, in 1765, John Harrison, an English watchmaker and carpenter, succeeded in creating such a chronometer."

It was long after midnight when the captain finished his explanations. He was very proud of his detailed knowledge. At sunrise, he disappeared into the darkness of the deep sea, leaving me behind, perplexed.

Islamic astronomers

The next morning at breakfast, a surprise awaited me.

"Anansi, are you wearing a hijab?! Since when are you a woman, and have you converted to Islam?"

"Oh, you silly white man. Not woman, not Muslim. Many Muslim friends in Surinam and Antilles."

Anansi was right. When the Dutch kingdom still included the Netherlands Indies, it was one of the largest Muslim kingdoms in the world. History may be forgotten quickly but the understanding gained in those days could become most valuable beyond today when tens of thousands of Muslims are migrating to Europe and the Netherlands.

"Anansi, let us play a little game and see what you know about Islamic culture, if anything. Let me give you a mini test. Who were Avicenna, Al Biruni, Omar Khayyam, Averoës, Idrisi and Ibn Battuta? Do you know the names of any of these great, great people?"

As I was rattling off the famous names of Muslim scientists, I realized how much I had learned about many of them throughout my life, and how familiar their names rang in my ears.

"I will give you a hint, Anansi. They were all polymath superstars. Never mind, let me play teacher again and tell you; once a teacher always a teacher. You better listen and remember. We are now in the West Indies because of their contribution to navigation and cartography.

Avicenna, or Ibn Sīnā, lived about the year 1,000. He was a Persian polymath and wrote books on philosophy, medicine, astronomy, alchemy, geography, geology and even psychology. His studies became the basis for all those who succeeded him.

Al Bīrūnī, who lived about the same time as Avicenna, was also a Muslim astronomer, mathematician, ethnographer, anthropologist, historian, and geographer of Persia, and navigation made him very famous.

Omar Khayyám of Samarkand followed about one hundred years later. He was a Persian polymath: scholar, mathematician, astronomer, philosopher and poet. Science in those days was all disciplines in one. Little specialization existed.

Khayyam's sonnets became famous even in the western world. As a schoolboy, I learned his famous bread and wine Rubáiyát by heart, never to forget.

> *Here with a Loaf of Bread beneath the Bough,*
> *A Flask of Wine, a Book of Verse - and Thou*
> *Beside me singing in the Wilderness -*
> *And Wilderness is Paradise enow.*

Avicenna, Al Biruni, and Omar Khayyam were the fathers of science in the Islamic Golden Age. Their influence traveled with the Umayyad, the aristocratic successors of Mohammed, to Andalusia, and on to Portugal and the Netherlands. For Khayyam, astronomy was identical to poetry, as in his song LIX:

> *Ah, but my computations, People say*
> *Have squared the Year with human compass, eh?*
> *If so, by striking from the Calendar*
> *Unborn to-morrow, and dead Yesterday.*

Later came Ibn Rushd (1126-1198), alias Averroes, who was born in Córdoba, Al Andalus, in present-day Spain, and died at Marrakesh, in present-day Morocco. He continued the exploration and design of navigation techniques based on what Avicenna and Al Biruni had started.

Idrisi, or Muhammad al-Idrisi, was a mapmaker born in Ceuta, just across from Gibraltar, then part of the Almohad Kingdom of modern Morocco. The most famous Tabula Rogeriana map was drawn by al-Idrisi for King Roger II of Sicily in 1154. It showed Africa, the Indian Ocean, and the Far East. Idrisi did not use astronomy and mathematical grids but gathered all kinds of information from travel logs, commercial shipping lists, and the cargo of Arab merchants and explorers.

Ibn Battuta (1304-1368/1369) was a traveler and another famous Moroccan diplomat. Battuta became the great explorer of his time and wrote about all his trips in his diaries, *Travels*.

Averroës, Idrisi, and Ibn Battuta were what you today would call Moroccans. Their mathematics, cartography, and geology made it to Andalusia, now Spain, and eventually to Lisbon, Portugal. And that completes the circle. In the 1470s Bartholomew, a brother of Christopher Columbus, was a mapmaker in Lisbon. With his knowledge of Islamic astrolabes, mathematics, and cartography, he joined his brother Christopher on that fateful voyage.

Guided by Islamic astronomers, Columbus made it to the Americas. In 1495, Christopher rewarded Bartholomew with the title of Adelanto, or Governor of Española. Bartholomew and his nephew, Diego Colon, the viceroy, founded Santo Domingo, now the capital of the Dominican Republic and our next destination."

Anansi may have been asleep throughout my entire exposé for all I know. But studying his cobweb was the key to devising navigation techniques, and he got that much! Proud spider!

That evening, I made a cobweb spider cake.

Cobweb spider cake

Ingredients
1 box chocolate cake, plus ingredients called for.
½ cup unsalted butter softened
1 cup confectioners' sugar

7 ½ oz. jar marshmallow crème
1 tsp. vanilla extract
1 pinch of kosher salt
3/4 cup heavy cream
1 ½ cup semi-sweet chocolate chips
1 tube store-bought vanilla icing

Instructions
Butter and flour two 9" cake pans.
Prepare cake batter according to the package instructions. Bake according to the package instructions and let cool.
Once cool, place the first cake on a platter.

The frosting
In a large bowl using a hand mixer, combine butter, confectioners' sugar, marshmallow crème, vanilla extract and salt and beat until fluffy and combined.
There was still plenty left over to make a second cake.

Ganache
In a small saucepan, heat heavy cream until it starts to bubble.
Place chocolate chips in a heatproof bowl and pour over the heavy cream.
Let stand for 2 minutes, then whisk until the chocolate and cream are completely combined.
Pour the ganache over the cake.
Draw a spiral out of frosting on top of the ganache and use a toothpick to draw cobwebs.

11 SANTO DOMINGO

The first permanent establishment of the New World and capital of the West Indies, the Colonial City of Santo Doming - the only one of the 15th century in the Americas - was the place of departure for the spread of European culture and the conquest of the continent. - UNESCO World Heritage Centre

Dignitaries

Paying my respect to Adelantado Bartholomew Columbus Colón and Viceroy Diego Colón, his nephew, was high on my priority list. Diego was the eldest son of Christopher Columbus and his wife Filipa Moniz Perestrelo. The year must have been 1511. The young men were at the height of their powers and success. The marriage of Ferdinand and Isabella in 1469 had forged a new kingdom, the Kingdom of Spain. A further expansion was realized as their daughter, Isabella of Aragon, married King Manuel I of Portugal in 1497, and became queen of Portugal. Global might came with the New World discoveries, and so did the establishment of viceroyalties. Unknown opportunities, wealth, and power were at their fingertips. Unfortunately, my meeting could only take place in my imagination.

Both dignitaries greeted me formally but with measured disdain, an attitude innate to Spanish colonial governors and nobles. For Spanish aristocratic rulers, all Dutchmen, Países Bajos sailors, were smelly, money-grabbing, herring-trading scum without sophistication, culture, or refinement. And to make it worse, early 16th-century Low Landers were rebels. The future threatened unrest due to this new breed of heretics. Heretics deserved to burn in hell.

Herring seller, by Gerard Dou, oil on panel, circa 1670-1675 ©
Hermitage St Petersburg

Adelantado Bartholomew Columbus Colón and his nephew were functionaries of the highest distinction in the viceroyalty aristocracy of New Spain.

After days at sea, the pavement under my feet moved like the waves and I was slightly seasick. As a drunken sailor, walking on an uneven conveyer belt, I staggered through the streets of historic Santo Domingo. The elegantly lantern-lit Calle de Las Damas was the first paved and lit street in the western hemisphere. It was still the place to see and be seen.

Entire families, chaperoning their young daughters and sons, were strutting up and down, ogling others. The city of Santo Domingo, even in modern times, was still Spanish in every way and fashion.

Rich mansions lined the streets. Military might was mirrored in Fortaleza Ozama, guarding the river entrance against the enemy and invading pirates. The Cathedral of Santa María la Menor shielded souls from wickedness.

Calle de las Damas in Santo Domingo - Athulf, German Wikipedia,
2002

At the palace, open porches faced a large, enclosed courtyard with fig trees and a whispering Moorish fountain in the center.

A dark-skinned slave boy served a basket of fruit and *Mama Juana*, a local rum drink mixed with red wine and honey, soaked in a bottle with tree bark and herbs. In 1510, the king of Spain had issued a permit to transport Africans to the New World to replace the indigenous Carib workforce that had perished from European diseases to which they had no immunity.

"Your Excellencies," I said slowly, "I cannot but marvel at the splendor of your grand city and its fortifications. Indeed, in such a brief period of time, only fifteen years, you have forged a true Spanish miracle, a miracle for God and King, out of nothing but heathen and wilderness."

The Spanish kingdom would soon be faced with enormous challenges, but my distinguished hosts could not have the faintest notion. They were proud, courageous men, heroes, discoverers, entrepreneurs; men who had changed the world forever.

Salt embargo

One of those challenges was the independence war in Protestant Holland that would last eighty years and exhaust the treasury of Spain to the point of bankruptcy. Those smelly Dutchmen, led by their treacherous stadtholder, Prince William of Orange, would try to separate from Catholic Spain. During that war, Spain imposed economic sanctions on the Dutch and their business in Hispaniola. Tragedy followed on Hispaniola in 1605, a hundred years after the founding of this glorious town. It is known in history as the *Devastaciones de Osorio*.

In the early 1500s, the herring and salt industry dominated the economy of Holland. The herring trade made the Dutch rich, very rich, especially after an invention that allowed fish conservation for extended periods of time. Sometime during the late 14th century, the Dutchman Willem Beukelszoon, or Buckles, developed a process that improved the taste of herring by saltwater curing, the so-called *Buckles' gibbing process*; a byproduct was long-term preservation. The gills and part of the gullet of the fish were cut out to eliminate the bitter taste, and the liver and pancreas were left, releasing enzymes that flavored the fish.

Willem Beukelszoon, circa 1380, by Hilmar Johannes Backer, print, 1821, Rijksmuseum Amsterdam

During the Age of Exploration, food preservation on board ships was an enormous problem. Long voyages, sometimes around the globe, or as far as Tasmania and Australia, resulted in vitamin C deficiency for crew members, and consequently scorbutus, or scurvy, then a deadly disease.

Citrus fruits were only available to a few. Pedro Álvares Cabral, a Brazilian-Portuguese nobleman, regarded as the discoverer of Brazil, confirmed Vasco de Gama's ideas about the curative effects of citrus fruit, but that knowledge did not result in any sustained agricultural efforts. Only in 1593 did the infamous British admiral Sir Richard

Hawkins promote drinking orange and lemon juice as ways of preventing scurvy. Drinking orange juice at breakfast became a tradition, but only for those who could afford it.

For food preservation the industry relied on salt. Foods to be preserved were stored in stone jars filled with alternating layers of solid salts. Processing plants using brine required massive amounts and salt was in short supply. Most imported salts were traded out of Portugal and Spain, and often bartered for wood. The Dutch shipped massive amounts of wood from Russia and traded it for salt in Lisbon.

In 1595, the Spanish, frustrated by the twenty-year rebellion of their Dutch subjects, closed all their ports to interlopers from Holland and Zeeland wishing to ship salt. The salt embargoes dramatically intensified the eighty-year independence war with Spain, Guerra de Los Ochenta Años (1568-1648). The livelihood and riches of the Dutch were under threat. Economic survival fed into tenacity and, in 1608, Spain was eager for a ceasefire, which lasted only twelve years.

Salt in Bonaire

Cutting the Dutch herring industry completely off from critical salt supplies triggered more piracy at sea, and an intensive search for new sources, as well as the fast growth of black markets.

When Portugal, then under Spain's rule, also restricted access to its salt supplies, the Dutch had no other option but to cross the Atlantic, in search of salt on the Venezuelan coasts and on Caribbean islands like Curaçao and Bonaire. The adventurous Dutch, not easily discouraged and ready to bribe their way around, located new salt supplies in the Spanish West Indies. Spanish settlers were more than happy to trade.

Beyond colonial administrators' control, many Dutch traders, pirates, privateers, and interlopers joined English and French colleagues, all trading salt on the coasts of Hispaniola. The herring industry in Holland and Zeeland kicked back into full swing, employing at its peak more than 40,000 people in Amsterdam alone. This stimulated shipbuilding, facilitating ever-larger transatlantic salt transports. Soon the salted herring trade in all European export markets was booming; thus, Holland became Europe's most powerful seafaring nation.

Herring dish, De Porceleyne Byl, porcelain, circa 1760-1790,
Rijksmuseum Amsterdam

At the time, the Dutch herring fisheries in the North Sea were the most sophisticated fishing operations in the world. The clandestine salt business run by Spanish colonial settlers, dealing with Dutch interlopers, became a get-rich-quick enterprise.

Spain became infuriated with its settlements on the northern and western coasts of Hispaniola Island that so radically undermined the economic sanctions. A military campaign of 1605 razed five of the thirteen settlements on the north coast to the ground. Villages were burned and pillaged by ruthless Spanish troops, including two settlements in what is now Haïti, La Yaguana, and Bayaja. The Spanish may have won the battle as the saying goes, but they soon lost the war.

This military intervention proved disastrous; more than half of the resettled Spanish colonists died of starvation or disease. More than 100,000 cattle got lost in the wilderness and countless numbers of slaves escaped. Many Spanish settlers fought back against the Spanish colonial troops and escaped to the jungle. Some even fled to the safety of passing Dutch ships. The Spanish military action became more and more counterproductive as English, Dutch, and French pirates were now free to set up bases on the islands in the settlements abandoned by Spanish colonists. Eventually, the colonists were forced to resettle closer to the city of Santo Domingo, under strict governmental control.

The northern and western coasts of Hispaniola, where cattle was now plentiful, became the new promised land for adventurers, runaway slaves and pirates. Spain never gained total control of these areas again.

Today's crime statistics in the Dominican Republic are such that visitors, outside the tourist enclaves of Punta Cana and Bávaro at La Costa del Coco, feel unwelcome and unsafe.

Once I had paid my respects to the historic sites of the glorious city of Adelantado Bartolomé Colón, and his nephew, it was time to move on. Too many Spanish descendants still had an axe to grind with western European sailors, and especially with the Dutch. We sailed eastward on our way to Puerto Rico, the Leeward Islands, the Windward Islands, and the Leeward Antilles.

Mona

Our next anchorage was halfway between the Dominican Republic and Puerto Rico, on the islands of Mona and Monito. They sit comfortably in the middle of the Passage between the two large islands. Shaped like beans with concavity to the north, they provided reasonable anchorage and a great harbor for pirates.

"You may never have heard of these islands, Anansi, but in the 16th and 17th centuries they played a major role in the discovery and development of the Caribbean by Europeans."

Anansi listened most carefully. Pirates appealed to his imagination.

Historians estimate that about 5,000-8,000 pirates were active in the Caribbean at all times between 1600 and 1750.

The island of Roatan, by the coast of Honduras, became a haven for pirates, far away from the Spanish and British privateers out to eliminate them. The island became a hideout for French, English, and Dutch pirates who would intercept and conquer Spanish cargo vessels en route to Europe, loaded with gold and other treasures. It is estimated that, by the mid-17th century, there were approximately 5,000 pirates living on Roatan and the Bay Islands.

West Bay on Roatan - West Brown Canada, 2016

Of those 5,000, about thirty percent were black pirates, mostly runaway slaves from the Spanish colonies. Also, many black pirates came from the Guinea Coast of Africa as well. Creole pirates and privateers in the Caribbean were also no exceptions. They numbered an estimated 1,500-1,800 at all times. They came from Negroland and Guinea, as Herman Moll, a cartographer in London, in 1729 called today's countries of Mali, Senegal, Burkina Faso, Ghana, and the smaller coastal republics.

Map of Negroland and Guinea, by Herman Moll, 1729 © University of Florida, George A. Smathers Libraries

It was the infamous black pirate Mateo Congo who captured a frigate in the Mona Passage in 1625. Mona Island and Passage, between Hispaniola and Puerto Rico, had proven to be a very strategic location for all those with opportunistic and ill intentions, and Mateo was certainly one of them. Ambushing regular traffic from those islands was a dream for any pirate.

The Portuguese had been active since the mid-15th century in most port cities in West Africa.

After Prince Henry the Navigator of Portugal set up business on the Guinea Coast in 1441, a Creole population quickly emerged. Extraordinary accounts of the expedition recounted many details presently lost in history. Using new ship types, larger and able to sail half wind, the expeditions pushed further onwards. Nuno Tristão and Antão Gonçalves reached Cape Blanco in 1441. The Portuguese sighted the Bay of Arguin in 1443, and built an important fort there around the year 1448. Dinis Diassoon came across the Senegal River and rounded the peninsula of Cape Verde in 1444.

Creoles were descendants of European, mostly Portuguese, sailors and traders and local women. Atlantic Creoles played a major role in the transatlantic shipping of slaves. Creoles grew up in multilingual and multicultural environments. Men worked as interpreters or go-betweens for Africans and Europeans; others worked as sailors, merchants, pirates, and traders. After Columbus discovered the Americas for the Spanish, and the Spanish King granted the transatlantic slave trade, many Creoles moved on and traveled to the Caribbean, North America or Europe.

Nanouma by Adrien-Henri Tanoux, oil on canvas, 1887

Christian slaves, Barbary Coast

From the 16th till the 19th century, the primary concern in Europe was not the transatlantic slave trade of Africans but the Barbary Coast abomination, the ruthless slave trade of Europeans kidnapped by North

Africans. African pirates raided coastal cities and bought and sold millions of so-called Christian, European slaves, kidnapped from England, France, Holland, Spain, Portugal, Italy, and Greece.

Muslim pirates of North Africa, called *corsairs*, used young men for galley slaves and women for resale to harems. Corsairs also pestered the regular shipping lanes across the Atlantic and along European coasts. They were out to seize famous passengers who could be traded for ransom.

Christians being sold as slaves at a square in Algiers, by Jan Luyken, etching, 1684, Rijksmuseum Amsterdam

Piet Heyn, later in his life a national naval hero for the Dutch, served as a galley slave for four years (1598-1602) and lost his father and uncle to the Barbary Coast slave traders. And later, Jacob Leisler of Frankfurt (1640-1691), who worked for the Dutch in New Amsterdam and later led the revolt in New York against the British, was captured and ransomed on his way from Europe to the New World. If the families of captives were not wealthy enough to pay the gigantic ransoms, church congregations across Europe often collected money.

An account of a British Parliament meeting of 1672 indicates that over one million Christian, English slaves were in African custody. England and France reacted with massive naval activity in the Mediterranean and along the North African coast. The Barbary Coast slave trade reduced, but never ceased until the late 19th century.

The new transatlantic slavery business looked so attractive that thousands of black African corsairs tried their luck and moved to the Caribbean. Either they actively participated in the transatlantic slave trade or pillaged the regular shipping convoys.

Torture of Christian slaves by the Turcs, by Jan Luyken, print, 1684,
Rijksmuseum Amsterdam

Jol

A Dutch admiral, Adriaen Cornelis Jol (1597-1641), nicknamed *Pie de Palo* for his pegleg, also used Mona Island and its passage as a harbor from which to launch ambushes. In 1626, Jol ambushed ships laden with goods on their way to Santo Domingo in Mona Passage. Earlier, Jol had also attacked San Juan and sunk four ships from Santo Domingo. The adventurous Adriaen Jol had quite a reputation. He crossed the Atlantic Ocean nine times and attacked the Spanish and Portuguese along the coast of Brazil and in the Caribbean. In 1637, the admiral, leading fourteen ships, boarded an African ship in Mona Passage carrying cedar lumber from Central America and stole part of her cargo.

Jol was also active as a buccaneer. He attacked Campeche, an important port in the Yucatan, looting the settlement in 1633. This wild and ruthless Dutchman brought back enormous treasure to the Dutch Admiralty and was lauded as a national hero. Today, Dutch football manager and former midfielder Maarten Cornelis 'Martin' Jol claims to be a direct descendant of the pirate.

Ethics

The ethics of warfare at sea, hand in hand with needless, cold-blooded killings, did not seem to conflict with various philosophical, legal, and theological discussions of those days. The Protestants at the Synod of Dort (1618) may have made a start on defining human rights.

Hugo de Groot, or Hugo Grotius, a Dutch jurist, laid the foundations for international sea law. In *The Free Sea, Mare Liberum* published in 1609, Grotius formulated the new principle that the sea was an international territory and all nations were free to use it for seafaring trade.

My Anansi feels a special closeness to Grotius, since he escaped from his prison in a book chest assisted by his wife, Elselina, much like Anansi once escaped his prison with the aid of his wife.

So, Passage Mona was a crossroad for African pirates, Dutch privateers and buccaneers, British and French slave traders, and the entire retinue of plundering scum that was out for Spanish gold and silver treasure fleets. Today, it is a forgotten, heavily polluted, very sad island, inhabited by poor Taino Indian descendants.

That evening, I could not think of a more appropriate time to prepare a salted herring dish following a recipe from 1730.

Salted herring

Instructions
First make a stock of soup with herbs, roots, and bread.
Season it with the same seasoning, but not too much salt.
Take six red herrings, broil them and beat them in a mortar.
Put to them some of your stock and strain and force them through your strainer. Prepare a ragout of old onions.
Strain them into the rest.
Take a little celery, endive, a little spinach, sorrel, and parsley; mince them and put them in brown butter till very tender.
Put all together and stove it up.
Put in fried French machete, dish it up, broil some more red herrings and lay them around your dish.
Garnish with sliced lemon and scalded spinach.

12 TREASURE

There's a pot of gold at the rainbow's end, guarded by a tricky leprechaun. - Melanie Radzicki McManus, *10 Myths About Rainbows*.

"Anansi, you have been very quiet there in your hammock, listening to my stories. Do you want to become an expert in island history, or are you brushing up on your own bag of stories? Tell me, why are you still on board?"

"Easy man! Treasure! Get treasure with you. I rich."

"So, you are piggybacking, a free rider, soon to become a freeloader! Why not? Now, let me ask you a question. Why do you think all these pirates put their jewels, gold, and silver in chests and buried them somewhere on a secret, deserted island, where only they could find it? Most of them knew very well that they stood a good chance of dying in the next battle and risk never seeing their treasure again. Why bury their hard-fought treasures?"

"Silly white man. Buried treasure for me. Pirates good for slaves. Slaves find all treasure. Treasures for Ashanti people, for all Anansis-in-the-world. You see, treasure reparation payment for suffering."

"Ha, very smart, Anansi, but I do not think so. Let us ask our ghost stowaway tonight. As the Flying Dutchman he knows the trading mentality of the VOC and WIC, and of those privateers, pirates, and buccaneers like no other."

That evening at midnight promptly, the captain appeared on the front deck, dressed in a sober black frock and a large hat. He looked like a Calvinist clergyman, straight from the pulpit of the Synod of Dort, about to open his Bible and deliver a sermon.

The captain spoke solemnly. "By the Grace of God, it was ordained that the lazy and worthless who dig a hole in the ground to hide their money, will be cast into outer darkness, where there will be weeping and gnashing of teeth; as is written Matthew 25: 14-30."

I recalled the story from Sunday school, and, once upon a time in Surinam, Anansi must have heard it as well: A master entrusted five, two and one *talents* - the unit of currency at that time - to his slaves and went on a trip. When he returned, he asked the slaves what they had done with the money. The first one had made another five talents. The next one, two, but the last one had put it in the ground and returned his talent to his master without even a little interest. This last, silly slave was punished for his lack of entrepreneurship.

And as if his message was not sufficiently understood, the captain hollered directly into the wind, "We harvest where we did not sow. We gather where we did not scatter seed."

"You see, Anansi, pirates were unable to invest their money in anything legal. After they had spent some of their money on possessions and debauchery, often at massively inflated prices, they had no other option but to dig a hole in the ground.

It is comparable to Pablo Escobar in recent history. Through cocaine trafficking, the gangster made 40 million dollars per month on a little island in the Bahamas. But the little island had very few businesses, and international money laundering had become very complicated. Soon, Escobar had no way to spend his greenbacks, so he hid them in barrels and dug pits into the ground. He took the money out of circulation and thus it became worthless currency. He finished up in jail and died a miserable death.

Pirates did the same. For a short while, they caused huge inflation through spending incredible amounts of money, and then without a productive society surrounding them to absorb it, they had no other option but to take it out of circulation by burying it."

Anansi was sitting up straight. Stories about endless riches could get even a crippled man to run a marathon.

Mansa Musa

"You not logical, in Africa gold, a lot of gold. Look at Ashanti king and family: Gold, gold, gold. King Moses, Mansa Musa I, Emperor Mali Empire: Gold, gold, gold."

Mansa Musa sitting on a throne and holding a gold coin, Catalan Atlas (detail) 1375 © Gallicia Digital Library

"Yes, something similar happened to Mansa Musa of Mali. Mansa Musa was a devout Muslim who in 1324 made a year-long trip to Mecca. His caravan had 60,000 men, including 12,000 slaves who each carried 1.8

kilos of gold bars and eighty camels, each carrying 23–136 kg of gold dust. Mansa Musa paid for everything. Feeding the entire procession of men and animals was already a giant undertaking. In addition, Musa gave gold alms to the poor along the arduous route, and he built a mosque every Friday, including in Cairo and Medina, and often traded his precious gold for worthless souvenirs.

Musa's pious generosity devastated the economies of the regions through which he passed. In the cities of Cairo, Medina, and Mecca, the sudden influx of large amounts of gold caused enormous inflation and devalued the precious metal for the next ten years.

More gold, used as currency, could not lift the productivity of those economies sufficiently, and, consequently, inflation ruined existing markets. The price of goods and wares doubled, tripled, and quadrupled, leaving millions unable to buy food. Mansa Musa's big heart caused enormous poverty. Pirates, buccaneers, and corsairs had the same problem; they could never find markets large enough to spend their money, so they were left with the option of burying it and waiting for later."

Anansi looked at me in disbelief and cried, "No man. Find treasure. You find treasure. A treasure for me!"

Spanish gold inflation

"Ai, dear Anansi, let me give you another example, the revolution that happened from 1500 till about 1650, when Spanish conquistadores poured enormous amounts of gold and silver from the Inca and Aztec empires into Europe. Inflation translated into spiraling prices, sometimes six-fold increases.

During the reign of King Philip II of Spain, there were five state bankruptcies: in 1557, 1560, 1569, 1575 and 1596. The Spanish blamed the Dutch after their declaration of independence that created the Dutch Republic in 1581, but that was only partly true - mostly it was an excuse. It is undeniable that the long war had some influence during the first twelve years of King Philip III's reign (1598-1621); the Low Countries' war alone cost over 40 million *ducats*. A *ducat*, Anansi, is a small gold coin, weighing about 3.5 grams, worth about US $170 in today's market.

By 1607, the Spanish government had a debt of almost 23 million ducats and had assigned all of its revenue to creditors for four years ahead. The Spanish lack of understanding of the effects of poring silver and gold into the economy was a much more significant and long-lasting reason for the hyperinflation than any war."

Anansi did not register or did not want to register this salient truth. His belief in money was too much shaped by childhood fairytales of great abundance coming from large amounts of cash, gold, and precious stones. Alas, many professors in economics, money-laundering narco traffickers and politicians still do not understand it either.

Piet Heyn

"Allow me to recount the story of the riches captured by Piet Heyn in Cuba. Schoolchildren in Holland still sing the praises of their 17th-century hero, Piet Heyn:

> *Piet Heyn, his name is curt*
> *but his accomplishments are so great*
> *but his accomplishments are so great.*
> *He did win the Silver Fleet,*
> *he did win the Silver Fleet,*
> *he did win the Silver Fleet.*
> *Did you hear about the silver fleet,*
> *the silver fleet of Espanã?*
> *They had so much Spanish money aboard,*
> *and apples of Orange.*

You may have heard the name Pieter Pietersen Heyn and tales of the Cuban conflict in 1628. Yes, he is the same person we met before, who served for four years as a galley slave for the Barbary corsairs.

Piet Heyn captured in gold and silver 11,509,524 guilders of booty, an equivalent of nearly two billion euros today. It was the largest plunder of the Eighty Years' War with Spain. Also, shiploads of expensive goods, such as indigo and cochineal, were reloaded onto Heyn's fleet before the remains of the Spanish galleons were set on fire and sunk; the entire raid was executed without any bloodshed. The capture of the treasure fleet was the Dutch West Indies Company's greatest victory in the Caribbean.

Terracotta bust of Piet Heyn, attributed to Hendrick de Keyser, 1636,
Rijksmuseum Amsterdam

The Cuban incident at the Bay of Matanzas was Heyn's retribution for years of suffering at the hands of the Spanish as a prisoner of war. Piet Heyn, his father and uncle, all sailors on merchant ships, were captured by the Spanish after a skirmish at sea, sold and traded as galley slaves to the Moors.

Between 1603 and 1607, Piet Heyn was held captive again by the Spanish when he was captured near Cuba. After eight years as a prisoner, Heyn lusted for revenge. In 1623, Heyn became vice admiral of the newly founded Dutch West Indies Company, the WIC.

The West India House in Amsterdam, headquarters of the Dutch
West India Company from 1623-1647

Heyn was a privateer and pirate far more than a naval officer. Even so, Heyn cared very much for his reputation. He was a strict disciplinarian who strongly discouraged disorderly conduct among his crews. But

121

pillaging whatever they could was part of the contract when sailing back and forth across the Atlantic.

With a small and undermanned expedition, Heyn sailed for the African west coast and attacked a Portuguese fleet in the vigorously defended bay of Luanda. Pleased with the precious loot Heyn brought back to Amsterdam, the WIC promoted Heyn to admiral and sent him out again, this time raiding Salvador and capturing over thirty richly-laden Portuguese merchant ships.

In 1628, Admiral Heyn, with Witte de With as his flag captain, set out to capture a Spanish treasure fleet loaded with silver from their American colonies and the Philippines. Admiral Hendrick Lonck and a squadron of Vice Admiral Joost Banckert, as well as the Jewish pirate Moses Cohen Henriques, joined Heyn on his voyage.

For weeks, Heyn and his fleet were hiding out in the Dry Tortugas, a small archipelago of seven islands in the Gulf of Mexico, just west of Key West. From the Tortugas, it was easy to spot sailing convoys heading for Havana. Heyn possessed valuable information from his many scouts about a Spanish treasure fleet imminently due in Havana harbor.

Heyn's strategy was to scare the convoy captains by chasing them. The threatened commanders would put out too far north of the Cuban north coast to catch wind and speed, and thus overshoot their target of Havana harbor.

From there, it was easy to drive them into the next bay, the shallow Bay of Matanzas. Thus the entire Spanish treasure fleet was caught in the Matanzas cul-de-sac and run aground. After some theatrical musket volleys from Dutch sloops, the crews of the galleons surrendered immediately, since many women and children of Spanish settlers were on board.

The Dutch did not take prisoners but ferried the Spanish crews and passengers to land, gave them supplies, and told them how to walk to Havana. The released were surprised to hear the admiral personally giving them directions in fluent Spanish. Heyn was well acquainted with the region since he had been held there during his internment."

Van der Decken had been silent for a while. Now with all that money being discussed, he obviously wanted to put a penny in the bag, so to say.

Duit of the VOC from Westfriesland, copper, 1792, Rijksmuseum Amsterdam

"We, at the VOC, minted our own money. We understood that money was symbolical, just to replace the cumbersome barter trade. Currency did not need to have any intrinsic value. The *duit* was a copper Dutch coin worth 2 *penning*, with 8-duit pieces equal to one *stuiver* and 160-duit pieces equal to one gulden. But in Dutch Indie, we had different values: 4-duit pieces were equal to one stuiver.

To prevent smuggling and speculation, the VOC ordered special coins with their monogram embossed upon them. Only those pieces were valid in Indonesia. It was also used in the Americas while under Dutch rule. The name of the coin was preserved for a long time in the *fourduitcoin* (or *plak*), because it was worth 4 duiten = half a stuiver (or 2.5 cent)."

Boudewijn Hendricks

"And, just for contrast, dear captain, let me tell you one more pirate story. You may know the cheese farmer and trader Boudewijn Hendricks, alias Balduino Enrico (circa 1625), former Burgomaster of Edam, a small town in Holland. You see how important the name Hendrick and its variations are?"

"Yes, I knew him," said Captain van der Decken. "He grew from a cheese farmer to become one of the great privateers of the Dutch West Indies Company. Edam cheese was a standard cargo for any ship on a long-distance sea voyage, since it was non-perishable. We all knew him well. Hendricks was a traveling salesman for Edam cheese, but in a much more hostile environment than we can possibly imagine. He was a salesman with a dagger and a gun to the head of his customers. I was told that on one of those occasions when he landed in the Puerto Rico area, he was no longer able to control his greed. Tales about Puerto Rico's gold deposits in ten rivers and the Sierra Luquillo were a temptation that could not be resisted by any pirate.

Waag (Weighing house) in Edam

So Boudewijn Hendricks attacked San Juan and besieged Fort San Felipe del Morro and La Fortaleza. But he came up empty-handed. He did not find what he was looking for; there was no gold. Before his expedition, he may have received intelligence from Pieter Schouten (circa 1622) of Vlissingen, another Dutch privateer who was employed by the WIC. Schouten was an intelligence agent, a spy, who collected extensive information before establishing WIC trading posts in the West Indies. The VOC and WIC shared intelligence and had become very good at systematically getting news from all kinds of sources. Extracting valuable information from prisoners was a skillful art, but often most unpleasant. Torture was often necessary. Some relished in the practice."

Van der Decken fell silent and was lost in gloom. There was much more he remembered, I was sure, much more that he had seen and witnessed but was not ready to share, not yet.

"Thanks, Captain. You are quite right. There are so many more stories between heaven and hell than we could ever share."

I allowed myself to also slide into melancholy. Talking about history is often realizing how little mankind has learned from it. Dreams about cities of gold, El Dorados, propelled countless luck seekers and adventurers into despicable and destructive situations, often at others' expense. Without tangible production to match currency, either in printed bills or gold or silver, there cannot be any real wealth. Speculation on nothing but hot air is a falsehood, born out of greedy dreams. The speculation in tulip futures and mania that followed in the Dutch Republic during the 17th century is one example. At the peak of tulip mania, in February 1637, some single tulip bulbs sold for more than ten times the annual income of a skilled artisan. At the same time as speculators were imagining great profits, the bulbs themselves were rotting away in the ground or shriveling up from draught in storage boxes. It was a trade in windbags - empty. Investors, small as well as large ones, were ruined by the fall in prices, and Dutch commerce suffered a severe shock. Today, the same is happening with Bitcoin and gold.

El Dorado

The fantasy about a city made of pure gold, El Dorado, hidden somewhere in the New World jungles of the Amazonas or on a treasure island, inspired many explorers. The rumor mill about gold and riches on the island of Puerto Rico started once Conquistador Ponce de Leon (circa 1506) took the first samples of gold from the river Manatuabon. During the first few decades of Puerto Rico's occupation by the Spanish, the gold produced was worth more than $4 million in Spanish currency.

But as we have seen before, Spain found out the hard way that using gold or silver as currency did not improve productivity and wealth in any community.

Wealth is created by improved productivity, not by increasing the amount of currency, like Venezuela, with inflation of 1,000 percent per year, is finding out. Venezuela's registration of quantities, as the nation with the largest oil reserves in the world, did not bring any wealth either. The Bolivar Forte, Venezuelan's currency, is now a worthless piece of paper, no matter the quantity of unexplored oil in the Orinoco basin. Studying history could have taught Venezuela that lesson.

A businessman

"Try to imagine, Anansi, the value of money and gold on a little island, an island without people. Just ask yourself what the value of money is, and what ownership means. Let me tell you the story of a businessman on an island, all alone.

A little island in the Caribbean belonged to a businessman. He was also the only person on that little island. The man was so busy governing and administrating his island that he did not even raise his head when I visited him.

'Twenty million and forty-six million and a half makes sixty million and a half, but I am short by six million after counting three times over. So, who has been stealing from me? Who is taking the sand off my beaches?'

'But you are the only person on this island,' I said. 'What is the purpose of counting your possessions all the time? Does not the sea bring sand every day and take it away on other days?'

'The purpose of counting is to be rich! I count everything, all day long, the sand on the beach and the stars in the sky. I own them all. I am extremely happy to be so rich,' the businessman hollered, and stared at me straight in the face.

'Interesting. But how can anyone own the stars?' I asked.

'Whom do they belong to?' the businessman grumbled. 'I do not know. To anybody, maybe. But now, they are simply mine, because I thought of it first. First, I started to manage all the stars by counting them and putting them in my ledger, properly: with name, date of birth or discovery, frequency, season, and brightness. Then, I had the notary draft a deed, and the deed determined that they were mine, and in forty-five years nobody has come forward to contest my claim. My deed is registered and filed with the Global Court where all deeds are registered. Just in case somebody forgets, anyone can go there and check it out.'

'Yes,' I tried, though it was clear that the businessman was not open to criticism. He was frozen in his greed. 'I perfectly understand now. Thank you. You are just like the colonials in history when they came to the Caribbean and made deeds that declared their ownership of these islands. Upon arrival they would actually post plaques, declaring islands to belong to the Spanish or English Crown. Once deeded, the kingdoms of England, France, Portugal, Spain, Denmark or Holland then owned these islands. The colonials also claimed that they owned the people who lived there, or they simply found people elsewhere, deeded them as their property, and shipped them over.'

My remarks were not appropriate as a visitor, but the businessman's attitude had triggered my rebellion. 'What happens when an owner forgets to make a deed and someone else declares his ownership? Or when the deed gets lost, or when the subjects have been already deeded by someone else?'

'Yes,' said the businessman, 'that happens, and that mostly means war. The strongest party always wins. It gets complicated when the people who thought that they were deeded as someone's property find out that their deed was invalid or expired, or simply canceled. Suddenly they are not owned by anybody but themselves. You see, I had quite a few of those people on my island. The debate with them became very complicated since they believed that I had to take care of them. Supposedly, there existed such a deed that declared them my property. In the end, they all left, but are still claiming damages against me. Never mind, now I own the sand on the beach and the stars in the sky, and they never disputed me. I am truly a rich person, now even a very rich person! Therefore, I have to continue to count and register the quantities in ledgers.'

I was overwhelmed by his bungled logic and was wondering whether there could be any deed that declared that someone owned me. Suddenly in a hurry, I moved as quickly as I could to check at the Global Court where all deeds are registered. There I declared, with a brand-new deed, that I, and no other person on this globe, own me. After all, when greed kicks in, everything becomes beyond the reach of morals, ethics, and reason.

"Are you not happy, Anansi, that we have come to the point in history where nobody can own another person anymore, that we are the owners of our lives?"

After all those riches, I decided to make the best chocolate mousse in my life.

Chocolate mousse

Ingredients
7 oz. dark chocolate (75 percent cocoa solids), broken into pieces
4 fl oz. warm water
3 large eggs, separated
1 ½ oz. golden caster sugar

Instructions
Place the broken-up chocolate in a large heatproof bowl, which should be sitting over a saucepan of barely simmering water.
Keeping the heat at its lowest, allow the chocolate to melt slowly - this should take about 6 minutes.
Remove it from the heat and give it a good stir until it's smooth and glossy.
Let the chocolate cool for 2-3 minutes before stirring in the egg yolks.
Then give it another good mix with a wooden spoon.
In a clean bowl, whisk the egg whites to the soft-peak stage.
Whisk in the sugar, about a third at a time.
Whisk again until the whites are glossy.
Now, using a metal spoon, fold a tablespoon of the egg whites into the chocolate mixture to loosen it,
then carefully fold in the rest.

You need to have patience here - it needs gentle folding and cutting movements so that you retain all the precious air that makes the mousse light.
Divide the mousse between the ramekins or glasses.
Chill for at least 2 hours, covered with cling film.

I think it's also good to serve the mousse with a blob of whipped cream on top.

13 BARTOLOMÉ DE LAS CASAS

First resident Bishop of Chiapas and the first officially appointed
Protector of the Indians: a 16th-century Human Rights Observer
and Champion of Caribbean indigenous populations. - Catholic-
Hierarchy.org. David M. Cheney

A Short Account of the Destruction of the Indies

Bartolomé pertained that the indigenous populations in the Spanish
colonies were systematically butchered, and their meat sold as food in
butcheries, carrying the seal of the Spanish king. He angrily protested
such barbaric treatment with long pamphlets and personal pleas to the
Crown. The counter argument at that time was that the indigenous
people were not human beings, and, as such, there should not be any
qualms about hunting and butchering them.

The Spanish court allowed Bartolomé to produce specimen of
indigenous people to prove otherwise. On one such occasion, he
produced an indigenous boy who was able to sing religious hymns with a
counter-tenor voice. The king was charmed but still not convinced. The
economic aspects also had to be considered. If the indigenous could not
be used for labor, who was going to replace them? History flip-flopped

the priest's intentions so that Bartolemé de Las Casas by misfortune became the main driving force behind the import of African slaves for use as labor over Carib Indians on the sugar plantations.

Bartolomé de Las Casas, artist unknown, oil oil wood, 16th century

Bartolomé was the son of Pedro de las Casas, a merchant, migrant and settler, who came over on board the ship of the Spanish royal governor, Nicolás de Ovando. De Las Casas and his family immigrated to the island of Hispaniola in 1502; thus, De Las Casas became a *hacendado* and slave owner.

The Spanish Crown had sent de Ovando to establish the formal *Encomienda* system. The Encomienda was a labor system rewarding Spanish and Portuguese conquerors. Settlers, like Pedro de Las Casas, got a land lease, no ownership, and usufruct of native workers. Usufruct combines the legal rights of use and fructus, or profit. In return, settlers paid a percentage to the governor and the Crown.

Bartolomé witnessed indescribable atrocities with the locals as the victims. You could say he became one of the world's first human rights observers. His entire life he protested against the injustices against the native populations.

The treatment of the indigenous populations was horrendous by all accounts. The mistreatment of the Indians resulted in the annihilation of millions. Some historians estimate that between 1500 and 1600, Spanish and Portuguese settlers and soldiers killed 20-22 million people. We will never know the exact numbers, but the unspeakable bestiality can be studied in great detail today in the scenes of Joos van Winghe, a Flemish painter, and Theodorus de Bry, an engraver. Their series of etched plates show what Bartelomé, as an eyewitness, described in his work Brevíssima relación de la destrucción de las Indias (*A Short Account of the Destruction of the Indies*).

Brevísima relación de la destrucción de las Indias, by Bartolomé de Las Casas, published in Sevilla, 1552

On November 20, 1542, after a lifelong protest, De Las Casas succeeded when the emperor signed new laws abolishing the Encomienda and removing certain officials from the Council of the Indies. The new laws made it illegal to use Indians as carriers except where no other transport was available. It explicitly prohibited all taking of Indians as slaves. Instead of indigenous Caribe Indians, Africans became the new labor of the New World.

Discussion

Back on board, heading for the Lesser Antilles with the Leeward in the north and the Windward Islands in the south, I continued my monologues with Anansi and Captain Hendrick van der Decken.

"Anansi, are you upset? You seem so very nervous, shaking in your web today. What is wrong?"

"White man, what you think!" Anansi exploded in anger. "I shocked by stories. You say, European came for salt to the Caribbean, and not slaves.

Cannot be true! Never hear a salt story, herring, and gibbing story before. You phantasy man. You whitewash slavery sins?"

Spanish atrocities committed in the conquest of Cuba in Las Casas's "Brevisima relación de la destrucción de las Indias", engraving by Theodor de Bry, after Joos van Winghe, 16th century

"No, no, Anansi, I said that many non-Spanish adventurers, merchants, and traders came for salt, initially. Later, they engaged in different kinds of commerce. The huge salt trade is not an alternative fact, but an openly known and registered event in history, for the entire world to check. Even today, you can see the mountains of salt on islands like Bonaire. So please, go and check it out."

For a moment, I was discouraged. Had Anansi not learned anything from our previous discussions? So many seem to pick out only those parts of a historical scenario that fit their political objectives. But it was not the right moment for sarcasm or highbrow jokes. Poor Anansi did his utmost to listen to most of my analysis already, and that was to be respected.

"I know it is grossly inconvenient for all those who use selected historical facts to push their own agenda of slave trade crimes and reparation claims. Those may be after the money and not after the facts. Publicly available are many sources of information. Libraries are full of thousands and thousands of shipping documents, tax assessments, loading records, diplomatic correspondence about armed conflicts, insurance policies, claims, financing liens, lawsuits, death certificates, crew lists, etc."

"Truth!" blasted Anansi. "White people, evil. Yes, rich Europe, only from sick black slaves!" Anansi yelled in protest, plugging his ears in preparation for my retort.

Portrait of a Woman, possibly Madame Claude Lambert de Thorigny (Marie Marguerite Bontemps, 1668–1701), and an enslaved servant by Nicolas de Largillierre, oil on canvas, 1696 © The Metropolitan Museum of Art, Rogers Fund, 1903

"If you do not want to listen to me, or listen to our ghost friend, that is up to you. But would you learn about the VOC bosses' interest in cinnamon, caneel or canel, canella, and other spices?"

"You two white men. White men know a lot. Anansi only smart survivor."

And with a sudden turn of emotion, he sarcastically added, "Go on, go on, always nice hearing your voice."

I praised myself for not making too many jokes with Spiderman. The topic meant walking on eggshells. However, my insights may help him understand some historical facts.

"Trade of slaves out of Africa to the Middle East and South East Asia had been happening since Pharaoh Hatshepsut, circa 1500 BCE, who imported slaves from Punt, today's Djibouti and Somalia. By the way, she was the only female pharaoh of Egypt's thirty-three dynasties, including the Persian, Greek, and Hellenistic period. She used a stick-on beard at ceremonies, but as far as slavery was concerned, her gender made no difference."

"Far from my bedside, my darling," said Anansi, in a better mood now. He sang something in falsetto that I could not make out.

Van der Decken added, "Some reported that, most reluctantly, the VOC got involved in annual deliveries of a contingency of slaves from the king of Ashanti to the Demak Sultanate in Semarang. Initially, the big money was not in the slave trade and slavery; the business cycle was too long. The seasoning, or training, of a captive often took three to five years before a slave could be resold. This was costly. Many slave-shipping operations had to file for bankruptcy as they simply ran out of cash. The entire supply chain from African coasts to American plantations took too long and was too capital-intensive."

I added my piece of trivia. "The Dutch West India Company (WIC), a leading transatlantic slave shipper from 1660-1713, filed for bankruptcy four times. Also, the British and Danish West India Companies filed for bankruptcies or reorganization to protect themselves from creditors.

Yes, slavery was terrible and we must thank God that slavery has been abolished in most of the world, but let's not pretend that one nation or one race had the monopoly.

In agricultural economies, slavery was a legal form of employment for thousands of years, in the entire world. Everybody and every nation was involved, not by exception but as a rule and by law, and everyone was the victim. It was only in the 19th century that those massive and impoverished populations, the proletariat, spun into enormous movements like the world had never seen before. And eventually, the prevailing economic philosophies of mercantilism, capitalism, socialism and communism competed in bloody world wars."

Spanish colonial labor arrangements, penal colonies

"Spanish and Portuguese conquistadors had successfully colonized the larger Caribbean islands and most of Central and South America. But make no mistake, conquest was no philanthropy; it was the quest for profit, thirst for gold, and lust for power that motivated conquistadors to risk their lives. Early on, Spanish settlers established large plantations for new agricultural products, like sugar, requiring vast numbers of workers.

But the Iberian invasion had decimated peaceful Arawak and other indigenous tribes. Many died from infectious European illnesses, like influenza and measles, for which they had no immunity; others succumbed to the hard labor on the plantations.

With a steadily increasing shortage of labor in the Spanish colonies, and other islands that were taken over by European nations, new migration routes across the Atlantic developed, with thousands of either voluntary or involuntary workers arriving in the Caribbean.

In the Lesser Antilles, the shortage of workers was at first compensated by indentured labor. Indentured laborers were more or less volunteers from Europe with work contracts for a lifetime, or a lengthy number of years.

The early proletariat, as they became known in the 19th century, was the result of a mismatch between rapid population and economic growth. The resulting misery in Europe, hunger, poverty and exploitation, was exacerbated by countless local wars, the plague, and lost harvests due to climate change.

The courts forced out countless misfortunates by imposing criminal convictions on vagrancy. Hired drafters and hustlers rounded up thousands of homeless street dwellers in London and Paris, who finished up on board ships within days, sold off to the New World. Most of the European settlers were initially no more than white trash, the scum of the earth.

The British developed Australia much the same way - it became a penal colony. An account says that between 1819 and 1848, over 50,000 male convicts passed through the Hyde Park Barracks, the Ellis Island of Australia."

Daily food for the enslaved

"Dr. Fitzroy J. Henry of Jamaica has published extensively on obesity in the Caribbean. He claims that obesity is the underlying cause of most deaths in the Caribbean and that the medical costs are overwhelming the local budgets. Diabetes, kidney disease, amputations, and premature death are common. Walking around the markets, most women are huge and slowly wobble up and down the streets.

The story of Saartje Baartman comes to mind, a Khoikhoi woman who, due to her large buttocks, was exhibited as a freak-show attraction in 19th-century Europe, under the name *Hottentot Venus*.

Saartje Baartman, hand-colored etching, artist unknown, 1810 ©
The Trustees of the British Museum, London

Steatopygia, in medical terms, is the state of having substantial levels of tissue on the buttocks and thighs. This build is not confined to the gluteal regions, but extends to the outside and front of the thighs, and tapers to the knee, producing a curvaceous figure. For many, this is the Venus ideal.

The Africans who came to the Caribbean also brought the genetic code for this kind of overweight. But like any kind of obesity, it requires enormous amounts of calorie-rich food. Sugarcane and lard became the staples of the slaves and the rest seems history.

It was not always that way. Many islanders, predominantly slaves, went hungry for decennia, and many children suffered from malnutrition. The daily menu of slaves, and indentured laborers, was far from a banquet. Records from St. Kitts and Nevis give some idea about the volatile supply and circumstances.

The volcanic soils of the two islands were very fertile, allowing plantation owners and managers to maximize profits from sugar crops. The plantation owners distributed North American corn to their slaves as well as salted herring and beef, while horse beans and biscuit bread were sent from England on occasion.

Losing cane land for growing food was not a proposition. The salted meat and fish were shipped from New England, along with timber and animals to drive the mills.

On the Stapleton estate on Nevis, records show that there were only thirty-one acres set aside to grow yams and sweet potatoes. Slaves on the plantation had five acres of provision ground, probably a little more on the rougher area of the plantation, at higher elevations, where they could grow vegetables and keep poultry.

Plantation owners provided their Africans with weekly rations of salted herring or mackerel, sweet potatoes and maize, and sometimes salted West Indian turtle.

The slaves supplemented their diet with other kinds of wild food. Some of them were fond of eating grasshoppers or locusts; others would wrap up cane rats in *bonano* (banana) leaves and roast them on wood embers.

Many enslaved Africans were permitted provision grounds and gardens in the villages or plantations to grow food. However, these were not enough to stop them from suffering from starvation in times of poor harvests.

It became so bad at times of failed crops that in Nevis, in 1682, a law was passed to force plantation owners to provide land for food crops, thus preventing starving slaves from stealing food.

In the year 1706, there was a severe drought that caused most food crops to fail. Many slaves would have died from starvation had not a prickly type of edible cucumber grown that year in great profusion.

In 1750, St. Kitts grew most of its own food, but 25 years later when harvests were meager, Nevis and St. Kitts had come to rely heavily on food supplies imported from North America.

At the outbreak of the American Revolution in 1776, trade was restricted between North America and the British islands in the West Indies, leading to disastrous food shortages. In 1777, as many as 400 slaves died from starvation or diseases caused by malnutrition on St. Kitts and on Nevis."

I suggested a menu of cucumbers that night.

Cucumbers

Ingredients
1 tbsp. salt
1 tbsp. celery seeds
2 cups sugar
1 cup white vinegar

Instructions
Mix the pickling solution in a medium to large sealable bowl.
1 medium onion, sliced
1 green pepper, sliced
Cucumbers, unpeeled, sliced

Add the vegetables to the pickling mixture and stir.
Use as many cucumbers as you desire, as long as the slices don't pile up above the liquid.
Cover the bowl and refrigerate.
Rather than make a new batch every time the pickles are eaten, simply add more vegetables to the remaining liquid.

It will keep for months, so you can enjoy your cucumbers long after harvest!

14 THE TRANSATLANTIC SLAVE TRADE

January 22, 1510: the start of the systematic transportation of African slaves to the New World. King Ferdinand of Spain authorized a shipment of 50 African slaves to be sent to Santo Domingo. - *A Chronology of Slavery, Abolition, and Emancipation in the Sixteenth Century*

The transatlantic slave trade is an unavoidable topic when touring the West African coast and the Caribbean, especially because today's reality is still shaped by what happened then, hundreds of years ago.

"Dear friends, Anansi and Hendrick van der Decken, since we are heading east, towards the Lesser Antilles, we need to have a serious tête-à-tête about the Afro-Caribbean population and what brought them to the Caribbean."

Transatlantic slave trade

"In public debate, on radio and television, I often think that so many arguments are soaked in the emotions of the moment. The public conversation about issues like historical slavery has become almost impossible to continue; bullying and intimidation determine the outcome in verbal battles, competitions of words, not the facts of what once was and what happened. Many historical facts are twisted for political gain, but they remain undeniable facts.

Anansi, in so many ways, you, as the fairytale Ashanti prince spider, are part of the soul of those who came across the Atlantic. You embody the spirit of their tales of joy, faith, fear, desperation, and hope. Your opinion is also shaped by incidents, accidents, and atrocities.

The biggest mistake man made is to look at the past from the perspective of the present; that is very misleading since ethics and morals have changed dramatically. Thus, the reality of the past comes out as a bizarre caricature in the light of today. We do condemn slavery in the past, but did a different mass employment system even exist?

Gravestone of Valens, with two slaves, 117-200 AD, Rijksmuseum van Oudheden, Leiden

What was and could have been the alternative? You may insist that the labor conditions should have been better, with fixed wages, vacations, and extra pay for overwork, but those are the conditions forged by the Industrial Revolution in the 19th and 20th century, by socialism and communism, ideologies that did not exist in the 16th and 17th century."

It was silent in my cockpit and I let it remain so. Let the words sink in a bit.

Then I continued, "Captain Van der Decken, you are in many ways the personification of Dutch traders and shippers of the 17th century, who, with the Bible held to their chests, sailed around the world for God and fatherland and for profit of the VOC and WIC. The roles of Dutch clergyman on a mission to save souls for eternity, and businessman out for profit were so intertwined that the distinction was often blurred."

And thus, I made a little trip through history, not so much focused on the individual horror stories, but more on the bigger social and economic picture of those days.

"It is silly to state that slavery started then and there, especially since the concept of slavery goes way back to biblical times. It is even sillier to claim that slavery was a form of punishment, or had only a criminal racial intent, to subjugate blacks or to mark them as inferior beings that were merely good as slaves. Slavery was the only, and preferred, way of employment in agriculture in most of the world from the beginning of time, and all races were enslaved one way or another.

On one of my Silk Road trips across Asia, I came upon the city of Khiva, in today's Uzbekistan. A plaque reminds the random visitor that more than six million slaves were auctioned on that spot in the 17th century; not a single one was black, they were all Caucasian and Asian. A massive proletariat of slaves, or serfs, powered agriculture in all of Asia and Russia.

Passageway used for slavemarket. East Gate of the Ichon-Qala in Khiva

Europe had a system of forced and indentured labor, especially in kingdoms with an elaborate country nobility. Debt bondage as barter for lease, domestic servants as a privilege of the landowners, shaped the customs. A slave was unable to withdraw unilaterally from any such arrangement; he became property to be bought and sold at the whim of his owner. Chattel slavery is the term used by many as a specific sense of legalized, *de jure* slavery.

In 2017, the world witnessed chattel slavery practiced in the ISIS state, in Iraq and Syria. Thousands of Yazidi women and children were sold at auction as sex slaves. Slave auctions are also held in Libya, where able men are sold out of refugee camps.

The expulsion from Spain and Portugal

The transatlantic slave trade was for many Europeans after the Middle Ages a starting point for a new social-economic era, often called the Age of Discovery. Large-scale industrialized agriculture was a new phenomenon, and a prelude to the Industrial Revolution of the 19th century. Traffic and trade developed on a global scale as never before.

Ferdinand and Isabella (1476-1516) Double Excelente, gold coin ©
Royal Collection Trust

In October 1469, King Ferdinand V of Castile united the Iberian Peninsula by his marriage to Isabella I of Aragon.

The Alhambra Decree, or the Edict of Expulsion, issued on March 31, 1492, was the beginning of the Golden Age of Spain, especially after the expulsion of all Jews, the confiscation of their properties, and the reconquest of Andalusia from the Muslims. Some 400,000 Spanish Jews were forced out of Spain and fled to Portugal from where they were also expelled, on December 5, 1496, by Manual I. King Manual's relationship with the Portuguese Jews started out well. At the outset of his reign, he released all the Jews who had been held captive during the reign of John II. Unfortunately for the Jews, he decided to marry Infanta Isabella of Aragon, the heiress of the united Spain, and widow of his nephew, Prince Alfonso.

Ferdinand and Isabella had expelled the Jews in 1492 and would never allow their daughter to marry the king of a country that still tolerated their presence. In the marriage contract, Manuel agreed to persecute the Jews of Portugal. In December 1496, it was decreed that all Jews must either convert to Christianity or leave the country without their children. The Crown and the Inquisition confiscated most of the Jewish properties. Columbus' exploration of the New World, in 1492, was financed with the capital confiscated from the expelled Jews.

Jewish pirates

Upon fleeing Spain and Portugal some of these Jews, suddenly without a nationality, especially the traders, shippers, and captains, became pirates and privateers, while others became interlopers; the early shippers of African slaves. Slave transports by interlopers, unregulated shippers, and traders, out to pick up any cargo that brought them a profit, started the Transatlantic Passage, as it is known today. The regular trade followed suit.

Privateers carried a *Letter of License*, granting the right to attack ships of enemy nations; they were licensed pirates. Jewish privateers often got authorization by Spanish rivals, such as the Seventeen Provinces of the Low Lands, a 16th-century precursor of the present Benelux, or the Ottoman Empire.

In those days, the Islamic countries were welcoming expelled Jews, especially in the Ottoman Empire. Thus, many privateers were recruited and became corsairs for the Sultan of Istanbul, or the Bey of Barbary Coast, today's Morocco, Algeria, Tunisia, and Libya.

Some famous Jewish names come to mind when talking about the expulsion. To mention a couple, Sinan Reis and Yaakov Koriel, who both became prominent Jewish pirates. Sinan Reis was a refugee whose family emigrated from Spain to the Ottoman Empire. He sailed as a Barbary corsair under Hayreddin Barbarossa. Some attribute to him the defeat of an imperial-Spanish fleet in 1538 at the Battle of Preveza, a city in today's western Greece.

Yaakov Koriel was born to a Jewish family. Under pressure from the Inquisition, his family converted to Christianity when Yaakov was still a child. They became Conversos, and were also called *Maranos* or *Morenos*. Yaakov became captain of the Spanish fleet until the Inquisition arrested him. He was freed by his sailors; most were also Maranos. Revenge became Yaakov's only goal in life. With three pirate ships, he soon plundered and murdered in the name of the Sultan.

Jewish privateers and pirates often solicited and received help from Creoles, the offspring of Portuguese sailors and local African women. The word *Creole*, from the Spanish word *Criollo*, was used in general for children of white parents born in the colonies. The Spanish then used it for slaves, and especially those not born in Africa. That is what gave the word *Creole* a negative connotation.

More about Creoles

In 1440, a Creole colony had developed quickly and steadily after Portugal established business with the West African coast. Prince Henry the Navigator of Portugal had set up extensive trading in West Africa around 1440, mostly with gold and cotton. By 1444, a cargo of 235 enslaved Africans had been shipped to Lagos in Portugal. And by 1460, the Portuguese were using enslaved Africans on sugar plantations in Madeira, a Portuguese island off the west coast of Africa.

The Portuguese built their first slave fort in 1481, on the coast of modern Ghana. Elmina castle became the headquarters of the Portuguese slave traders, later taken over by the Dutch. Interestingly enough, Creoles as corsairs also captured millions of European slaves for the North African provinces, in the so-called Barbary Coast Christian slave trade from 800-1900.

Barbary Coast was the marketplace for millions of European slaves, captured or traded by corsairs. The African west coast, southwards from Casablanca, was the territory of Barbary corsairs. So you can see that the more we invest ourselves in Caribbean history, the more complex the players become.

Map of Barbary Coast in 1590

The next act by the mighty rulers of the Spanish and Portuguese empires came, as I mentioned before, with the expulsion and the Reconquista of 1492, driving all Jews as well as Almoravid and Umayyad Muslims, Moors, out of Andalusia. The Moors left behind tens of thousands of slaves wandering free, or awaiting resale; by 1500 the European markets were totally saturated with abandoned black slaves, all soliciting employment as highly-trained domestics. Therefore, initially, the trade of black slaves to the Caribbean was not successful. Local markets were quickly oversupplied and African blacks needed extensive training periods versus Europeans, who came as experienced indentured labor.

A new impulse for the slave trade came with the demand from the New World and the failure to employ the indigenous population of the Americas. In the early 16th century, the new Spanish colonies were desperately short of labor and offered good money to anyone who was ready to provide workers. Responding to the demand, in 1510 King Ferdinand issued a Royal Consent to what became known as the Asiento, the right to transport and sell African slaves to the Spanish colonies in the New World by other nations.

Interlopers, privateers, and pirates as slavers were succeeded by officially-licensed Portuguese and Spanish slave shipping and trading companies. Eventually, these Iberian companies shipped as many as seven million African slaves across the Atlantic. After 1510, the trade was opened up to all other nations under the Asiento. Transatlantic slave trading became a lucrative business for many nations, like England, France, Holland, Flanders, Denmark and Sweden.

African chiefs and kings accommodated eagerly and sold off their slaves, prisoners of war, and criminal delinquents. The international transatlantic slave trade was born and the Asiento functioned intermittently from 1543 till 1834.

Employment perspectives

In most of the world, slavery was the standard model for mass employment till major structural changes took place in the 19th century.

Slavery in Europe in one form or another in large-scale agricultural models was more or less the standard. The Europe, Asia and Africa that the Roman Empire had left behind were organized into a class society of nobility, military, priesthood, and peasants. Over 90 percent of medieval people were peasants.

An aristocracy led by a king, often as a hereditary absolute ruler, governed the countries and owned most property; the aristocracy was made up of the nobility. The military, clergy, and city dwellers formed their own classes, with duties and privileges, and often their own courts.

Town and city dwellers often paid hefty duties to their rulers and local nobility for privileges, either in money or labor. The large group of penniless country peasants paid their dues to the aristocracy only in the form of indentured labor for life, or slave labor. The growth of towns with craftsmen, traders, and artisans changed that picture. Towns became increasingly more powerful and the accumulation of capital allowed them to become independent of the aristocracy.

Privateers, pirates, buccaneers, filibusters, and corsairs

All seafaring European and many West African nations eventually participated in the Asiento. But many poorly-defended shippers fell victim to the opportunistic behavior of outlaws. The world got to know these freeloaders, who at times fulfilled regular contracts, by many fancy and romantic names, like privateers, pirates, buccaneers, filibusters and corsairs.

Privateers and buccaneers usually carried some kind of a consent, or license, issued by authorities; others were outlaws and acted strictly at their own risk. Piracy was ruthless, with thousands of pirates swarming all over the trade destinations. Piracy was so frequent that soon all trade ships were outfitted with heavy guns. Around 1700, most ships carried aboard 50-100 guns. A leisurely cruise across the Atlantic was no longer possible.

The Ottoman Empire employed millions of slaves; all of Egypt and Syria consisted of slaves, the so-called *Mamluks*. A giant slave revolution even brought Mamluk slaves to power, in Syria and Egypt, for nearly 200 years.

Africa was a major source of slaves for the Ottomans, but they also sourced them from Europe and the Balkans. Race was not much of an issue, though Ottoman Muslims maintained that blacks were an inferior race. While it is commonly believed that Caribbean slaves were only black, we also learn from history that that's not entirely true.

Trade with Africa

Local chiefs and kings of West Africa became enthusiastic players in the revamped slave-trading business after 1510. At one point in time, the kings of Benin, Congo, and Dahomey were known as the richest people in the world.

Deals did not close overnight. It took many diplomatic missions from shipping nations to negotiate contracts with African kings. For instance, the king of Luanda, today in Angola, kept a Dutch delegation hostage for eight years until the king issued his permission, on the condition that he could join the voyage to Recife, Brazil. The story goes that upon arrival, the king was also sold as a slave.

Nearly 2,000 castles, factories, and forts, large and small, either converted or purposely built by the Portuguese, Swedish, Danish, Dutch, British, and French formed the holding pens on Africa's west coast before the human cargo was loaded onto ships. It could take quite some time, often months, before a sufficient number of captives were collected to fill a ship hold.

Slave Trade by John Raphael Smith, after George Morland, print, 1762-1812, Rijksmuseum Amsterdam

Cape Coast Castle is one of about forty slave castles on the Gold Coast of West Africa, now Ghana. It was originally built by the Swedes for the trade in timber and gold but was later used in the transatlantic slave trade. Other well-known slave castles were Elmina Castle and Fort

Christiansborg, a Danish fort. Gorée Castle, on a little island in the harbor of Dakar, became infamous for its 'gate of no return', which was the last stop before crossing the Atlantic Ocean. The Dutch Admiral Michiel de Ruyter set up his offices in Gorée.

Ship physicians checked the captives before shipment. Licking and tasting the captives' skin was an approved method; sweaty or sour-smelling persons were distinguished and discriminated against. The sick and elderly were refused; prime cargos were teenagers.

To claim, as some black advocacy groups do, that the 12 million transatlantic slaves who were shipped across over time were transported against the will of Africans, and were only the victims of ruthless raids by white Europeans, is not supported by the facts. The slave trade in Africa was an established and extensive economic system for thousands of years. Long before any European set foot ashore, Africa knew the trade in slaves.

African leaders not only supported the slave trade but also benefited from it. They pocketed enormous amounts of money that made them amongst the richest individuals of those days. Europe may have abolished slavery and the slave trade, but Africa never did. Hundreds of thousands are still bought and sold every year.

Signing abolition agreements issued by the United Nations or humanitarian organizations is still a symbolic act, but done more to appease western donors of foreign aid - it means very little in real life.

Slavery was also a widely accepted system for dealing with an inventory of prisoners of war and convicts. It is not surprising that the locals put up so very little resistance. Generally, in Africa, it was an accepted practice that prisoners would be sold as slaves.

Once the convicts and prisoners-of-war ran out in Africa, the Tuareg were employed as hunters to carry out raids. The Tuareg people are a large Berber group in the Sahara desert, and they operate in a vast area from southwestern Libya and southern Algeria to Niger, Mali, and Burkina Faso. The Tuareg enslaved the entire Bella tribe in their operations. In the recent skirmishes in Timbuktu, these tribes formed the Jihadi rebels, killing countless innocents and ransacking the monuments of the old city.

The Tuareg tribe, as slave hunters, had quite a reputation already. Rounding up people for the slave trade was their most lucrative commercial activity. Since the demand for slaves developed and grew with the progress of the Muslim world, Tuareg slave traders were in high demand.

Timbuktu, the major exchange market in the Sahel, became known all over the world. From the Timbuktu market, millions of captives marched in long caravans across the Sahara, toward the Mediterranean for shipment. The new ports along the West African coast reinvigorated the Tuareg slave-trading business.

When I visited Loropéni I could still find the artifacts left behind by countless prisoners. Loropéni is a thousand-year-old fortress in Burkina Faso, near the borders of today's Côte d'Ivoire, Ghana, and Togo, which was revamped to hold as many as 15,000 captives from Tuareg raids.

Koumbi Saleh, or Wagadu, the former capital of the Ghana Empire, and presently an extensive archeological site in southeast modern Mauritania, became another storage place for prisoners and crossroad of trade.

Moorish slaves

The Spanish aristocracy financed Columbus' expeditions to the New World, and once successful, claimed their share. In the colonies, Spain set up structures based on colonial aristocracy, so very familiar to Europe since the Romans. Gradually, slavery became a part of it, as it had always been in feudal Europe.

The economic system of the Muslims, even in Spain, was almost entirely based on slavery; after 1500, the Spanish assimilated Islamic slavery and its Andalusia adaptations into their legal structure.

The Encomienda, a legal system designed during the Reconquista of Muslim Spain for the extraction of tribute and free labor from Muslims and Jews, also became the applicable law in the colonies.

Once the British got involved in global empire building, they did exactly the same as the Spanish; a colonial aristocracy was created, and peasants had to work for free; they were serfs, slaves, or labor indentured for life. Class mobility was possible but in minimal numbers; one was born into a social class. The Vatican not only consented but also participated in the trade. The pope insisted that all captives be baptized and given Christian names, for which service the Vatican collected considerable fees.

In the 1950s, an American black activist, Malcolm X, with the Christian family name Little, after the ship captain's at the time of such baptism of his ancestors, protested. He declared that he preferred an X rather than the slaver's name.

The Spanish and Portuguese were the clear frontrunners of the business; they shipped about seven million Africans across the Atlantic. The British and French became serious players towards the end of the 16th century. The Dutch were still excluded until after the Peace of Westphalen (Münster) of 1648.

The Asiento, the right to transport slaves to Spanish South American colonies, got into Dutch hands in about 1662, through Bastiaen Willem Coymans, a scion of a banker-trader family of Haarlem and Amsterdam, in a joint venture with the WIC, only to be lost again in 1672.

Willem Coymans' operations used the island of Curaçao as their main shipping port; it became the Amsterdam of the Dutch Caribbean. The capital investments of building forts, holding yards, and training plantations were enormous, and progress extremely slow; it often took years between transatlantic transport, seasoning, and the sale of a slave in the New World. Soon Curaçao felt itself to be in competition with St. Eustatius, another Dutch Caribbean island trading post, with transshipment, an instant clearing market. Another Coymans family member took on a new Asiento assignment in 1685, but the direct Dutch involvement in the Asiento ended by 1713, with the Treaty of Utrecht; all Dutch Asiento rights were relinquished and went to England.

In 1750, Coopstad & Rochussen, a joint venture between trading companies of Rotterdam and Middelburg, were amongst the many that managed subcontracts for the English, which more or less replaced the activities of the WIC, but in much smaller numbers.

The demand in the market for cheap labor on the sugar plantations was too strong to be ignored by shippers of any nationality.

The slave trade into the US

Contrary to what most of us were taught in school and by countless movies and books on slavery, the United States of America only imported directly in total 388,000 of the 10.7 million Africans who made it across the Atlantic alive. For further reference, please see Professor Henry Gates, Black Studies, Harvard University.

Of the 12.5 million shipped across, at least 10.7 arrived alive. Most of them ended up in Brazil. The most common cause of death during the voyage was dehydration. The ships were unable to carry sufficient drinking water for crew and cargo for six to ten weeks. Dehydration had the convenient side effect that the captives in the ship hold were weak and quiet. Many unfortunates died, and the payout risk for the insurance companies became so high that they insisted on the presence of a physician on board at all times. The installation of water-distilling equipment became mandatory. Small water distillers became the standard equipment on board all ships - it was relatively easy to use seawater for the distilling process.

The Caribbean absorbed millions of African captives for seasoning, a training period which could last as long as two or even three years, before passing them on to other destinations. Furniture workshops in the Caribbean produced highly-skilled labor. Slaves sold as cabinetmakers would fetch top prices in, for instance, Virginia.

Skilled slaves had become so very expensive that financing became an issue. Many financing operations were set up issuing mortgages for the purchase of slaves, who were then often shared by several owners. Cooperative ownership of skilled slaves in small workshops or factories became common.

The entire transatlantic slave-trading period lasted about 250-350 years. On average, 30-40,000 people per year were transported from Africa to the rest of the world. By today's standards when it comes to forced migration, these numbers are small. The United Nations reported that 2014 had the highest level of forced migration on record: in that single year, 59.5 million individuals migrated because of 'persecution, conflict, generalized violence, or human rights violations', as compared with 51.2 million in 2013 (an increase of 8.3 million), and with 37.5 million a decade prior.

The transatlantic slave trade was brutal and inhumane and stirs up strong emotions in many blacks as well as whites in the West. Especially today, with morals and ethics inspired by humanism, humans sold as cattle is beyond comprehension.

The apathy of the present descendants of transatlantic slaves towards the slave trade in West Africa and the Sahel today is hard to understand. No significant voice of protest has been raised against any of the horrendous slave-trading activities in Africa, the Middle East, and Asia.

Presently, descendants from small Caribbean islands and Afro-Americans in the US are seeking reparations from those who supposedly benefited illegally from the historic slave trade. International lawsuits are writing history, since laws apply to the time they were issued, seldom retroactively. Slavery and the slave trade were legal by law at the time in all the participating countries. It may take many more years before final judgments will be passed.

The moral and ethical aspects at the time are interesting to get to know, but to many of us they are unfathomable. Learned, emotional, and political publications with pro and con arguments fill libraries around the world.

The Dutch WIC had a unique case in Jacobus Josias Capitein when it came to morals and ethics. We will meet him later on."

My fellow sailors remained silent.

15 POWERFUL CLERGYMEN

De servitude, libertati christianae non-contraria. How slavery is
not in conflict with Christian freedom. - Jacobus Capitein

Some kind of ISIS-like state of mind existed in Christianity during the
Middle Ages and lasted until the Age of Enlightenment and the French
Revolution.

The Inquisition could arrest, torture and kill at will in the name of the
Lord. Slavery and racial prejudice were easily mixed with divine
devotion, and almost everything became permissible with the blessing of
the Church.

John Gabriel Stedman's 1796 narrative of a five-year-expedition of
revolting negroes in Surinam portrayed unspeakable atrocities and
torture that have impressed the world through today.

John Gabriel Stedman by Reinier Vinkeles, after Tardieu, etching
1751-1816, Rijksmuseum Amsterdam

The battle of words that rages on in public debate and the media when it comes to black history and its slavery legacy is one not only of bigotry but also magical thinking. The Melanin Movement, an Afrocentric movement based on the theory that black people have superior mental, physical, and paranormal powers because they have more melanin in their skin and brains than whites, is one of many examples. The Movement members argue that black people have more melanotropins, or B-MSH, in their system and that would contribute to the superiority of people of color over whites. Therefore, only blacks are able to communicate with the vibrations of the divine. In fact, whites are not human beings but more mechanical things.

This movement is as prejudiced and irrational as white supremacists. Fanatics amongst them are full of such irrational notions and bizarre fantasies. The Santeria of Cuba, Voodoo of Haïti, and Rastafarianism of Jamaica are full of magical thinking. The intensive hatred of many of its members allows radicalization, as we have seen with the Black Panthers in the US. Old and new Black Panthers and Malcolm X were, and are, with raised fists, ready to kill.

Recently, ISIS has shown the world that in the name of religion, the most inhumane and atrocious acts can be sanctified. From slave trade to decapitation or any other unspeakable crime against humanity, all is fine as long as you do it 'in the name of God'. Effortlessly, twisted arguments are offered as truth. Children, the weak, and the poorly educated are brainwashed. Distinguishing religion from magic is almost impossible; the two seem inseparable.

Before the era of Enlightenment that started sometime in the 18th century, philosophy and political ideology in Europe were dominated by religion, by Christianity. Superstition and magic were deeply rooted in all aspects of the beliefs of the faithful, also in the state religions of Roman Catholicism and Protestantism.

Thus, the clergy had an enormous hold on the society and economy. Everything was related to biblical and ecclesiastical values. Even after the reformation, society remained intolerant of any other interpretation but the prevailing religious mantras of whichever flavor of Christianity happened to be in power. The Inquisition and church law prosecuted trespassers and persecuted heretics.

The Catholic Church and its Inquisition took care of all matters when it came to morals and ethics; civil law simply took care of the executive side.

After the reformation, moral leadership was no longer as homogeneous as it had been under Roman Catholic rule. In 1553, Calvin of Protestant Geneva managed to equal the Catholic Inquisition in cruelty when he had Servetus, a prominent scholar, arrested when passing through Geneva. Servetus was condemned to death and burnt alive for a heresy related to the baptism of children. His sin was that he had written in a pamphlet that paedobaptism was an invention of the devil, an infernal falsity for the destruction of all Christianity.

Protestant churches differed greatly in how to apply religious teachings to everyday life. The position towards the slave trade and slavery gradually changed, but mostly afterwards, as a whisper in the corridors, not with moral leadership and never in a united way.

The position of a priest, minister, or clergyman became one of great public respect, influence, and power. Their opinions set policy for years, also when it came to slavery.

Jacobus Elisa Joannes Capitein (1717-1747)

In the 18th century, in the middle of an intense moral debate over slavery and the slave trade, the Dutch West Indies Company, in search of religious justification for their trade, benefited greatly from the efforts of a black clergyman, Jacobus Elisa Johannes Capitein, once an African slave himself.

Portrait of Jacobus Elisa Johannes Capitein by Pieter Tanjé, print, 1742, Rijksmuseum Amsterdam

Jacobus, Ashanti by birth and enslaved as a child in the Ashanti kingdom (Ghana), became a free man in Vlissingen (Holland) when he set foot ashore, as was the rule in Zeeland. The Republic of the Low Lands only knew slavery in its far-away trading posts, not at home. Although rulings concerning blacks in the home countries may have differed somewhat in the autonomous states, Holland and Zeeland, the outcome for Capitein was that he could study and live like a free man.

With the help of a Dutch sponsor who had bought the young man as a house slave but soon discovered his intellect, Jacobus studied theology at Leiden University. He became the first black man to be ordained as a Protestant minister in Holland.

On March 10, 1742, Jacobus Josias Capitein defended his thesis for his doctorate. The title was provocative but great marketing for the WIC's slave trade. Capitein delivered sermons in academic settings, as well as from the pulpit in churches. The churches were full. Not only was it a great novelty to have a black Dutch minister read these biblical texts to the congregation, it also made a great impact. Often, people wanted to touch his black skin and cropped hair just to have the feel of it or to see if it was real. Jacobus Capitein turned into a kind of county fair attraction.

Title page of the Dutch edition of Capitein's dissertation, 1742,
Rijksmuseum Amsterdam

Jacobus' book appeared under the title *De servitude, libertati christianae non contraria* (How slavery is not in conflict with Christian freedom). It ran through five Latin and Dutch editions within one year and became a real bestseller, not only read by the clergy but often prominently displayed in the offices of WIC-affiliated businessmen.

In the thesis, Capitein presented a lengthy exposé of biblical slavery cases and concluded that slavery was a divinely preordained order to be respected. He also promoted slavery as the grand solution for the countless vagabonds who polluted the towns and villages and committed crime.

Soon, in all major cities of Holland and Zeeland, under Capitein's supervision, the biblical texts were studied extensively and used as directions on how to deal with slaves. Exodus 21 appeared to be Capitein's and the WIC's favorite:

Laws about slaves
Now, these are the rules that you shall set before them. When you buy a Hebrew slave he shall serve six years, and in the seventh, he shall go out

free, for nothing. If he comes in single, he shall go out single; if he comes in married, then his wife shall go out with him.

If his master gives him a wife and she bears him sons or daughters, the wife and her children shall be her master's, and he shall go out alone. But if the slave plainly says, 'I love my master, my wife, and my children; I will not go out free,' then his master shall bring him to God, and he shall bring him to the door or the doorpost. And his master shall bore his ear through with an awl, and he shall be his slave forever.

When a man sells his daughter as a slave, she shall not go out as the male slaves do. If she does not please her master, who has designated her for himself, then he shall let her be redeemed. He shall have no right to sell her to a foreign people since he has broken faith with her. If he designates her for his son, he shall deal with her as with a daughter.

If he takes another wife to himself, he shall not diminish her food, her clothing, or her marital rights. And if he does not do these three things for her, she shall go out for nothing, without payment of money.

Capitein was awarded for his stance with an appointment as missionary minister at the Dutch Elmina Castle, where he arrived on October 8, 1742, at the age of 25.

Elmina Castle in the Atlas Blaeu-Van der Hem, circa 1665-1668

During one of my visits to Ghana, after taking a look at the dungeons, I wandered around the grounds surrounding the fort at Elmina and tried to read the names on the tombstones in the cemetery. Gravestones told the story of colonial administrators who succumbed to tropical disease or isolation. Many names in the graveyard sounded so familiar, as if they could have been neighbors in Amsterdam, New York, or Curaçao. There was no marked grave or tombstone for Jacobus.

Elmina Castle was a hellhole for the black captives as well as for the WIC staff and soldiers who served the WIC administration. Yes, a hellhole in every respect. The castle acted as a depot where slaves were brought in from different kingdoms in West Africa. Slaves were often held captive in the castle for months. Up to 1,000 male and 500 female slaves were shackled and crammed into the castle's dank dungeons, with no space to lie down and very little light. Without water or sanitation, the floor of the dungeon was littered with human waste and many captives fell ill. The men were separated from the women, and the captors regularly raped the helpless female slaves.

The famous black clergyman arrived in a hell even worse than Dante's inferno, or the diabolical scenes in Hieronymus Bosch's pictures.

It had been Jacobus' dream all along to convert the locals of Ashanti to Christianity. He tried for several years but without success. The Ashanti were not interested in Christianity. When the WIC refused to give their permission for Capitein to marry a local girl, he married the Dutch Antonia Ginderdros instead. He founded a school and an orphanage and taught the children of Opoku Ware I.

No matter how often I visited Elmina and read Jacobus' story, I could never totally feel and experience the delusion that had driven this young man in his plight and later in his madness. Very much in contrast to Jacobus Josias Capitein's unfortunate destiny was that of Olaudah Equiano (c. 1745-1797), alias Gustavus Vassa, a prominent African of Nigeria, who settled in London.

Liberalism had progressed in London and a freed slave could settle and live there, and be active in the British abolition movement; naturally, he had to be a devout Christian and upstanding citizen.

Equiano had worked and traveled for twenty years as a seafarer, merchant, and explorer in the Caribbean. His last 'owner' was Robert King, an American Quaker merchant, who allowed Equiano to trade for his own account and purchase his freedom in 1766. In London, he even became part of the Sons of Africa, an abolitionist group composed of prominent Africans living in Britain. To this day, he remains an icon, a great emancipation hero in abolition history.

It is a foregone conclusion that in the 17th and 18th centuries, slavery and the slave trade were condoned if not morally supported by Catholics as well as Protestants. In the second half of the 18th century, Evangelicals, Protestants of the second reformation, led the abolition movement. Quakers, Baptists, and Presbyterians prevailed, and eventually slavery and the slave trade were ended but more for economic reasons than ethical and moral ones; human rights had not been invented yet, let alone were being implemented.

World economy changed in the 18th and 19th centuries. Mighty colonial empires collapsed or became independent. The collapse of the Spanish Empire, the independence of the American viceroyalties of New Spain, Peru, and Mexico had once again changed the demand for slaves in the markets. Slavery continued in most of the colonies, but the supply from the local Afro-American population provided sufficient workers, so overseas transports became unnecessary.

New social systems of mass labor were a novelty that gained in popularity towards the end of the 19th century. For employers, this meant flexible employment contracts, predetermined conditions of working hours, and fixed salaried compensation. Long term, these new provisions turned out to be more efficient, and cheaper.

The Industrial Revolution, with mass-market production, was only possible with a large, flexible labor pool. The status of the labor force in industrial agriculture fell behind and was one of the last vestiges of exploitation.

In Cuba, I observed the blacks of today, mostly descendants of former slaves. In spite of Castro's communist labor laws, they are still concentrated on the sugarcane plantations. It shows that racial and cultural segregation remains a determining factor in the often self-imposed suffering amongst slave descendants, through today. Many seek and find a victim role and almost eagerly gravitate towards it. They become frozen in time, like the mannequins in a wax museum.

Edward Wilmot Blyden (1832–1912), photograph, Dalton and Lucy,
Booksellers to the Queen, Library of Congress Prints and Photographs
Division Washington, D.C.

Edward W. Blyden of St. Thomas

Another most influential clergyman was Edward W. Blyden of St. Thomas. The island of St. Thomas is presently part of the American Virgin Islands. The Dutch West India Company established a post on Saint Thomas in 1657. The St. Thomas Reformed Church was an offshoot of the Dutch Reformed Church, and Protestantism dominated the island's culture. Religious zeal and making a profit went hand in hand for the Dutch.

I searched for whatever I could find about Blyden on the island of St. Thomas but did not get beyond a terminal that was named after a namesake. How is it possible that with such a strong sense of black history a man like Blyden is nearly forgotten? Blyden is widely regarded as the father of Pan-Africanism and is noted as one of the first people to articulate a notion of African personality and the uniqueness of the African race.

His major work, *Christianity, Islam and the Negro Race* (1887), promoted the idea that practicing Islam was more unifying and fulfilling for Africans than Christianity, though Blyden remained a Christian priest. In 1858, he was even ordained as a Presbyterian minister and appointed principal of Alexander High School. He had been brought up in St. Thomas under the powerful influence of Rev. John P. Knox, the pastor of the Dutch Reformed Church. Rev. Knox, impressed with Blyden's scholarly potential, became his mentor, and through him, Blyden decided to answer his calling and became a clergyman.

Historical events on the island of St. Thomas played a major role in Blyden's life. The aggressive expansion policy of the megalomaniac Danish king Frederik III resulted in a takeover of St. Thomas Island in 1666, and by 1672 he had established control over the entire island through the Danish West India and Guinea Company. The new Danish colonial economies of St. Thomas and the neighboring islands of St. John and St. Croix depended solely on slave labor and the slave trade. In 1685, the Brandenburgisch-Afrikanische Compagnie took control of the slave trade on St. Thomas, and for a brief period the largest slave auctions in the world were held there.

Two hundred years later, Africanism sprung from this culture. Edward Wilmot Blyden was born on August 3, 1832, in St. Thomas, in what is now the US Virgin Islands. As the father of Africanism, black re-migration eastward became depicted as the best solution to the African migration that once happened westward; the idea was very popular at the time, but poorly executed. Today, many seem to have forgotten that Africanism ever existed and was regarded as the ultimate solution to the African transatlantic migration.

In January 1851, as a nineteen-year-old, Blyden made the Atlantic crossing, first from the British Caribbean colony to New York and then as a passenger on board a steamer from New York to the Grain Coast. "Those are the lions' mountains," he shouted in excitement when his ship approached the African coast. The majestic rock pillar formations rising out of the Atlantic by the Grain Coast of West Africa had to be the home of lions, the king of animals, Blyden can be assumed to have thought. Many others must have had the same experience because the name Sierra Leone stuck, although the country never had any lions. For Blyden, it hardly mattered; he had finally come home, back to Africa.

Part of the Grain or Pepper Coast, thus called by European traders for its abundance of Malagueta pepper, became a British colony and is today the country of Sierra Leone. The new colony was destined for re-migration of Afro-Caribbean blacks of the West Indies after abolition. Large numbers of liberated but destitute Africans were stranded on the streets of London. Their numbers posed a security and health risk to the city, leading to urgent action by political leaders. The vagabonds were packed up and shipped out, but this time back to Africa.

Re-migrating Caribbean and American blacks to Africa was logical and natural to Blyden and his followers. Going back home to Africa became Blyden's calling. His powerful message related to a strong feeling of kinship with all black people. Thus, Blyden became one of the founding fathers of Africanism.

Blyden challenged the prevailing notion of black inferiority, initially spread by Muslims and increasingly popular in Europe and North America. He argued black equality and used examples of little-known but successful persons of African ancestry. Between 1856 and 1887, Blyden, a prolific writer, authored four influential books: *A Voice from Bleeding Africa* (1856); *A Vindication of the African Race; Being a Brief Examination of the Arguments in Favor of African Inferiority* (1862); *Africa for the Africans* (1872); and *Christianity, Islam and the Negro Race* (1887), as well as numerous articles. In each of his publications he promoted and defended Africanism and re-migration as the one and only solution. But in Africa he was preaching to the converted, and in Europe and the Americas his ideas died and were forgotten. The world changed, and so did the demand for Blyden's solution of re-migration. For a while, though, he was successful.

Following the abolition of the slave trade in 1807, the English navy, trying to enforce the new slave trade embargo, delivered thousands of intercepted Africans destined to become slaves back to Freetown. Liberating them from illegal slavers was relatively easy, but relocating them was a challenge. Soon, these new immigrants created a Creole ethnicity called Krio, speaking Krio language. Another solution was to resell many of the intercepted and so-called liberated Africans, not as slaves but as apprentices. At $20 a head, to be paid to the English Admiralty, they became apprentices to white settlers in Nova Scotia and to Jamaican Maroons. Others were forced to join the British navy.

The re-migration from the United States developed in a similar way to what had happened in the British colonies. In the US, abolition movements gave birth to the establishment of Liberia, a similar colony to the British Sierra Leone. Liberia in West Africa was exclusively designated for black re-migration. Monrovia, the capital, was named in honor of US President James Monroe, a prominent supporter of re-migration and the colonization of Liberia. White slaveholders of the South, opposed to having free blacks living in their midst, preferred to assist in the financing of the new black colony in Africa.

The first ship that departed from New York was the Mayflower of Liberia on February 6, 1820, destined for Liberia, West Africa, and carrying eighty-six settlers.

The love of liberty brought us here became the dictum of the 13,000 persons who crossed the Atlantic (1817-1867) with the financial support of the American Colonization Society (ACS). The first Caribbean ex-slaves and re-migrants to Liberia came from Barbados; their numbers grew from five hundred to one thousand. 620 came from Trinidad and Tobago. About 345 followed from Saint Vincent and the Grenadines. Yet another group, about 350, came from St. Kitts and Nevis, 483 from Grenada, and 400 from Saint Lucia. For a while, it looked like re-migration was a winner.

But integration with the local population did not happen easily. The early settlers practiced their Christian faith, sometimes in combination with traditional African religious beliefs. They spoke African American vernacular English, and few ventured into the interior, or mingled with local African peoples. They developed an American-Liberian society, culture, and political organization, strongly influenced by their roots in the Caribbean and the United States, particularly the Southeast.

The settlers in Monrovia, Liberia, built up an agricultural plantation economy in the style of the American South; they clung to American fashion and manners. It did not take long before re-migrants became black plantation owners, living in antebellum mansions. On the local markets, they purchased local slaves to work their plantations, like they had been purchased themselves. Afro-Americans who had re-migrated to Africa had nothing against slavery or the slave trade.

The clandestine slave trade, especially in the immigration state of Liberia, became so prevalent that West Indian blacks preferred to emigrate from Liberia and settle in Freetown, Sierra Leone, out of fear of recapture. In spite of these attempts to escape the recurrent ordeal, many were kidnapped and sold back into slavery elsewhere in Africa by leaving Liberia and Sierra Leone, especially when they were trying to go back to their original villages. Re-migration to Africa, something that appeared so logical and natural to Edward Blyden, became an unfortunate mishap in global history.

In 1934 in the US, Elijah Muhammad took Blyden's cue that practicing Islam was more unifying and fulfilling for Africans than Christianity and created the Nation of Islam (NOI). After a falling out between Elijah and Malcolm X, the latter, one of the movement's initial charismatic leaders, departed from the NOI to become a Sunni Muslim.

Elijah Muhammad's grandson, a black history scholar, came to visit me once. He denied that a link between Blyden's ideas and his grandfather existed. Also, for Muhammad Junior, Blyden did not really ever exist.

Liberia and Sierra Leone are not only failed nations today but also known for their military coups, ruthless dictators, and the ravages of Ebola.

Nikolaus Ludwig von Zinzendorf

A totally different approach from Blyden's African re-migration came from early eastern European Evangelists who often promoted slavery as a God-given reality of which the conditions should be improved; they were never out to correct an error of history or humanity, but rather worked within the system. They set up and took over plantations and made the work profitable without atrocities.

Noblemen of Courland, western Latvia, and Brandenburg got into the action for profit or ideology or maybe both. Reichsgraf von Zinzendorf und Pottendorf (1700-1760) was such an inspiring example. Nikolaus Ludwig von Zinzendorf was a German religious and social reformer, and bishop of the Moravian Church of Jan Hus and founder of the Herrnhuter Brüdergemeine. Initially, Herrnhut was a village Von Zinzendorf built on his estate to shelter refugees from the religious persecution of neighboring states.

Piety and an ascetic lifestyle were the thrust of Zinzendorf's gospel, not dogmatic teachings and scriptural interpretation; his morals were based on Lutheran or Calvinist Protestantism, but he rejected theological debate over exegesis that often resulted in endless quibbles. Von Zinzendorf became a true mystic, increasingly more averse to formal preaching and theological arguments, and one of the first Evangelical born-again Christians. The count made enormous progress with his

165

missions in Greenland, the Caribbean, and South America, which exist to the present day.

At Amaliënborg Castle in Copenhagen, I searched for clues to understand what had motivated the peaceful Danes to so suddenly take up the trading of slaves in the Caribbean. It was certainly not religious fervor or a calling to save the souls of the heathens from the devil. The only answer I could find was greed. The kings of Denmark wanted to be recognized as real players in the European arena of power and money.

At the coronation of the Danish King Christian VI in 1730, Von Zinzendorf met two Inuit children converted by the Danish priest Hans Egede at his mission in Greenland. He also met a freed slave, Anthony Ulrich, who told Von Zinzendorf about the terrible oppression of the slaves in the West Indies. That touched something in the good count. Soon, he set up a Caribbean as well as a Greenland mission. The combination of Greenland and the Caribbean seems odd now, but to the Danes it was natural. The failure of the Danes to bring Christianity to their Greenland colony, Caribbean trading posts of St. Thomas and St. Croix, and the West African slavery forts, created an opening for Von Zinzendorf's missionary work.

Hernhutters were way ahead of most social and theological emancipatory developments in Europe and the US. They promoted interracial marriages, women ordained as priests, and total racial and cultural equality.

Zinzendorf's heaven still featured a white Jesus sitting on a throne amidst Inuït, Caribbeans, Indians, South Africans, Europeans, and Maori, but the idea of racial equality, even in the life hereafter, was revolutionary and for too many deeply shocking. After a while, the Danish king stripped Von Zinzendorf of his royal decorations, and Von Zinzendorf had to retreat, almost an exile, to his estate.

In spite of some failures and disappointments, Von Zinzendorf's connections with Danish royalty resulted in Moravian missions in the Danish-Norwegian sphere, spanning St. Thomas and St. Croix in the Caribbean, the African Coast and Greenland and Denmark.

In 1732, St. Thomas saw its first Moravian mission established, and in 1733, so did Greenland. It did not take long before seeing Inuits on the streets of Charlotte Amalie and Caribbeans in Nuuk became an ordinary event. The mission's plantations, worked by slaves, prospered.

From St. Thomas, Von Zinzendorf's Evangelism, as well as devout entrepreneurship, spread to Costa Rica, Guyana, Honduras, Jamaica, Nicaragua, Surinam, Trinidad, Tobago, Barbados, Antigua, St. Kitts, and the Virgin Islands, including St. Croix, St. John, St. Thomas, Tortola and Grenada.

The Herrnhuters community in Zeist, the Netherlands, became a tourist attraction. The Herrnhuter congregation did not become the European frontrunner when it came to emancipation. Maybe it was piety or Moravian modesty that prevented congregation members from being more proactive in terms of social and economic development of the Caribbean region. They were not vocal about ending the slave trade or slavery economies - to the contrary. In their eyes, slavery was a divinely ordained social and economic order, to be respected.

How Von Zinzendorf's followers became absorbed by the concept of slavery and improving labor conditions recalls the famous story of the white Moravian slaves. A freed slave, Anthony Ulrich, told Von Zinzendorf about the terrible treatment of the slaves in the West Indies and specifically on St. Thomas and St. Croix. Ruthless overseers, hired as some kind of contract managers, extorted the slaves and stole from the absentee European plantation owners to gain larger profits for themselves.

Von Zinzendorf's staff, Johann Leonhard Dober and David Nitschmann, followed up on Anthony 's call for help. They volunteered as Moravian slaves in the transatlantic slave trade. Their intent was never to end slavery but to go and show the workers how a master/slave relationship should be like.

The story goes that when asked by a Danish court official who was to issue their exit visas how they would support themselves, Nitschmann replied, "We shall work as slaves among the slaves."

"But," said the official, "That is impossible. It will not be allowed. No white man ever works as a slave."

"Very well," replied Nitschmann. "I am a carpenter, and will ply my trade."

Told that that was not allowed either, Dober and Nitschmann then sold themselves to a slave owner and boarded a ship bound for the West Indies. As the ship pulled away from the docks, they sang as faithful and fearless martyrs at the stake,

May the Lamb that was slain receive the reward of His sufferings.

Anansi, the only audience in the auditorium of my history class, moved restlessly in his banana-leaf-supported silk-thread hammock and yelped, "Only wisdom in Anansi, no need for thesis, books and university. Here in Caribbean or there in Africa, everywhere! You learned white man, but what you know about Anansi and Pot of Wisdom? And look at my magic, Anansi is a Prince as a spider, present in the whole world. Who wants to hear all that clergymen were saying? Never suffering was changed. We celebrate abolition, and freedom, not history."

16 MEN-OF-WAR, AND THE MEN WHO SAILED THEM

Kill one man, and you are a murderer. Kill millions of men, and you are a conqueror. Kill them all, and you are a god. - Jean Rostand, *Thoughts of a Biologist* (1938)

Age of Exploration

Captain van der Decken, or rather his ghost, jumped to attention when I announced that an account of the Age of Exploration would follow. During this time, the courageous Portuguese, Spanish, Dutch, Danish, Swedish, French, and British started to explore the globe, and reach for far-away cities of gold and exotic goods. The VOC made it its business to explore and exploit Asian trade. The route was around the Cape of Africa, the Cape of Good Hope, a rocky headland on the Atlantic coast on the Cape Peninsula, South Africa.

"The Cape was a nightmare for ages," recounted the captain. His face went blank. A host of bad memories seemed to shut him up for a while.

I found an account by a Chinese explorer trying to get from east to west. On the 1450 Fra Mauro map, the Indian Ocean was depicted as connected to the Atlantic. Fra Mauro names the southern tip of Africa

Cape of Diab. Fra Mauro was an Italian monk and cartographer of Venice. His detailed and accurate maps of the world were the best of his time; his masterpiece is known as the Fra Mauro map.

Map of the world by Fra Mauro. Copy made by W. Fraser in 1806 © The British Library, London. The map is orientated with south at the top.

Mauro is hard to decipher, but around 1420 a ship from India crossed the Sea of India towards the Island of Men and the Island of Women, off Cape Diab, between the Green Islands and the shadows. It sailed for forty days in a south-westerly direction without ever finding anything other than wind and water. According to the sailors on board, the ship went some 2,000 miles ahead until, once favorable conditions came to an end, it turned around and sailed back to Cape Diab in seventy days.

The junks that navigated these seas carried four masts or more, some of which could be raised or lowered, and had forty to sixty cabins for the merchants, and only one tiller. They could navigate without a compass because they had an astrologer who, with an astrolabe in hand, gave orders to the navigator. As you may recount, our dear captain followed the opposite course.

Since it ended in failure, it was obvious that it was not an easy story for him to tell:

"As we approached the tip of Africa, we failed to notice the dark clouds and did not hear the screams of terror from our man in the lookout as I sailed straight into a fierce storm. After hours of battle with nature, our ship hit treacherous rocks and began to sink. I was not ready to die and screamed out a curse: I will round this Cape even if I have to keep sailing until doomsday! Since that day, I, Captain van der Decken, and my crew have sailed the oceans, doomed never to reach a port."

And then the captain fell silent again, leaving me with the feeling that he had not told his entire story. What was he hiding? I would find out sooner or later. I tried to fill in the gaps and continue where the captain left off.

"The desire of European monarchs to find an alternate trading route to China and India was the driving force for exploration. The argument was that either a Northwest Passage along the coast of North America or a Northeast Passage along the coast of Siberia should exist. Soon, Dutch and Danish expeditions scouted the icy seas of the Arctic.

It was an exciting time, especially because in the 17th century, the Age of Exploration, the seas were full of dangers, mostly due to pirates and warring parties.

View on deck of VOC ship, by Jan Brandes, work on paper, 1778, Rijksmuseum Amsterdam

Trading nations had little choice but to set up protective mechanisms and institutions. Long before a navy existed, ships had to rely on an onboard arsenal, ranging from swords and knives to sophisticated heavy guns.

Hiring others for protection and sailing in a convoy was common for ships carrying valuable goods. Privateers, WIC corsairs, and buccaneers would eagerly offer their services, but often turned on their clients and hoisted the pirates' flag.

The terms privateer, corsair, buccaneer, filibuster and pirate were used interchangeably, but formally, there are some slight differences. Pirates were the lawless of the sea that pillaged and sacked anything they could get their hands on. Deception was just one of their weapons. Privateers were legitimized pirates with some form of governmental approval. A nation would issue some kind of a Pirate Letter, an official permission to attack enemy ships and to give protection to traders if contracted. During the Eighty Years' War between the Republic of the Low Lands and Spain, the Republic issued a lot of pirate licenses to anyone who was ready to attack the enemy, the Spanish fleet. A corsair was a privateer in the Mediterranean and along the African Atlantic coast. Filibusters, or filibustiers, were French privateers.

Dear Anansi, to give you some notion of the people who did the business and shaped the society in the Caribbean, I will tell you the stories of four Dutch and three English privateers, or pirates."

Boudewijn Hendricksz

"My first actor is Boudewijn Hendricksz, also known as Bowdoin Henrick to the English, or Balduino Enrico to the Spanish, who was once a privateer for the Dutch West Indies Company. We already met him briefly earlier on, when discussing the Mona Passage.

You may remember that Hendricksz and his family were already prominent in their little hometown of Edam and nearby Volendam in Holland; at least prominent enough to become mayor, or Burgomaster. Edam was a small shipping and trading town on the outskirts of Amsterdam, known since the Middle Ages for its cheese production.

Lengthy sea voyages during the Age of Exploration demanded easy-to-transport food products that remained edible for a long time. Dutch merchants kept their ships stocked with large quantities of Edam cheese. Hendricksz was Edam's traveling salesman, but with a sword and a gun. Volendam, at the Southern See, a sea inlet that once gave access to the harbors of Hoorn and Amsterdam, was a fishing village specializing in smoked eel. Smoked eel could also be carried on long-distance sea voyages without the risk of spoiling.

For Hendricksz, the middle-class trading towns were too small, so he ventured out into the world and became a Dutch corsair for the WIC. His task was to attack Spanish ships and fleets, and Barbary Coast pirates in the Mediterranean and off the Atlantic coasts. As we have learned already, Barbary Coast pirates preyed on all commercial traffic, and kidnapped millions from Europe's coastal towns and villages.

Hendricksz did well and brought his WIC sponsors and financiers great profits. The West Indies Company, pleased with the proceeds, awarded him with the official title of admiral. Since no formal navy existed, admiral was more of an honorary title, issued from time to time by governing authorities, especially during times of war. The word admiral comes from *Emir-al-Bahr*, commander of the sea, and arrived in Europe during the Crusader period. With the Admiralty Ordinance of January 8, 1488, Emperors Maximilian and Philip the Fair tried to build on Burgundian precedents and extend their authority over maritime activities. A navy was born, at least on paper.

An admiral's function was to set strategy, harmonize actions, organize mission and expeditions and lead sea battles. Mostly, an admiral would put together a convoy or fleet made up of privateers, trading ships, and, at times, an official, purpose-built admiral's ship, sometimes with a few additional support ships.

Maintaining a convoy was also essential for social control; occasionally a single battleship plundered richly-laden trade ships sailing under the same flag, the very ships they were supposed to protect.

Sea battles with square-rigged tall ships were always terrible wars of attrition. Full follies of gunfire ravaged enemy ships completely and wrecked their enormous, exposed exterior of sails, masts, and rigging. Seaman could have their limbs torn off by cannon fire in seconds. Dynamite often exploded too early die to the primitive firing systems of the large guns. It was nearly impossible to stay in one piece as a fighting seaman.

Man-of-war

A novelty in the 17th century was the man-of-war, an ocean-going warship carrying square-rigged sails that permitted tacking up the wind. Those ships were most heavily armed, often with as many as 50-150 cannons.

Man-of-War, by Willem van de Velde the Elder, drawing, 1622-1707, Rijksmuseum Amsterdam

The sizes of the guns varied from 8-42 pounders. Even 68 pounders were no exception. Each gun was manned by four to six gunners, plus the boys hauling bullets and dynamite from the storage holes. In addition, hundreds of deckhands hoisted and trimmed sails, rescued masts and booms, or hauled in entering hooks. Ship holds were filled with heavy guns and enormous loads of iron or stone bullets and giant amounts of explosives. No longer were holds the confined world of galley slaves, driven nearly to death by overseers with cracking whips to gain speed to ram enemy ships.

Slave-manned galleys had been the standard in the Mediterranean for more than two thousand years. The man-of-war made the galley with rowers, master, and slaves obsolete very quickly. This was an enormous change. The man-of-war demanded teamwork, whereas the galley with rowers depended on slaves.

Spanish tall ships in battle continued the traditional Mediterranean way of enter opponents' ships by trying to run their bow over an enemy's side and invade the deck. The direction of the wind and the position of both ships were essential in such maneuvers. Pirates with entering hooks, dagger knives clenched between their jaws, swarming out over the decks of enemy ships is still the most popular shot in any pirate movie. An opponent who was attacked could always try to baffle such an attack by edging away. In the meantime, the art was to fire with the broadside to cripple the opponent's spars, like booms and masts, as well as the bowsprit and spinnaker pole.

The large numbers of crews on such ships demanded intensive and extensive teamwork, and many teams had to work in concert. It was always a team of a sailing master, navigator, master gunner and captain of marines that ran a warship. Teamwork required more equality between then men. The weakness of the Spanish ships remained in their social structure of deeply embedded class distinctions - today we would call it the corporate culture. Nobility ruled, also on a ship; the common sailor had no say, he was just dirt.

In contrast, Protestant ships, especially of trading nations like Holland and Denmark, had very few class distinctions. If you did not know your business or were unable to follow orders, you were out. Pretense had no place in the Protestant commercial culture and navy.

The Spanish and British lost many battles due to pompous and pretentious officers. Ship designers were well aware of these disadvantages, and the Spanish and British took shelter by building ever-larger ships with heavier guns. Legendary are stories about British shipbuilders on the shores of the Thames whose products became so large and heavy that they sank into the mud. The Spanish armadas also had a history of running aground.

Boudewijn Hendricksz was a common man, a hands-on manager who understood teamwork and therefore became a most successful admiral. The Dutch West India Company had ordered Hendricksz to rescue Bahia, Brazil, that was held by the Dutch but had been attacked by the Spaniards several times. Bahia was a northeastern Brazilian state, and its capital, Salvador, was an important hub for slaves arriving from Africa.

Hendricksz was given thirty-four ships with heavy artillery and no fewer than 6,500 sailors and soldiers. Holland produced around 30,000 ships from about 1600 till 1700, though it could take as long as five years to complete one vessel. Thousands of carpenters and specialized sail makers found employ at the ship wharves, and the customers were international.

By the time he arrived in Brazil, the Spanish had already expelled the Dutch from Bahia. Without delay, Hendricksz split his fleet in three. One part returned to Holland with the costly supplies and ammunition destined for the garrison of Salvador; the other two attacked, respectively, the Spanish Caribbean colonial town of San Juan de Puerto Rico and the Portuguese African trading post of the Castle of Elmina. They were both decisively defeated.

Puerto Rico assault

Seventeen ships commanded by Hendricks himself went to Puerto Rico with the intention of capturing it. On September 24, 1625, Hendricksz arrived with 2,000 men in the bay that formed the harbor of San Juan de Puerto Rico.

Hendricksz' fleet was made up of privateers, ready to loot and plunder. The ship names gave a good impression of how a fleet was put together in those days, and who were the greedy investors. The ships like the *Leyden, Utrecht, Nieuw Nederlandt, Hoop van Dordrecht, Hoorn, Medemblik, Vlissingen,* and *West Kappel* were sponsored by their towns in Holland and Zeeland. An expedition on San Juan promised enormous profits and booty. *Koningin Hester* and *Jonas* were both ships managed by Jewish pirates who had temporarily signed on as WIC privateers.

Recovery of San Juan de Puerto Rico by Governor Juan de Haro, by Eugenio Caxés, oil on canvas, circa 1634-1635 © Museo del Prado, Madrid

Once in Puerto Rico, Hendricksz devised a bold plan. At 1 p.m. on the 25th of September, the entire Dutch fleet sailed directly into San Juan's harbor. San Juan's Spanish governor - naval and military veteran Juan de Haro y Sanvitores - had been in office for less than a month. Hendricks sent a message to the governor, ordering him to surrender the island immediately. Governor De Haro refused.

The Dutch exchanged some shots with the harbor castle, inflicting superficial damage and killing four Spaniards before gaining safe anchorage within the roadstead off Puntilla Point, beyond the range of de Haro's artillery. However, shoals prevented an immediate disembarkation of troops. The delay allowed Spanish civilians to flee inland, while the governor marshaled his slender strength within San Felipe del Morro citadel. A land battle followed, which left sixty Dutch soldiers dead and Hendricksz with a sword wound to his neck, which he received from the hands of Amezquita, who was considered one of the best swordsmen on the island.

Hendricks, upon his retreat, left behind one of his largest ships and over 400 of his men. He then tried to invade the island by attacking the town of Aguada. He was again defeated by the local militia and abandoned the idea of invading Puerto Rico.

For a privateer to lose a battle was no big thing, but to return home without loot and treasure was an unfathomable dishonor. As such, Hendricksz went on to Santo Domingo, where he engaged another fort, and later sailed on to ransack the island of Margarita.

On February 22, 1626, he arrived at Pampatar, which he took easily, and disembarked in a village now called Porlamar. But these limited successes were not enough to make up for the giant losses in Puerto Rico. So Hendricks decided to head to Havana. However, after his scouts brought back intelligence about Havana's defenses, he decided that it would be madness to try to take it.

He then traveled on to Matanzas and landed in Cabañas. In Cabañas, Hendricksz fell ill and died on July 2, 1626. His fleet returned to Holland, with only 700 of the 2,000 men he had started out with.

The legacy of Boudewijn Hendricksz is that of a brave, national hero. His role in the battle of San Juan during the Eighty Years' War, in which he tried but failed to capture San Juan from Spanish forces, was lauded as beyond the call of duty.

He was a man who never gave up and rather died trying than to go home empty-handed. He was just a cheese salesman and a true Flying Dutchman."

At this point, Captain van der Decken voiced his observations. "I said it earlier. You may have an excellent memory, my young friend. But something I can tell you from my experience. Take a rest, and a drop a little more often."

Oorlam of very old Genever

"I recommend an Oorlam of very old Genever, with a pickled Volendam smoke eel snack, and diced Edam cheese. Bols and Levert & Co at the Wildeman distillery have been producing it since 1575 and 1690, respectively."

17 ANOTHER THREE DUTCH AND THREE BRITISH PIRATES

"Hey, Hey, Hey, we're the Buccaneers." - Tampa Bay
Buccaneers, *Hey, Hey Tampa Bay* (1997)

Jost van Dyke

Jost van Dyke was not a rock star, though the annual New Year's Eve happening may suggest as much. Hundreds of pleasure yachts, large and small, and thousands of Van Dyke fans flock to the little island named after him just north of Tortola in the British Virgin Islands.

The party reaches its climax in the middle of the night, when the huge crowd, carrying giant picnic baskets and countless bottles of champagne, blasted in the New Year. At twelve o'clock, the sky lights up with tens of thousands of fireworks and an ear-deafening thunder that lasts for hours and is reminiscent of a 17th-century siege and naval attack. It is all in honor of a rogue Dutch pirate with a most dubious reputation.

Yes, today, the Virgin Archipelago, with its rich Spanish, Dutch, Danish, English, French, and American history is welcoming travelers who like to overindulge, as it was once the home of outlaws and fortune seekers. Little or nothing remains of the Dutch Virgin Islands, only a tiny key, with the name of the once famous and infamous Dutch privateer, Jost van Dyke.

Jost Van Dyke, British Virgin Islands

At midnight, as usual, Captain van der Decken stood firmly on the deck clinging onto the forestay, his thumbs under both lapels of his bleached-out, salty uniform as he recalled Jost van Dyke.

"Oh yeah," Van Decken rang out with his sonorous voice that carried far over the water. "I recall former times of sound and glory! Jost van Dyke was the rascal amongst us. He ignored God and all His commandments as he acted out his lust in games of debauchery on two small hideaway islands, just north of Tortola. Like the sinner Emperor Tiberius of Rome once acted out his immorality on Capri, Van Dyke played in his Caribbean garden of forbidden delights."

Jost van Dyke Island and Little Dyke's, now known as Little Dix, were Jost's secret refuge, ambush harbors but also playgrounds. Jost was licensed by the Dutch West Indies Company, and thus eventually became the 'Patron of Tortola', later part of the British Virgin Islands. He moved his trading operations from a sheltered harbor, Soper's Hole, to the only town on the island, now called Road Town.

In White Bay on Jost Van Dyke Island, over dinner and a bottle of wine at Sandcastle, the one and only place to dine, an aristocratic British lady whispered in my ear tales of Jost's sins with women, and even more unspeakable, with young deckhands. Officially, of course, no records remained to substantiate any such claims.

"Haha, times have changed, haven't they?" I returned her soft whisper with full volume. "Jost van Dyke would have been featured as an LGBT poster boy today."

My companion was shocked.

"My dear," I continued, ignoring her embarrassment, "think of the Virgin Islands pirates of today. They are off-shore money managers, or, according to some, money launderers, all based in Road Town, the capital of Tortola. It is one of the largest and most competitive offshore corporate finance centers in the world, processing hundreds of billions of dollars every year, especially out of Hong Kong and other Asian domiciles once under the British flag. Supposedly, in anticipation of the 1997 transfer of British Hong Kong to China, more than one trillion dollars flowed through Road Town."

"Possibly," my decorous lady murmured, "possibly, but anyhow. In the 17th century, it was not yet that sophisticated. I learned that Van Dyke first set up docking, offices, and warehouses in Soper's Hole, the west point harbor of Tortola, and traded cotton and tobacco with friendly Spaniards in Puerto Rico. The Spanish also mined copper on Virgin Gorda, an island to the northeast." She sipped her white wine and then pulled rank.

"My husband was a historian, you know. He researched on behalf of the Royal Historical Society. Last year he deceased."

"Yes, I understand as much going through the historical archives," I said, hijacking her whispered gossip, ignoring her dead husband. "The once-friendly mining settlers later became treacherous partners for Jost van Dyke in the conflict with Puerto Rico. Van Dyke took an enormous risk when he supported Admiral Boudewijn Hendricksz' attack on San Juan, Puerto Rico. His once-friendly Spanish trading partners turned against him in anger and were out for compensation and revenge. After Boudewijn's failed attack, Van Dyke's former partners retaliated by attacking his businesses on Tortola. In the process, an expedition of Spanish traders and privateers laid waste to most of the island's fortifications and factories and destroyed its plantation settlements, all WIC and Van Dyke assets. They acted in the name of God, morality, and the King of Spain; thus, unspeakable sin and evil were removed from the face of the earth."

She looked surprised. Most visitors have no notion of history, let alone the details of Jost van Dyke's sordid life.

"Jost van Dyke barely escaped, running for his life. Somehow he made it to his secret escape harbors, hurt but alive. Once peace returned to the region and the Spanish retreated, Van Dyke moved stealthily back to Tortola, but his and the WIC's substantial investments in large stone warehouses east of Road Town were lost."

Spruce Goose

Sailing southwest from Jost Van Dyke, we anchored for the night in Van Dyke's Soper's Hole, west Tortola. For hours I searched for the remains of Jost van Dyke's offices and warehouses, but to no avail. The pirate's assets had disappeared and only a whispered legacy remained.

In the early morning, I was woken up by the heavy sound of the eight prop engines of eccentric billionaire Howard Hughes' *Spruce Goose*. The *Spruce Goose* was the monumental folly that never flew; only once did it lift itself from the ocean runway 30 feet into the air. Howard Robard Hughes Jr. (1905-1976), a modern time Jost van Dyke, was an American businessman, investor, pilot, film director, and philanthropist, known during his lifetime as one of the most financially successful individuals in the world.

H-4 Hercules "Spruce Goose"

Howard, once the owner of Trans World Airlines (TWA), did not believe in the future of jet engines, therefore he continued the development of huge planes with propeller engines. Prop-water planes were for him the future of aviation. The Hercules H-4, under the name the *Spruce Goose*, was a prototype of his dreams. Some collector of historic planes, using Tortola as his private playground, bought and restored the plane and was attempting a run over the water of Soper's

Hole. The giant plane never lifted from the sea. The *Spruce Goose* was much like the Dutch Virgin Islands; neither ever got off the ground. But back to the story of Jost van Dyke. Once the show was over I was able to finish my Danish-Caribbean expose.

"In the years that followed Jost's demise, competition was strong. Not only the Spanish but also the English and Danish were eager to take over Van Dyke's businesses. Van Dyke and the WIC were directly in a contest with the newly established Danish West Indies Company in St. Thomas and St. Croix. The Danish king was so devoted to the project that he named the capital of St. Thomas after his wife, Charlotte Amalie. The Caribbean project became part of the royal family."

VOC Senior Merchant, by Aelbert Cuyp, oil on canvas, circa 1640-1660, Rijksmuseum Amsterdam

Van der Decken had fallen silent, attentively listening to my accounts. He was a proud man, cast in the straightjacket of Protestant morality and VOC trading ethics, which left little room to play. When he stepped away from the front stay, he seemed a little hunched over, as if he were carrying a load of guilt on his back. He looked transparent in the earliest spark of the morning light. I thanked my captain for his cryptic discourse on Van Dyke and his kind attention, but he no longer heard me as the first rays of the morning sun came over the horizon. The strange turn of history during the Danish episode puzzled me. I contemplated these strange events.

The Danish king was trying his hand at the slave trade, ruthlessly but productively. Even Van Zinzendorf's evangelical plantation, linked to the Hernhutters' mission, became a great commercial success for him. A shock reverberated across Protestant Europe, when the Lutheran king,

Frederick III of Denmark, suddenly established an absolute and hereditary monarchy as a result of the military defeat of Sweden. It was an anti-cyclical event in the minds of many who believed that political evolution had reached the end of history, as Voltaire put it in the 18th century and Fukuyama in the 21st century.

Frederick III decreed the colonization of Greenland, the Caribbean and Christiansburg, in today's Ghana. Osu Castle, renamed Fort Christiansborg, near Accra, Ghana, became the Danish African West Indies Company's principle hub for slave-trading activities. The Danish West India Company took control of St. Thomas in 1671, after Frederick's successor, King Christian V, decided to secure the island for the increasingly more profitable slave trade and sugar plantations. From 1672-1733, the Danes gained more control of the nearby islands St. John and St. Croix.

For the Dutch, business did not work out that well. In 1672, the English got away with huge loot in their most treacherous attack on the Republic, in alliance with France and several German bishops. Amongst many other territories, Tortola and the Jost Van Dyke islands were lost to the British, which still holds. England also annexed Anegada and Virgin Gorda.

Many treasure hunters have searched every cave and crevice on Jost Van Dyke Island and Little Dixie but to no avail. Jost's riches remain as aloof as the man himself. Will Jost van Dyke ever be vindicated by history? Not likely, unless someone finds his pot of gold.

Almost as an afterthought, Sweden also got into the slave-trading business by buying Saint Barthélemy from France. Denmark received large revenues from its West Indian colonies and was the envy of Swedish King Gustav, the new ruler of Sweden in 1771. He wished to re-establish Sweden as a great power in Europe, and trading colonies were part of that image. It was a total disaster."

Simon Bérard, the Swedish consul general in L'Orient, the only town, reported that:

It (Saint-Barthélemy) is a very insignificant island, without a strategic position. It is very poor and dry, with a very small population. Only salt and cotton is produced there. A large part of the island is made up of sterile rocks. The island has no sweet water; all the wells on the island give only brackish water. Water has to be imported from neighboring islands. There are no roads anywhere.

After all this Dutch, Danish, Spanish, British and Swedish back and forth, I drank a Painkiller at the Foxy beach bar.

Painkiller drink recipe

Ingredients
2-4 oz. of Pusser's Rum
4 oz. pineapple juice
1 oz. cream of coconut
1 oz. orange juice
Grated fresh nutmeg

Instructions
In a cocktail shaker filled with ice.
Add the first four ingredients and shake.
Pour into cocktail glasses over ice and top with grated nutmeg.

Gerrit Gerritszoon

Another Dutch adventurer came from the northern city of Groningen: Gerrit Gerritzoon, alias Roche Braziliano. He was a pirate. Gerrit came to Recife with his family as a consequence of the treasures by Piet Heyn.

Roche Braziliano, from The Buccaneers of America, 1678

185

The enormous amount of loot that Piet Heyn captured in Matanzas in 1628 changed the map of the Dutch Republic forever. The WIC share of the loot was so large that it paid for all military expeditions of the aspiring Stadtholder Prince Frederick Henry for one year or more.

Prince Frederick Henry was the successor of his half-brother Prince Maurits, who had died childless in 1626. The ambitious new Stadtholder was eager to expand the Republic with part of the Spanish Netherlands, part of modern Belgium and Luxemburg. So he moved on 's Hertogenbosch, or Bois-le-Duc. It had been besieged several times by Prince Maurits, but he had failed to bring it under his control. Conquering the provinces of Brabant and Limburg were Frederick Henry's first objective. With Captain John Maurice of Nassau at his side, Frederick Henry captured Bois-le-Duc, the capital of Brabant and the seat of the bishop on September 14, 1629. The sixth bishop of the duchy, Michael Ophovius, had to abandon his seat and live out his days in exile in Brussels.

Frederick Henry and John Maurice were related, as the latter was the grandnephew of William the Silent, Prince Henry's father. John Maurice was later known as João Maurício de Nassau-Siegen, count and prince of Nassau-Siegen. Stadtholder Prince Frederick Henry rewarded his nephew by recommending him for the post of governor of Dutch Brazil for the West Indies Company in 1636.

The next year, Johan Maurice landed at Recife, at the port of Pernambuco, and embarked on a glorious and most profitable career; one day, he would even return to The Hague as king of Brazil.

In contrast to the Portuguese colonial hierarchy, the Dutch community in Brazil was more egalitarian. *Dienaaren*, those employed by the WIC, soldiers, bureaucrats, Calvinist ministers, *vrijburghers* or *vrijluiden*, settlers, merchants, artisans, and tavern keepers made up the community.

This form of society was a novelty to the locals, used to a strict Spanish and Portuguese hierarchy, and that made John Maurice an instant hero to the peasants. Most aristocratic privileges were annulled by decree of the count. Soon, the vrijburghers formed a solid economic pillar of the colony, with most trade being under their control.

The business practices of settlers and planters were not always in accordance with Calvinistic ethics. The fast-growing slave trade, with a constant stream of arrivals from Africa, was a dubious development. Short-term hired overseers often resorted to extreme cruelty to squeeze out the maximum return for themselves. Even a hundred years later, Voltaire wrote about the atrocities in his satirical *Candide*.

Count John Maurice became very wealthy, mostly from his share in trading salt, sugar and other colonial ware. He left to the world two ornate palaces in Dutch Brazil and one in The Hague, still known today as Maurice's home (*Mauritshuis*), where he displayed his riches. The Mauritshuis museum is so embarrassed about the count's dealings that they removed his bust from the entrance hall after protests from the Surinam community in The Netherlands.

With John Maurice, the well-to-do trading family Gerritszoon of Groningen, Gerrit Senior, his wife, and their 17-year-old son, Gerrit Gerritzoon, arrived in the Dutch colony in Brazil. Gerrit Junior, soon nicknamed Roche Braziliano, or The Brazilian Rock, quickly rose to prominence. Initially, Roche was a docile God-fearing boy who was eager to bring the blessings of Dutch colonialism to Brazil. First, he became a privateer in Bahia, operating out of Salvador. In spite of his young age, being a privateer for a few wealthy WIC investors was not enough for him.

One day, on board a WIC privateer's ship, Gerrit led a mutiny, took over as captain, and adopted the life of a buccaneer, using as his home port the pirate's nest of Port Royal, Jamaica. Roche managed to buy a buccaneer's license from some corrupt governor and luck was on his side. On his first real raiding trip as a buccaneer, he captured a ship of immense value, and brought it back safely to Jamaica. In a short while, Gerrit gained a reputation as a ruthless man, and debauchery and drunkenness ruled his life. According to one account, Braziliano would threaten to shoot anyone who refused to drink with him. Another tale recounts how Gerrit once roasted two Spanish peasants alive on wooden spits after the farmers refused to hand over their pigs.

Eventually, Gerrit was caught and sent to Spain, where he managed to escape. Full of bitterness and eager for revenge, he resumed his criminal career and bought a new ship from fellow pirate François l'Olonnais, and set up business with the well-known British privateer Sir Henry Morgan.

After 1671, Roche Braziliano was never seen or heard of again. The author Alexandre Olivier Exquemelin made Roche Braziliano famous, or rather infamous. Alexandre Olivier Exquemelin (c. 1645-1707) was a French, Dutch, or Flemish writer and himself a buccaneer. He is best known as the author of a 17th-century book on piracy, published in Dutch as *De Americaensche Zee-Roovers*, in Amsterdam in 1678.

Hiram Beakes

Sex, romance, and true love played out with Hiram Beakes. Beakes was a scion of the ruling family on the island of Saba. His story of licentious sex that turned into true love, stolen gold, ruthless murder, and suicide is something no author could have made up; the Hiram account is true history.

Beakes was born as the second son of the councilor of the island and had a privileged and protected youth. Naturally, like any young man, he was eager to venture out into the world. By the grace of his father, he mustered onto a crew as an apprentice on a trade ship, *The Adventurer*, on the shuttle route Saba-Vlissingen.

In 1764, the 19-year-old sailor crossed the Atlantic and set foot in Vlissingen for the first time. Upon arrival, he made a courtesy call to pay his respects to his employer, Mr. Snyder and his wife. Mrs. Snyder was a brunette of Antwerp and only half the age of her wealthy husband. The lady had a roving eye. Hiram, hardly more than a boy, was instantly lost to the lust of the lady, and became the object of great intrigue for the sophisticated woman. The lady played the boy. Caution and discretion were hardly her trade. When Mr. Snyder suddenly died, supposedly from having been poisoned, accusing fingers immediately pointed at the young man and his mistress. Hiram and Snyder's widow were charged with murder but due to a lack of evidence, or perhaps appropriate payments under the table, the couple was acquitted.

The traumas and intricacies of passion, love, murder, and public scandal were too much for the young man. The cautious adolescent matured quickly and turned into a reckless outlaw. Almost overnight, the spineless lover boy became a foolhardy daredevil. Out of revenge, Hiram stole the ship *The Adventurer* from his former patrons and employers. Once re-rigged, and with beginners' luck, Hiram used the boat in a raid on a Chilean vessel, laden with 200,000 small gold bars. Hiram brutally murdered the Chilean crew in the most despicable manner.

The loot of *The Acapulco* was large enough for Hiram to buy a *Lettre de Marque*, a pirate license, from the governor of Gibraltar. Thus, a new pirate was born. Under the adage 'dead men tell no tales', Hiram pillaged, plundered, and murdered six days a week, but not on Sabbath, the Day of the Lord. Every Saturday he collected his entire crew on deck for a solemn religious service, begging the Lord for forgiveness of their many sins.

Hiram suffered intensely under his deadliest of all sins, fornication. His carnal pleasures with Mrs. Snyder went against the ethics that he had grown up with and held dear. After all, Leviticus left no room for misinterpretation: *None of you shall approach anyone to uncover nakedness. I am the Lord.*

Pirate or no pirate, one time when plundering a convent on the Balearic Islands, Hiram sensed what was about to happen; licentiousness of his crew would inevitably result in the debasing of the nuns. As captain and commander, he intervened by marrying all nuns to his crew, so, at least, the orgy about to happen could be condoned as marriages consummated in sanctity.

One day, when his shame and anger fell silent, the love-starved Hiram decided to return to Zeeland, marry his mistress, and head back for his home harbor on the island of Saba. But upon arrival in Vlissingen, he learned that the criminal courts of Holland and Zeeland had prevailed upon his mistress. She had been convicted and hanged for attempting to poison her child, the love child he had fathered.

Hiram lost his mind. Loyal to his faith, he followed in Jesus' footsteps in driving out the demons that had taken possession of his soul. He carefully followed Matthew 8: 31 that reads: 'And the demons begged him, saying, If you cast us out, send us away into the herd of pigs.'

At home, on the island of Saba, Hiram had lived on a rock in the ocean with sheer cliffs, but Vlissingen had nothing like that. Like the demons in Matthew, who were sent into a herd of pigs that jumped off the cliffs, Hiram had to settle for second best and threw himself off the dike at the Schelde river. He suffocated in the mud of the sandbars at the bottom.

Yes, it is a sad story about a young man who had everything and wasted it all.

British pirates

After four Dutch fellows, let us move on to England's most famous privateers.

English privateers and pirates were so very different from their Dutch counterparts. After all, England had a long tradition of nobility; none of them were cheese farmers, settlers, or former galley slaves. The officers of the poop deck lived a life of distinction, with pages serving at the dinner table, set with fine linens, silver, and crystal. In naval architecture, a poop deck - from the French word for stern, *la poupe* - is the highest deck that forms the roof of a commander's cabin built in the rear, or aft.

It was the heavenly dwelling for the top echelon of officers. Their lavish dinners contrasted sharply with the conditions for the crew, who subsisted on substandard stores of rotten meat and weevily biscuits. Ships of English privateers in the 16th century were hardly more than floating concentration camps, manned by miserable and frequently coerced sailors subject to brutal and arbitrary disciplining at the whim of sadistic captains. Mutinies were frequent.

Sir John Hawkins was Queen Elizabeth's slave trader as well as her supposed lover. He was commissioned by the queen to form a fleet. Hawkins insisted that his navy would not only have the best ships in the world, but also the best quality of seamen. He petitioned and won a pay increase for sailors, arguing that a smaller number of well-motivated and better-paid men would be more effective than a larger group of uninterested men.

Hawkins as a shipwright made important improvements in ship construction and rigging. A great invention was sheathing the underside of his ships with a skin of nailed elm planks sealed with a combination of pitch and hair smeared over the bottom timbers, as a protection against the worms that attacked the wooden hulls in tropical seas. He also introduced detachable topmasts. Masts were stepped further forward, and sails were cut flatter. His ships were 'race-built', being longer and with the forecastle and aftcastle (or poop) greatly reduced in size.

The English, and specifically Hawkins, entered the transatlantic trade at the earliest hour. The triangular system made sure that ship holds were always full; iron and guns from England to the African coasts, slaves from Africa to the Americas, and sugar and salt back to Europe. Sir John Hawkins was soon the most important player in the second part of the 16th century and became the chief architect of the Elizabethan navy. Hawkins was also a large slave trader, merchant, navigator, shipbuilder and privateer. Privateers or pirates were expected to fight the queen's battles with Spain and Portugal at their own cost and risk.

His first three voyages were semi-piratical enterprises. Queen Elizabeth I needed the revenues and demanded her cut. She donated to Hawkins' fleet a large old ship, called *Jesus of Lübeck*, once the flagship of her father, King Henry VIII. It became the first British slave ship to reach the Americas.

Hawkins' voyages became legendary. His third journey began in 1567. A report mentions that Hawkins and Drake obtained slaves from traders in Africa, and also augmented the cargo by capturing the Portuguese slave ship *Madre de Deus* (Mother of God) and its human cargo. He took about 400 slaves across the Atlantic to sell in Santo Domingo, Margarita Island, and Borburata. Hawkins was the role model for his younger second cousin, Francis Drake. They sailed to the West African coast together, privateering along the way. Towards the end of the century, they even joined forces in an effort to capture San Juan, Puerto Rico.

Trading and raiding were closely related, according to Hawkins. Success in the trade depended on African allies. The amount of violence he and his men used to secure the captives and force them into submission was extraordinary enough that he made special mention of it on several occasions. Hawkins wrote about his third voyage in detail in *A True Declaration of the Troublesome Voyadge of M. Iohn Haukins to the Parties of Guynea and the West Indies, in the Years of Our Lord 1567 and 1568*.

Sir Francis Drake

Sir Francis Drake was a sea captain, privateer, navigator, slaver, and politician of the Elizabethan era. Today, the Sir Francis Drake Channel, named after the famous British privateer, is the central passage through the Virgin Archipelago. It is ironic that amongst colonial islands built up to facilitate the slave trade, a slaver is still honored today. In spite of public protests, the name has not been changed and the government of the British Virgin Islands is not about to do so. They proudly honor the pirate responsible for the migration of millions.

Drake and his equally famous role model, Sir John Hawkins, organized a rendezvous in 1595 in Virgin Gorda. Twenty-six ships anchored in the sound and used the large hill, at Bitter End, to practice their attack on San Juan, Puerto Rico, a town with an abundance of riches just waiting to be taken from Spain. Bitter End is still a very popular destination in the luxury yachting world; its moorings are always taken and the clubhouse is standing room only.

Queen Elizabeth I of England also awarded Francis Drake a knighthood in 1581, after he circumnavigated the globe. Drake carried out the second circumnavigation of the world in a single expedition. It took him three years, from 1577 to 1580. Only the Dutchman Oliver van Noort competed with him for that honor. Drake's exploits made him a hero to the English but a pirate to the Spaniards. King Philip II even put a price on his head, offering a reward for his capture, dead or alive, of 20,000 ducats, about £4 million (US $6.5 million) by modern standards.

Drake became second-in-command of the English fleet against the Spanish Armada in 1588, with the title of vice-admiral, and died of dysentery in January 1596, after unsuccessfully attacking San Juan, Puerto Rico.

Sir Walter Raleigh

The biggest scoundrel of them all was Walter Raleigh. Even his contemporaries thought so, and Walter spent thirteen years locked up in the Tower of London. Sir Walter Raleigh was an arrogant liar who sold glitter rock for gold and also had elaborate flirtations with the queen, who was very jealous. In 1591, he secretly married Elizabeth Throckmorton, one of the queen's ladies-in-waiting, without the queen's permission. He and his wife were sent to the Tower.

In 1594, Raleigh became obsessed with the rumors about a 'City of Gold', *El Dorado*, in South America. He published an exaggerated account that contributed to the legend. All of England rallied behind him to outfit an expedition to rake in the riches. When Raleigh could not find any in spite of extensive torture and murder of local chiefs, he loaded his ships with glitter rock and tried to fake it back home. Ultimately, it landed him in the Tower again, though under a different pretext. After he lost the protection of Queen Elizabeth I, who had passed away, Raleigh was again imprisoned in the Tower, this time on drummed-up charges that he was part of the plot to assassinate King James I.

Sir Walter Raleigh, artist unknown, oil on panel, 1598, collection of the author

To the Spanish, Raleigh was the most hated of all pirates. He had the reputation that he could kill without blinking an eye. His legacy is that he popularized tobacco smoking in England. His name also lived on as the Raleigh bicycle and a Mexican cigarette brand.

This lengthy account of the lives of famous buccaneers justified sipping a Sir Walter Raleigh, a mean concoction.

Sir Walter Raleigh

Ingredients
1 ½ oz. brandy
1 tsp. Curaçao blue
1 tsp. grenadine
1 tsp. lime juice

Then I had a Sir Francis Drake Gimlet that tasted somewhat lighter.

Sir Francis Drake Gimlet

Ingredients

3 tbsp. Caorunn Gin
½ tbsp. coriander (cilantro) Bianco Vermouth
2 tbsp. rhubarb and ginger cordial
1 tbsp fresh lime juice
1 egg white
A coriander or flat parsley leaf to garnish (optional).

Mix and enjoy!

Sir John Hawkins has no drink accredited to his name; he may have been a great British naval hero but blood drips from his hands till this very day.

After a few more buccaneer drinks, Anansi, Van der Decken and I sang along to a recording of *Shores of Hisponiola* by Nancy Kerr, a British folk musician.

18 ST. EUSTATIUS AND THE GOLDEN DOOR

A journey to Statia is a journey back into the time of the Golden Rock. It is a journey, directed by the hand of Providence, to the Golden Door that millions of desperate Jews and oppressed peoples from around the world, would find open to them in the years to come. - *The Jews of St. Eustatius*, J. Klinger

Gold, a lot of gold, was awaiting us on Statia, but also disaster, blood, sweat, and tears. The voyage from the Virgin Islands to the next cluster of small islands, St. Maarten, Saba and St. Eustatius, was smooth sailing.

St. Eustatius, or Statia, is a tiny island that has changed flag twenty-two times. From the very moment Europeans saw it in their spyglasses and set foot ashore, everything went wrong for Statia.

The European names for the Caribbean islands are very confusing and have been for a long time. The Leeward Islands are to the north of the Lesser Antilles, and the Windward, the south; not to be confused by the Leeward Antilles, the islands off the coast of Venezuela. The Leeward Islands and the Leeward Antilles are hundreds of miles apart.

Confusion has ruled ever since Columbus came to the area and named his discoveries after saints. Also, several poorly charted small islands in the Leeward Island chain got their names accidentally transferred to another island. With all these tiny little islands, it is understandable that cartographers got confused.

That is how St. Martin got its name; initially, the present island of Nevis was called St. Martin. Supposedly, the initial name of the island of St. Eustatius was Santa Maria del la Niebe (St. Mary of the Snow), or something to that effect. The name is neither correct Italian nor Spanish, and one wonders about the concoction. White clouds, on the rock's peaks, are suggestive of snow. Columbus was from Genova and spoke some kind of Italian, probably mixed with Spanish. The island he named with the Spanish name *Nuestra Señora de las Nieves* eventually became *Nevis*, by a process of abbreviation and Anglicization.

How Santa Maria del la Niebe became St. Eustatius is even more of a mystery. Sint Eustatius is the Dutch name for the legendary Christian martyr, known in Spanish as San Eustaquio, and in Portuguese as Santo Eustáquio or Santo Eustácio. Abbreviated, it became Eustace, or Statia.

Eustace was a Roman general named Placidus serving under Emperor Trajan. While hunting, Placidus saw a crucifix lodged between a stag's antlers and this made him and his family convert to Christianity. But God does not take in new souls so easily; therefore, harsh tests to his faith followed.

Eustace's wealth was stolen; his servants died of the plague; when the family took a sea voyage, the ship's captain kidnapped Eustace's wife, Theopista; and as Eustace crossed a river with his two sons, Agapius and Theopistus, the children were taken away by a wolf and a lion. Like the prophet Job, Eustace lamented but did not lose his faith.

But surprise, surprise, Placidus was then restored to his former prestige and reunited with what was left of his family. Emperor Hadrian did not like it at all and condemned Eustace to death for heresy. He, his wife, and his sons were roasted to death inside a bronze statue of a bull, or an ox, in the year 118. However, the Catholic Church historians reject this version of the story as completely false.

What the relation between the island and Eustace could have been is a mystery. Eustace, or Statia, has more historical monuments per square mile than any other island in the Caribbean, enough for every history buff to make up his own hypothesis.

Some wondered if there had been a dramatic family dispute on the island that necessitated calling on Saint Eustace. Eustace was the saint for family trouble, and as we know from the legend, he certainly had his share.

In 1636, eighty Dutch families migrated from the Republic of the Low Lands and settled on the Island. The fledgling Protestant reformation in Europe, which started with Martin Luther's theses at the Wittenberg chapel in 1517, had matured by 1618. A distinct vacuum still existed for all legal family affairs, such as birth, death, baptismal and wedding registrations. The Catholic Church had fulfilled these functions for centuries, and their services were not immediately taken over by civil authorities or the Protestant churches.

The Synod of Dordt of 1618 in the Dutch harbor city of Dordrecht, where most European Protestant churches congregated, tried to design robust institutions for these functions, as well as rules for financial assistance for the poor and elderly. From these institutions many banks originated, especially in the United States.

Predestination versus free will dominated the religious discussion in Dordt. Predestination prevailed. There was a lot more at stake this time – it was not just the typical quibbling of Protestant clergymen. The beheading of the 72-year-old secretary of state of Holland, Johan van Oldenbarnevelt, for his support of the Armenians, the free-will advocates, demonstrates this point.

The decapitation of such an internationally-respected and recognized statesman like Van Oldenbarnevelt sent shock waves through all of Europe and the Caribbean.

Were the verdict and execution political, the result of plotting by the ambitious Stadtholder Prince Maurits who had eliminated his political opponent so that he could be crowned king? Or was a Protestant inquisition in the making, as brutal and ruthless as its Catholic counterpart?

Johan van Oldenbarnevelt just before his beheading, etching, 1619,
Jan Luyken, 1698, Rijksmuseum Amsterdam

Fear for their own position may have ruled the early settlers of the island. There were so many threats, coming from all possible directions. Were the settlers on Statia of 1636 secretly all Catholics who feared persecution and family discord? Calvin, the great reformer of Geneva, had a reputation that he had set up an inquisition equal in cruelty to that of the Catholics. In 1533, John Calvin had burned his theological opponent, Michael Servetus, at the stake.

Maybe the Statia immigrants were secretly Jewish and feared having treacherous Morenos or Conversos in their midst? To get access to trade or to elude expulsion, at times Jews converted to Christianity. Dark-skinned Morenos, Portuguese Creoles, were often like chameleons; they could be either Jewish or Christian. You could never tell with whom they sided.

Another threat was the rumor that the governor of Curaçao and New Amsterdam, Peter Stuyvesant, was out for very personal revenge. He had lost his leg in a 1644 campaign on nearby St. Martin. Plundering a successful and wealthy settlement by under false pretenses was not uncommon. Envy of others' wealth was a problem, as could be seen in the case of the Jewish traders and pirates on Statia.

Anti-Semitism

One of those targets was Moses Cohen Henriques, but he put up a ferocious fight.

198

Jewish privateers and pirates controlled most of the commerce from New Amsterdam to Dutch Brazil, with Statia as a comfortable halfway harbor. Anti-Semitism among the French, British and Dutch grew out of jealousy and in equal proportion to Jewish wealth and influence. On several occasions, the Statia Jews had to appeal for protection from their brethren in Holland, leaders of the Dutch Jewish community, and significant shareholders in the Dutch West India Company (WIC). It was the WIC that ultimately controlled many Caribbean Islands, including Statia, and the WIC had many wealthy Jews as shareholders. After a lot of haggling, Honen Dalim, Statia's synagogue, was built in sight of the large Dutch Reformed Church and the walls of Ft. Orange, under the express condition that the exercise of the Jewish faith would not interfere with that of the Gentiles.

Statia became the Golden Rock and, for many Jews, a Golden Door to the New World. Thousands of ships called at Statia's harbor every year. Hundreds and hundreds of warehouses, crammed with goods and slaves, lined the shore below the walls of Fort Orange. It was a treasure trove with very little protection, waiting to be attacked.

In 1781, Edmund Burke, a prominent British statesman, wrote in his report on the island:

It has no produce, no fortifications for its defense, nor martial spirit nor military regulations... Its utility was its defense. The universality of its use, the neutrality of its nature was its security and its safeguard. Its proprietors had, in the spirit of commerce, made it an emporium for the entire world... Its wealth was prodigious, arising from its industry and the nature of its commerce.

It's not surprising that it had to be a Dutch pirate who turned on his countrymen. In April 1665, Gerrit Gerritzoon, alias Roche Braziliano, was ordered by Governor Thomas Modyford of Jamaica to raid Statia with a fleet of privateers. The order read: '... capture Eustatia, Saba, and Curaçao, and on their homeward voyage, visit the French and English buccaneers at Hispaniola and Tortuga.'

The enormous wealth of Statia beckoned hundreds of pirates to participate. A charge by 350 of them easily overwhelmed the island's outnumbered and surprised Dutch garrison. Gerritszoon won complete control over the island in a matter of days; he and his pirates murdered, looted, and pillaged what they could. They seized 910 slaves and considerable booty, renamed the island New Dunkirk, and deported 250 residents to Barbados.

Somehow, Statia always recovered. Just over one hundred years later, in 1776, the devil himself arrived on the Golden Rock in the shape of British Admiral Sir George Rodney, a privateer in the tradition of Sir John Hawkins. Earlier that year, eighteen ships, heavily laden with provisions and ammunition from Statia, ran the British blockade and reached rebel ports in the revolting North America, still officially British colonies. The British were furious.

When a small American Brig, the *Andrew Doria*, flying the Grand Union Flag of the newly self-declared independent nation of the United States, arrived in Statia's harbor on November 16, 1776, Statia was propelled into an international conflict.

The first salute

Isaiah Robinson, captain of the *Andrew Doria,* was looking to buy gunpowder and military supplies for the continental army. The *Andrew Doria* fired a thirteen-gun salute upon arrival, one for each former British American colony. According to protocol, Governor Johannes de Graff ordered an eleven-gun reply. Thus, Statia fired the first salute of international recognition of the American rebel government in the British colonies, a salute that echoed around the world.

When British Admiral Sir George Rodney received word of this historic salute, he considered it the last straw. The British declared full war on Holland and its colonies on December 20, 1780.

Admiral Rodney arrived on February 7, 1781, with fifteen British ships-of-the-line with more than 1,000 guns. A ship-of-the-line was a new type of naval warship constructed for line battles at sea. It was the heaviest and biggest naval war machine available in those days.

Rodney also brought support ships, five frigates, and smaller craft. The British armada transporting 3,000 ground troops and their supplies were significant. The siege that followed resembled Gerrit's attack of 1665 but was even more extensive. After only a few rounds the Dutch garrison at Fort Orange, numbering only sixty-one men, surrendered.

The British captured almost 200 ships in the port, all the warehouses along the waterfront, and most of the population.

Statia was easy prey. In 1780, a terrible hurricane had razed most of the island to the ground and killed at least 4,000 people. Our modern concept of international aid after a natural disaster took on quite different proportions with Admiral Rodney, who regarded it as a prime opportunity to plunder what he could. The wealth that Admiral Rodney ultimately stripped from Statia equaled more than 15,000 pounds, an incredible sum.

As if that wasn't enough, Rodney ransacked the Jewish quarters and turned Jewish graves upside down. The rumor was the Jews had sewn precious stones and gold coins into the inseams of their clothing and put money in coffins during fake funerals. Rodney hated Jews in general and particularly those he found on Eustatius, as he reported in his log. Burning with hate, he destroyed the synagogue and burned down Jewish homes and properties. He wrote:

They (the Jews of St. Eustatius) cannot too soon be taken care of - they are notorious for the cause of (revolution in) America and France.

Rodney arrested 101 adult Jewish males, brutally locking them up in warehouses without food and water for days. He also deported the heads of over thirty Jewish families to neighboring islands. From the Jews alone, Rodney confiscated over 8,000 pounds sterling in cash, an enormous sum. That amount did not include Jewish goods, ships, and property. Rodney made sure to impoverish the Jews. Jews were easy prey; they had no army and no navy.

The admiral happily wrote to his family with promises of a new London home. To his daughter, he promised the best harpsichord money could purchase. He confidently wrote of a marriage settlement for one of his sons, and a soon-to-be-purchased commission in the foot guards for another son. He wrote of a dowry for his daughter to marry the Earl of Oxford. He noted he would have enough to pay off the young prospective bridegroom's debts.

Rodney's formal orders were to destroy the depots of St. Eustatius. Thereafter, he was to return north as soon as possible, to aid the British forces fighting the American revolutionary armies. The admiral ignored those orders. Rodney was too busy looting and counting his profits.

Almost two months after Rodney captured St. Eustatius, he diverted a significant part of his fleet to carry his fortune from Statia back home to England. The delay it caused cost the British the war in Virginia, the runaway American colony. The independence war was lost for England, and the American Revolution prevailed. Ironically, the Jews of St. Eustatius, who were lost to the anti-Semitic greed and hatred of a British admiral, helped win the American Revolution.

America will never forget!

Andrew Doria in the harbor of St. Eustatius by Phillips Melville, oil on canvas, 1776, Courtesy of the U.S. Navy Art Collection, Washington

God's wrath

The hurricane of 1780 is hardly ever mentioned in the historical records, but it must have played a major role in all events. Only a few sketchy reports state some of the facts. The storm tore through the islands and gained the name the Great Hurricane, killing between 20,000 and 22,000 people. The islands were battered for almost a week

Barbados, Martinique, and St. Eustatius felt the brunt of the ferocious hurricane. The storm obliterated almost all of the houses, as well as uprooted trees, hurling them across the sky.

The hurricanes of 2017 were equally devastating, but modern advance warning systems prevented large casualties. The damage was, however, beyond imaginable scope. Barbuda, an autonomous entity together with Antigua, was totally destroyed and all people evacuated; no one remained on the island. Dominica, officially the Commonwealth of Dominica, a sovereign island country, was 97 percent destroyed. Its prime minister, Roosevelt Skerrit, made a desperate appeal for help to the annual meeting of the United Nations in New York. Dominica is part of the Windward Islands in the Lesser Antilles archipelago.

St. Eustatius was cut off from food and fresh water supplies. When Dutch marines delivered large amounts of emergency aid to the island, they were met with threats by a local politician and member of parliament, Mr. Clyde Van Putten.

This delusional politician urged on a cheering crowd to murder and burn the bodies of the Dutch marines on the humanitarian mission and dispose of them in the streets of Statia. In the tradition of the twenty-two invasions Statia has lived through, the poor man believed that foreign troops were invading and occupying his little island. Time had stood still for him: 1780 or 2017, what was the difference?

I did not feel like drinking hurricane cocktails, but in case you feel compelled, here are some recipes. Created in the 1940s, this super-boozy rum-based concoction will get the party started - no matter where you are:

Hurricane cocktail

Ingredients
2 oz. white rum
2 oz. dark rum
1 oz. lime juice
1 oz. orange juice
2 oz. passion fruit juice
½ oz. Simple syrup
½ oz. grenadine

Or maybe another one:

Rum Swizzle

Ingredients
4 oz. Gosling's Black Seal Rum
4 oz. Gosling's Gold Rum
5 oz. pineapple juice

5 oz. orange juice
2 oz. grenadine or ¾ oz. Bermuda Falernum
6 dashes of Angostura Bitters

Instructions

Into a pitcher ⅓ full of crushed ice, add Gosling's Black Seal Rum,
Gosling's Gold Rum, pineapple juice, orange juice, grenadine or
Bermuda Falernum, and Angostura bitters.
Churn vigorously or mix in a cocktail shaker.
Strain into a martini glass.

19 ISLANDERS OF ALL KINDS

The Caribbean: a peculiar ethnic demography describes the presence of Asian Indians, Africans, Chinese, Syrians, Lebanese, Jews, Portuguese, Europeans, Amerindians, and various mixes and combinations. Despite this ethnic heterogeneity, structurally there is a bipolar dominance of persons of Asian and African descent. - Kellogg Institute for International Studies

Settlers and migrants

The Caribbean is not a melting pot of races and cultures, at least not like the United States. It is rather a mosaic of individual entities, living together on an island but strictly segregated. It is also quite common to find the same families in power, the same social hierarchy, century after century.

These powerful families often have a picture of reality that is heavily skewed, as it was influenced by their traditions and experiences over time. Some may behave as if abolition never took place, or as if they were still second-class citizens as underlings in a colony of some European nation. A St. Maarten politician presented such a picture:

My name, my reputation, and determination to do more for St. Maarten, are constantly covered in a fog, a fog not of my doing. The Dutch, or as I call them, the Gestapo on St. Maarten...

"Dear Anansi, are you still there? Listen to what I just heard on the radio. A politician of St. Maarten, and supposedly a former prime minister, is claiming to be a victim of the Dutch Gestapo, of colonial persecution. A few years ago the man was prosecuted for corruption of some kind. Supposedly, he funneled too much money into the wrong, or his own, pockets. Now he calls his criminal prosecution persecution and seeks revenge by calling on black anger against former Dutch colonists and slave traders. The newsreader added:

The victimization of St. Maarten by the Dutch is extended to Mr. Heyliger personally.

Just to be very clear, Anansi, my definition of prosecution is 'the institution and conducting of legal proceedings against someone in respect of a criminal charge'. And of persecution, 'all efforts of hostility and ill treatment aimed against a group or a person, especially because of race and political or religious beliefs'. These are two very different things.

Anansi, you know better than anyone that politically-inflated language is very common in the Caribbean. It is obvious that Mr. Heyliger has little or no notion of the Nazi Gestapo; and if he knew, it would be totally shameless to use such atrocities to his political advantage in a public broadcast. The ideological objective of Holland is, according to Heyliger, to make St. Maarten an outpost in the Caribbean. In other words, *autrement dit*, St. Maarten or St. Martin has become a place for the detention of outlaws and misfits of administrative Holland and France, a place for political outlaws.

But, what's new? No matter how outrageous and bizarre the claims of Mr. Heyliger, he and his people are not ready to budge for any authority, not even the Dutch Crown, or the French President. This attitude of Heyliger is not new, Anansi. To the contrary, it has been consistent with European settlers for hundreds of years.

In 1664, the prominent Dutch families on Saba were the Heyligers, Zagers, and Van der Pools. After the second Dutch-Anglo war, settlers with the same family names as today refused to swear allegiance to the

English when the island changed flags. Over a period of hundreds of years, many of the island families formed powerful clans, firmly in control of their properties and their island. They never shied away from dissent and obstruction to any government or authority. Mr. Heyliger's clan is a perfect example. Herewith, a little bit of family history.

The founder of the Heyliger family in the West Indies was Guilliam Heyliger (1650-1734), who evidently was on St. Eustatius in 1670 when he married Anna Ryckwaert. The family lived primarily on six of the Leeward Islands: the Dutch islands of St. Eustatius, St. Maarten and Saba and the Danish (now US), Virgin Islands of St. Thomas, St. Croix and St. John."

A steady snore came from above. Dear Anansi had sunk into a deep sleep, bored by my passion for the storms and sunshine of the fascinating Caribbean islands.

Major-General Sir Thomas Morgan

"It was the British Major-General Sir Thomas Morgan who forcefully evicted these original Dutch settler families of St. Eustatius and Saba to St. Maarten on behalf of his British overlords.

Morgan was what we would nowadays call a mercenary. All of the Caribbean was crawling with such people. Later knighted, Thomas Morgan was a Welsh soldier, an opportunist, and adventurer. He pledged allegiance to any flag that was ready to employ him. Thus, he played a decisive role in another affair of the Dutch and the Spanish, during the battle of the Slaak, or the Volkerak, on September 12-13, 1631.

Morgan fought on the side of the Dutch Republic. His opponent was Count Jan van Nassau-Siegen, on the side of Spain. Because he had recently converted to Catholicism, Count Jan was an embarrassment to his Nassau relatives, who were Stadtholders in Holland, Zeeland, and Friesland. To make things worse, he pledged allegiance to King Philip IV of Spain.

The disloyal count fought for the Infanta, Isabella Clara Eugenia. At the time, she was the governor of the Habsburg Netherlands for King Philip. Jan van Nassau lost the battle.

*Portrait of Jan VIII (1583-1638), Count of Nassau-Siegen, studio of
Jan van Ravesteyn, oil on panel, circa 1614-1633, Rijksmuseum
Amsterdam*

This victory for the Dutch Republic marked a turning point in the
Eighty Years' War. Control over the Volkerak, the mouth of the Rhine
River, established the Republic as a sovereign shipping and trading
nation.

A short while later Morgan fought again, but this time on the side of the
British against the Dutch Republic. He was the person in charge of the
deportation of settlers, like the Heyliger family, who were banished to
St. Maarten.

So, the Heyliger family has been on St. Maarten for a very long time.
After 350 years, they refuse to pledge allegiance to yet another crown.
Only with obstinate opposition did they manage to maintain their
existence and independence.

What goes around, Anansi, comes around. So, here is another lesson of
history that both noble gentlemen adhered to: Never bite the hand that
feeds you."

A slight vibration of the spider web suggested that my Spider-Prince
took notice of this at least.

Vagabondage

"Dear Anansi, let me now tell you a bit more about the background of those early European settlers in the Caribbean. The Caribbean was never a real penal colony but the British certainly used it for undesirables. For many white people in Britain and Ireland, the West Indies meant slavery or indentured labor. Vagrants, petty criminals, rebels, and, above all, the Irish, had little hope of escape or freedom. Nor did they have a happy ending in a return home

Deportations began under James I, as part of a general initiative to relocate the poor, vagrant, or criminal to places in the new empire desperate for labor. The 1603 royal decree on vagabondage listed both the East and West Indies as probable destinations, as well as Newfoundland and continental Europe.

In the late 1620s and early 1630s, hundreds were sent to Barbados, Bermuda, and St Christopher's, most described as rogues or vagrants. The legal basis of these shipments was rather vague. Many people volunteered to go rather than await trial and be sentenced. Others fled, with little time to leave London on their own initiative, and running the risk of being re-arrested if they did not do so.

And then there were those sentenced to deportation after criminal trials. Often, it was a matter of death sentences commuted to exile in the West Indies. After the Restoration in 1660, it became more common for judges to pardon criminals sentenced to death by sending them to the Caribbean.

Some prisoners turned into celebrities in the process, like Mary Carleton, the 'German princess' of Kent. She was a marriage swindler who used false identities, such as that of a German princess, to marry and defraud a number of men. Convicted for bigamy, she spent two years in Jamaica after being pardoned from the gallows and deported. Mary evaded any 'barbarous slavery' on her arrival, and was greeted as a celebrity according to popular pamphlets written after her death.

In 1685, 353 convicts left London and Bristol when the annual intake of white migrants was about 1,000. They were only slightly outnumbered by indentured servants. Demand for white labor declined steeply in the

1690s, in favor of blacks, and Jamaica refused to take any more convicts after 1717.

One more major factor in establishing a population in the Caribbean was the forcible deportation of 'rebels' in Britain and Ireland in the civil wars. One such rebel wrote:

The voyage was an experience of standing room only below decks with 100 others. 22 died on the way in a prison of crying and dying, and there were disease and death among the crew and passengers too.

Most of the white population of the Caribbean does not have roots to be proud of; their ancestry is checkered."

Anansi had not made a peep and was taking in the story. "What about Jews?" Anansi squeaked. "Caribbean, so many Jews!"

So I told him whatever else I could remember about the Jews in Recife, Essequibo, and the Caribbean Islands.

Jews

"After the expulsion from Spain and Portugal, Sephardic Jews moved to friendly Muslim and European countries, such as Morocco and Holland. In those days, Muslims were often more friendly towards Jews than they were towards Christians. Jews were ready to pay the Jizya, the special tax for non-Muslims. Protestant Holland also guaranteed freedom of religion and thus welcomed Jews, although with limitations and only sequestered in a ghetto.

Some Jews moved to Brazil, but the Inquisition did not allow them any religious freedom. Children of Jewish settlers were forcibly separated from their parents to be raised in Christian environments. In secrecy, Jews practiced their religions and educated their children, nevertheless.

In 1630, the Dutch sailed for Recife, northeast Brazil, and conquered it for the fledgling Dutch Republic. They had the help of many secret Jewish settlers in Brazil.

Since 1492, the Sephardics, cursed by everlasting diasporas, went from Spain through other countries around the Mediterranean, and Portugal, and since mid-16th century the wool-trade cities in Flandres. Pulled out in 1579 by the Union of Atrecht, they finally found some rest in Dutch trade cities like Amsterdam. In spite of the freedom of religion decree in the Union of Utrecht, of the same year 1579, their first official Amsterdam synagogue rose only after 1614, due to the hesitating, not to say detesting zealot calvinist town-authorities.

At least 600 Jews of Amsterdam moved to Recife, a 'Holy Jewish Community' that quickly expanded into about three or four thousand by 1642. Unfortunately, by 1654, the Portuguese re-conquered their lost territories with a siege and battle that lasted on and off for ten years; they prevailed in 1664.

A new Inquisition removed or killed all those who would not profess to being Catholic. Many Jews returned to Amsterdam, or moved to Surinam, Essequibo, Curaçao, Statia, or New Amsterdam, all under Dutch control. Officially, the British welcomed Jews in Jamaica and Barbados, though with smoldering hate. Surinam became the most successful recipient, since no British were ready to settle in this unwelcoming and impenetrable jungle. With the promise of citizenship, 10 acres of free land, and trade routes to Barbados, some Jews were enticed by the British.

A negative was that they were not allowed to trade slaves and had to live in the Jewish ghetto. Trading slaves was the big business at the time, and being excluded from that trade was bad news. The community in Barbados became successful. Also, the Jamaican community became wealthy, which sparked envy and legal restrictions and even petitions for expulsion. It took until the 19th century for equal rights for Jews to be established.

Some Jews settled in the French colonies, but in 1683 King Louis XIV ordered all Jews to be expelled. Though the order was mostly ignored, life was restricted and owning property was only by exception. The Danish were to some extent welcoming wealthy Jewish traders to St. Croix and St. Thomas. The Jews on Curaçao did by far the best. The first Jews in Curaçao were Sephardic Jewish immigrants from Amsterdam and Antwerp as well as Portugal and Spain.

These early settlers founded the Mikvé Israel-Emanuel congregation, which has the oldest continuously-used synagogue in the Americas. Supposedly, the first Jew to settle in Curaçao was Samuel Cohen, a Dutch Jewish interpreter. He arrived on board a Dutch ship in 1634.

By the mid-1700s, the community was the most prosperous in the

Americas and many of the Jewish communities in Latin America, primarily in Colombia and Venezuela, resulted from the influx of Curaçao Jews. In the 20th century Ashkenazi Jews from Eastern Europe immigrated to Curaçao, establishing their own traditions and a school. As of 2013, the Jewish population is only around 350. Of course, there is so much more to learn about this small but extremely interesting group of people who managed to succeed, whatever the challenges. Many are a great source of inspiration to other ethnic and religious minorities."

A priest

"To understand the islanders even better, Anansi, let me take you along on a visit to the mosaic of little islands and little minds. On a little island lived a priest. He was all by himself and I decided to pay him a visit. From afar, I could make out the contours of his church; not just an average church, but a huge cathedral, dwarfing everything else on the island.

People on other islands told me that the priest built his church as large as the Notre Dame of Paris, or even the Saint Peter in the Vatican. Nobody knew how he got the money, but he did and it was his life's achievement. The priest was a Franciscan friar, a celebrant of poverty.

'Father,' I said when I set foot ashore, 'so nice to meet you. Your church is magnificent, but where is the congregation?'

The priest pondered over my question and then mumbled, 'My life is in the name of Saint Francis of Assisi and my congregation is that of the fishes and the birds. Like Saint Francis, I preach to them every day and pray for them. I am just a friar, a lesser brother, sworn to poverty.'

'But dear Father, if your congregation consists of only fishes and birds how could you build this church? You must have access to quite a bit of money to construct this huge cathedral. I would hardly call that poverty.'

'All good things come from above, my son,' said the priest as he strode along the beach. After a long silence he explained, 'For many years, very kind Colombian people would visit with a boat, a very fast speed boat. On each occasion, they left behind a suitcase for my safekeeping. And then, all of a sudden, the visits stopped, and I never saw my dear friends again. After waiting for years, I decided to open the suitcases and they were full of money. That is how I built the church.'

The priest's bare feet touched the foaming water and his frock got wet at the fringes. Then he spread out his arms and sermonized.

St. Francis Preaching to and Feeding the Birds, by Giotto, fresco, early 14th century, Church of St. Francis, Assisi.

'My little sisters, the birds, ye owe much to God, your Creator, and ye ought to sing his praise at all times and in all places.'

Chanting softly, the priest continued his prayer for the birds. 'He has given you, my little sisters, fountains and rivers to quench your thirst, mountains and valleys in which to take refuge, and trees in which to build your nests; my little sisters, study always to give praise to God.'

Afterwards, in serene silence and side by side the priest and I walked from the beach to the portico of the giant church. Two lovebird pigeons cuddled on the path in the hot sand; they made no attempt to scurry away when we passed.

The air was filled with strong fragrances. The Ylang-Ylang exuded the most sensual of all floral scents, sending insects and birds into a frenzy. Tiny green and purple hummingbirds hovered incessantly over yellow parrot beaks.

'Father, do the birds congregate in your church out of piety?'

Pigeons and hummingbirds flew in and out of the dark minster, nosediving at rocket speed from the nests they had built near the highest point of the cupola.

'Yes, my son, the birds come for confession. The most rambunctious ones always nestle right inside the church, right over the altar. Birds know by instinct that they need blessings of the Lord. The poor animals cannot help it, but they fornicate all day long, and therefore I administer the sacrament of matrimony to them, so they can go and multiply in peace and in the name of the Lord.'

'Father, I hear that so many people are alone, like you, but also that on the next island is a young couple, all by themselves. Do you know them?'

'Yes, my son. Before they took the next island as their home, they came to me for a blessing and I blessed them saying the words of the Holy Scripture, as written in Genesis 9:5:

As for you, be fruitful and increase in number; multiply on the earth and increase upon it.

And that, my son, is a little over nine months ago. You better hurry up and go see them.'

Indeed, on an even smaller island this very young couple could be found. Someone told me that they suffered from the *Blue Lagoon* delusion. I decided to pay a visit to the young couple, as the priest had suggested."

A young couple and a baby

"'This is our island, and you are not welcome here,' was the first thing they said when I landed my dinghy at their beach.

They were very young, fifteen, maybe sixteen years old, beautiful children of nature, and very much in love - but scared of the world outside.

'Don't you want to get rescued?' I asked. 'You are castaways, aren't you? Castaways always get rescued, but if you prefer a different version of the script, let me know. I will be most happy to accommodate.'

I was so sorry for my sarcasm, but could not help myself.

As the young couple did not understand anyway, they diddled for a while before the lady of the household caught my sheet, and tied up the dinghy.

'Dear Grace, Holy Mary, you are pregnant and making headways with it,' I said to the woman, as friendly as I could possibly be since the man remained hostile. If he had had a gun he would have shot me for sure.

'Dear, oh dear, you better get into the pushing position.'

She was nervous and clearly did not know what to do next, or what to expect.

You better get out of here, get off the island before I throw you out!' yelled the young man.

I tried to reason with them. 'Come on lady, get it done! Man, sober up, your wife is about to give birth! Your wife is very pregnant and about to deliver any minute. Look, my friend. Are you not scared of the risks you are running? Never mind, it will only take thirty minutes, maybe an hour. That is, if all goes well.'

He swore at me but did not deny any of what I said. A cocktail of anger and fear was the reason for his behavior. He was unpredictable and I sensed danger.

'Childbirth is a natural fact and not a disease, and we do not need a doctor or anyone,' pleaded the young woman.

I noticed her blistered face and the sores of countless insect bites covering her legs and arms. Her stringy bleached and braided hair hung off her skull like an old rag.

'I am a hippy, drippy mom. My first child will be born far away from beeping machines and hospitals full of germs. Women have been giving birth in the wild for thousands of years, and so will I. I will go to the river and my child will be born in the water of the creek.'

By now, the young woman was delirious and rambled on and on.

Suddenly, with the most clearheaded of voices, the mother-to-be said, 'I remember my mom often telling us about when a local lady had her baby and how at the time she was due to give birth she simply found a nice spot, pushed out the baby, breastfed it, and wrapped it in a carrier cloth, tied the child to her back, and went about her business. That stuck with me and is one of the reasons I wanted to give birth to my child in the wild.'

So, after that little epiphany, we walked to the creek, only minutes away, expectant father, mother, and me, and she picked a spot where she could squat down and allow the process to take place.

The boy was angry and nervous. He yelled and threw stones at the fish that were long gone from the creek, and continued to threaten me.

'Push as if you're having a bowel movement,' I said. 'Relax your body and thighs and push as if you're having the biggest bowel movement of your life!'

I yelled, getting caught up in the excitement, 'And talking about bowel movements, put all your concentration and focus into the pushing, not into worrying about whether you'll be emptying your bowels or passing urine while you're at it.'

I mumbled, 'Dear, all delivering moms seem to be worrying about dirtying themselves and a little pee, but who cares?'

To the great dismay of the young man, I continued my little pep talk, 'You are sitting in a creek on an island where no one lives. Believe me, nobody in the world cares. Just forget about me! Do your thing. Dearest girl, it's warm and sunny and in the middle of nature. I can't think of a nicer place to bring a baby into the world.'

The young man looked more and more confused as he watched. Shock, disbelief, fear, and joy were the emotions expressed by the stunned partner, who seemed to have little or no notion about becoming a father. He covered his mouth and face in distrust before slowly backing away from his wife. It was just too much for the young man.

The young girl was blissfully unaware of her boyfriend's reaction.

The youth, and that is what he was, a teenager, continued to wrap his arms around himself and slowly backed into the dense jungle as the mother handled the bloody newborn.

'It's a boy!' I shouted triumphantly, but nobody seemed to hear.

The shocked father plucked up the courage to meet his newborn, though still refusing to exchange glances with the mother. There was shame between those two.

I wondered whether he was the real father, but who really cared at this point.

That was my encounter in the wild, on an island where nobody lived but a young couple. This was the standard in the Caribbean for many generations already; so many live in total isolation, abandoned and alone in delusion.

All men of distinction have a *baisite*. Most baisites, by-sites, shadow women, live, so to speak, on-an-island-where-no-one-lives. And the baisites bear children, outside children, children out of wedlock. Nobody talks about it, and life goes on.

Recent data show that around 75 percent of births in the Caribbean are out-of-wedlock, in what is nowadays neatly classified as single-parent families.

Sexual relations between unmarried people are very much the norm in, for instance, Jamaica. Slaves could buy their freedom and one easy way to get the money needed was prostitution. This is not seeking justification for women exploiting their bodies, just putting some historical context into the Caribbean picture.

So, getting outside children was an easy way to own a few children who could be put up for sale as slaves, by their slave mother or father. Thus, many slaves owned other slaves, and many slaves set up businesses buying, breeding, and selling slaves.

Children who were born out of wedlock in Jamaica could not inherit property until Michael Manley piloted the act to abolish the illegitimacy law in 1975, so that *No bastard no deh* again. It would not force fathers

217

to act in any particular way, but it set new legal standards for the children.

As the song goes,

Bastard!
Consider that bastard dead
Bastard!
Won't get screwed again.
Whoa! Whoa!
Bastard!
Make it quick, blow off his head.

Crime

Single mothers have a hard time, especially when fathers disappear without providing for the child. Lower-class black women substitute the breadwinner's role with higglering, women's informal work. Higglers hawk everything from farm products to illegal imports. It is the higgler who will try the higher price and the haggler the lower. In the higgle-haggle interphase an entire subculture of irregular trade formed in all of the Caribbean, threatening regulated markets.

If grandparents do not take care of bastard children, and the biological father is absent, as is usually the case, there is hardly any choice. Entry into the narco industry is fast and easy. Not only mules and couriers can be recruited quickly, but entire bolita factory-like workshops are set up overnight. Children's after-school activities are often in such environments.

The associated issues are all too apparent. Crime has become part of everyday life and often the only way to survive. Ask boys in school what they would like to become in life, and many will say that they dream of a music-video-style future in the rap-narco industry, with unlimited amounts of money to spend on women, partying and drugs. Crime rates in the Caribbean run at twenty to thirty times that of the US or Europe, ranging from petty crime to murderers for hire.

Once with friends, I was having a Friday afternoon beer. We were at a beach, only twenty meters from the very spot where a populist, nationalist and racist politician was assassinated on May 5, 2013, with five bullets at 5 o'clock in the afternoon. 5-5-5, it could hardly get more symbolic.

The hired assassins were arrested and convicted soon enough, but none of those who put out the contract on the politician were ever arrested. Like never before, the self-governing crime world of the Caribbean became apparent.

According to the latest statistics (2016), Honduras, with 92 murders per 100,000 people, and Jamaica, with 40.9 murders, are among the nations with the highest murder rates in the world.

Other destinations in the Caribbean region with murder rates significantly higher than the United States include: US Virgin Islands: 39 murders per 100,000, St. Kitts and Nevis: 38, Guatemala: 38, Colombia: 37, Belize: 30.8, Trinidad and Tobago: 35, Bahamas: 27.4, Puerto Rico (a Commonwealth of the United States): 26, Mexico: 24, Dominican Republic: 25, St. Lucia: 25, St. Vincent and the Grenadines: 22, Panama: 22, Dominica: 22, Curaçao: 22.

Crime has no ethics, as many found out in the aftermath of the 2017 hurricanes Irma and Maria. Looting and plundering devastated what was left of the national pride of St. Maarten. A press release read as follows:

The lawlessness that prevailed in the first days after the storms - when some people moved from scavenging food for survival to pillaging appliances, jewelry and cellphones - shattered the image many residents had of their island.

Every day, when the sun sets, friends gather in small clusters for a drink at the beach. By coincidence, it may be at the very beach where a murder was committed, but what difference does that make? Sunsets are sunsets, beaches, beaches, and friends should always be respected.

So one day, or any day, as they stand around, talk about nothing, laugh, drink, and eat, someone will bring along a stew of goat meat. As a giant fireball sets in the ocean, a tropical night with all its enticements is not far away.

The Banana Stoba was delicious. In case you are interested, here is the local recipe:

Banana Stoba

Ingredients
1 lb. salted meat
3 yellow plantains
½ lb. sweet potatoes
½ lb. pumpkin
2 tbsp. oil
2 tbsp. butter
1 onion
2 celery stalks, cut in 1-inch long pieces
4 cinnamon sticks
10 allspice, whole
10 cloves
Whole sugar, according to taste

Cut meat into 2-inch cubes
and soak overnight in the refrigerator.
Next morning, discard the water.
In large pot, put meat cubes, add water.
Cook over medium heat till the meat is tender.
Set aside.
Peel the plantains, and cut into 3-inch pieces.
Skin the sweet potatoes, and cut into 3-inch cubes.
Remove the hard skin, seeds, and stringy portion from pumpkin, and cut
into 3-inch cubes.
In a large pot, heat oil and butter, sauté the onion, and add celery,
cinnamon sticks, allspice, and cloves.
Add water, meat, and cook for 10 minutes.
Then add the plantains, sweet potatoes, and pumpkin.
Cook over medium heat until the vegetables are done.
If too watery, scoop out the vegetables and continue cooking until
reduced to a thick sauce.
Return the vegetables to the sauce and stir gently.
Add sugar according to taste.

20 ESSEQUIBO, DEMERARA, AND
BERBICE

Turbinado, demerara and so-called "raw" sugars are made from crystallized, partially evaporated sugar cane juice and spun in a centrifuge to remove almost all of the molasses. The sugar crystals are large and golden-coloured. - From Wikipedia, the free encyclopedia

---

"Dear Anansi, Hollywood movies love to show the cracking of whips by cruel European settlers and overseers, ruthlessly and needlessly punishing and abusing African slaves. But in Essequibo, Demerara, and Berbice the plantations were, more or less, under control of and run by its slaves. A unique situation existed in those coastal plantation states of South America that were considered part of the Caribbean.

European settlers were far outnumbered by slaves. One account tallied 345 white settlers and soldiers and 5,000 African slaves and Amerindians. Slave revolts easily upset the control of the colonial settlers and, de facto, the slave plantations were partly in the hands of slaves, and sometimes overseers, some kind of interim managers on a commission basis. The inhuman treatment of slaves by European settlers and their overseers to establish at least a little control was unspeakable in. Corporal punishment was still the norm in the civilized world."

Map of Guyana (East Coast)

"Barrebiesjes"

"Didn't you tell me, Anansi, that some of your relatives were living in Berbice, Essequibo, and Demerara? I asked around in Europe, the US and even on many Caribbean islands but very few people had ever heard of Berbice and Essequibo, or Pomeroon, as the Spanish used to call it. They said that no countries exist with those names and accused me of pulling their leg. That makes me a bit sad; I was not teasing or making things up. Only the Dutch seem to have an expression in their language, 'going to the Barrebiesjes', which means 'going to hell'. Nobody I asked was about to relate that expression to the former colony, Berbice.

The background of what is today called Guyana is one of colonial exploitation, slavery, and revolt. The first forts and settlements on the Essequibo River, built by the West Indies Company of Zeeland, date from the 1590s. Initially, settlers exploited the regions as Nova Zeeland, even before the colonialization efforts by the VOC in Asia.

The Dutch preferred trading posts to colonialization. Settlers, mostly from Dutch Recife, came to the Guyana coast and established the first settlements along the Essequibo and Berbice Rivers, introducing the industrial cultivation of sugarcane in the 1640s all along the coastal plain and the banks of the great rivers. By 1658 sugar was being prcduced in Guyana and within three years the first shipments sailed for Holland.

Over 300 sugar estates also had 300 stills to distill rum! The big breakthrough came in the 1650s when the British planters introduced the pivotal process of distilling. This proved so popular that by 1670, every sugar estate had a small still attached to it. In the same year, the local sugarcane producers formed an exporting co-operative, and by the 1700s there were well over 300 independent estates involved in producing their own unique rums from the molasses - a byproduct of sugar production.

In 1745, Demerara, or in Dutch, Demerary, was separated from Essequibo. One year later, the director-general of Essequibo and Demerara, Laurens Storm van's Gravesande, began to grant land on the banks of the Demerary River. In 1748, a map produced for him listed 38 plantation owners in the colony.

The post of commander of Demerara, a deputy to the director general, was created in 1752, and filled by Van's Gravesande's son, Jonathan. His surveyor Laurens van Bercheyck's 1759 map of the Demerary River listed 118 plantations. In only fifteen years' time, nearly 60 new plantations had been set up. Even with as little as a few hundred slave workers per plantation, it was an enormous undertaking and accomplishment.

In 1816, the British took over. Essequibo and Berbice are the largest rivers in today's Guyana."

Sugar

"Sugar had become very popular in Europe. New sugarcane plantations, often with thousands of African slaves, popped up along the big rivers in the South American tropical region. The Spanish and French were eager to buy shares in these new investment opportunities. More and more settlers, attracted by the high profits of rum production, built extensive plantations along the Essequibo, Demerara, and Berbice.

You can still find demerara sugar in a store. The name Demerara comes from the Arawak word *Immenary*, or *Dumaruni*, meaning 'river of the letter wood'. Demerara sugar is so named because it originally came from the Demerara sugarcane fields.

Sugar has been produced from sugarcane for thousands of years. It was a popular luxury item in the Middle East and traveled to Andalusia with the Umayyad. Jews, expelled from Iberia, picked up the sugar culture from the Moors, the Almoravid culture of North Africa. They brought it back to the Iberian Peninsula, starting in Madeira. The Spanish quickly adopted the practice, and the Portuguese took sugar to Brazil.

By 1540, there were 800 cane sugar mills in Santa Catarina Island, just off the south coast, and another 2,000 on the north coast of Brazil, Demerara, and Surinam. About 3,000 small sugar mills, built before 1550 in the New World, created a record demand for cast iron gears, levers, axles, and other implements. Through piracy, the Dutch obtained the know-how of sugar refining from the Spanish. That knowledge was in high demand throughout the Dutch colonies across the West Indies. In addition, Portuguese Jews, who turned out to be very familiar with the complicated production system, happily introduced it to Dutch Brazil.

The new business quickly attacked large investment in Holland and England. For instance, in 1750, Dordrecht had 13 sugar refineries, Rotterdam 25, and Amsterdam 25. Many Dordtars had shares in sugar refineries and sugar plantations in Surinam, Berbice and Demerary, and also in the sugar plantations on the West Indies of Tobago, St. Thomas, and St. Croix.

The rise of the sugar industry became the first major impulse to develop mold making and iron casting in Europe. In many ways, sugar mill construction, industrialized agriculture, became the forerunner to the Industrial Revolution in the early 17th century.

Guyana was more or less a Dutch colony until 1815. The Dutch had a very limited grip on the area due to many revolts and uprisings. Most of their settlements were located along the lower courses of the Demerara river. Its main town was Georgetown. The public may have erased these not-so-flattering stories about slave colonies, but they did exist for hundreds of years. The sweet tooth that Europe developed came with a hefty price tag.

Only recently a new country was founded, combining all these river areas: Guyana, situated north of Brazil, east of Venezuela, and west of Surinam. Guyana has the world's second highest percentage of rainforest. The state manages 84 percent of the forests and has a population of largely former black African slaves and indigenous Amerindians. Guyana has officially zoned very large parts of their country for nature conservation.

This new reputation for conservation is the country's pride. When Guyana's minister received the decoration of the Order of the Golden Ark from the World Wild Fund president, Prince Bernard of Orange, for his environmental protection program, it was a happy day of celebration for the entire country.

Voltaire, the most enlightened French philosopher and author of the 18th century, was also a plantation shareholder, though he never shied away from talking about the brutal treatment of the slaves on the sugar plantations."

Candide in Surinam

"In Voltaire's satire of the same name, Candide had the following encounter in Surinam.

As they drew near the town, they saw a Negro stretched upon the ground, with only one moiety of his clothes, that is, of his blue linen drawers; the poor man had lost his left leg and his right hand.

Illustration in Voltaire's Candide

'Good God!' said Candide in Dutch, 'what art thou doing there, friend, in that shocking condition?'

'I am waiting for my master, Mynheer Vanderdendur, the famous merchant,' answered the Negro.

'Was it Mynheer Vanderdendur,' asked Candide, 'that treated thee thus?'

'Yes, Sir,' said the Negro, 'it is the custom. They give us a pair of linen drawers for our whole garment, twice a year. When we work at the sugar canes, and the mill snatches hold of a finger, they cut off the hand; and when we attempt to run away, they cut off the leg; both cases have happened to me. This is the price at which you eat sugar in Europe.'

From today's perspective, the entire operation was very small. In 1762, the population of the Dutch colony of Berbice included 3,833 enslaved blacks, 244 enslaved Amerindians, or indigenous people, and only 346 whites.

A few thousand black African slaves developed a life and existence in the plantation areas with some degree of satisfaction. Most of the uprisings concerned the cut of the profits to be paid to the plantation workers.

Rebel slave, engraving based on the drawing of (1744-1797) and a picture by William Blake, Paris 1799.

Although there was some oversight by the Dutch settlers, most of the plantations were more or less self-governed. When the situation became too dire, revolts broke out till a new equilibrium brought stability. Every revolt left behind a trail of atrocities. Europeans, mostly French, Spanish, and Brazilian shareholders, employed overseers who often treated the laborers ruthlessly. Brutal treatment led to many revolts, uprisings, and bloodshed.

On 23 February 1763, slaves on Plantation Magdalenenberg on the Canje River in Berbice rebelled. Cuffy, an enslaved man at Lilienburg, is said to have organized rebels into a military unit. Other key figures among the rebels included Atta, Accara, and Accabre with a little over 2,000 maroons in the territories of Berbice, Demerara, and Essequibo.

A gruesome incident followed when the authorities struck back. The dead bodies of rebels were mutilated; hands were severed and taken to Governor Van Gravesande, who had them nailed to posts as a warning. The governor marked with small crosses on a map in his office the places where he had ordered the limbs to be nailed to posts. Eventually, he called for the help of the Indian tribes to prevent the rebels from retreating inland. He also sent word to, amongst others, the St. Eustatius colony. On May 3, the governor of St. Eustatius sent two ships with a total of only 154 soldiers.

Most governors and commanders did not last very long. They died from malaria or dysentery, or exhaustion from living under constant threat. For instance, Jonathan Samuel Storm van 's Gravesande died after just one year in service in 1761, and his successor, Laurens Lodewijk van Bercheijk, in 1765. And the next one, Jan Cornelis van den Heuvel, only lasted for five years."

More about Maroons

"There were thousands of runaway slaves in the Caribbean and South America, mostly identified as Maroons. As early as 1512, many runaways tried to make a living in the dense rainforest of the Amazon basin beyond the reach of European settlers and Amerindians.

Maroons in Panama, Jamaica, Guyana, and Surinam formed small nations and settlements. Clandestine life in their Maroon states, or catering to the informal economy of piracy and war, became their lot in life, which has continued till today. Maroons, who at times sided with the colonial powers, constantly threatened plantations in Essequibo and Berbice. They took opportunistic action in their own favor, but often flip-flopped and sided with unhappy slaves.

In the 16th century, the British privateer Sir Francis Drake enlisted *Cimarrones* during his raids on the Spanish. Cimarrones were runaway slaves in Panama. He noted in his log:

A black people that about eighty years past fled from the Spaniards their masters, by reason of their cruelty, and are since had grown to a nation, under two kings of their own.

Jamaica already had Maroons in 1655, some as pirates and others in hiding in the forest, and sometimes banded with Amerindians. The Maroons raided and pillaged plantations and harassed planters. They grew into a force to be reckoned with, but, especially on the small islands, they had little chance of lasting success. By 1700, Maroons had disappeared from most of the smaller islands. Many governors entered into treaties and agreements with established Maroon settlements to guarantee some degree of security and stability.

Visiting Maroons in their villages, often in very remote areas of the jungle, I have always been surprised by the strong similarities between Maroon and African art and music. Memories and traditions passed on by many generations have not faded the specific designs, artistry, and rhythm. Some, like our Anansi, claim a cultural heritage of the Akan people in West Africa. The Akan people reside in the southern areas of the former Gold Coast region, today's Ghana and Ivory Coast. The Maroons have talking drums much like the Akan. Talking drums, the hourglass-shaped barrels, most with two or even three heads connected with leather tension cords in different tones, can mimic human speech. It is a simplified version of a language that develops as a means of communication between two or more groups that do not have a language in common.

The Maroon version is at times identical to the Akan but has its own interpretation, sometimes with a kettle version copied from the European military marches.

Music, dance and mystic religious rituals in rhythms and rhymes shaped the Maroon culture. The music of the Maroons remains a unique blend of African, Native American, and European musical traditions. Even some of the modern lyrics are fascinating.

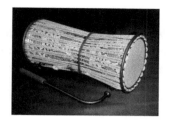

Talking drum

Let us finish with some great Maroon lyrics, ***Songs About Jane*** (2002) and ***It Won't Be Soon Before Long*** (2007)."

Delicious local Guyanese Creole cooking can also not be passed up, especially the *metemgee*, a Guyanese Creole stew.

Metemgee

Ingredients
6 oz. beef, cubed, optional
6 oz. pork or salted beef, cubed, optional
8 oz. saltfish
2 cups chicken stock (or water)
2 cups coconut milk
1 lb. sweet potato, peeled, cubed
1 lb. yams, peeled, cubed
1 lb. plantain, peeled, cubed
1 tsp. fresh thyme, finely chopped
2 habaneros, seeded, finely chopped
1 red onion, cut into rings
1 lb. okra, sliced
1 cup flour
2 tbsp. butter, small cubes
1 tsp. baking powder
½ tsp. salt
2 tbsp. sugar
2 tbsp. water

Instructions

Dust the beef and pork with flour and sauté.
Soak the saltfish in warm water for about 15 minutes. Drain.
Remove skin and bones and discard.
Squeeze the fish dry.
Grate the coconut.
Pour one pint of water over it, squeeze well,
and strain to extract the coconut milk.
Arrange the peeled plantains and seasonings in layers over the meat, with the saltfish on top.
Add the coconut milk and cook, covered, until almost tender, about 30 minutes.
Place onions and okras on top of the saltfish.
Steam, covered, for 10 minutes.
Add dumplings and steam for another 8 minutes.

For the dumplings

Rub flour and butter together.
Add baking powder, salt, and sugar.
Add enough of the water to make stiff dough.

21 THE DECLINE OF THE WIC, THE RESCUE, AND MODERN-DAY SLAVERY

The majority of modern slavery victims are between the ages of 18 and 24 years old. 1.2 million children are enslaved through forced labor and exploited in the sex industry each year. In 1850, the cost of a slave, if converted in today's dollar value, would be $40,000. The cost of a modern-day slave is $90. - *Abolition Media: Modern Slavery Statistics*

"Yes, Anansi, Essequibo, Berbice, and Voltaire's account of Surinam are unfortunate stories. Maybe I should not have told you."

"Oh no, I pleased," Anansi chirped excitedly. "My friends, Cuffy, nephews Atta, Accara, and Accabre. All big heroes! My family famous man!"

Anansi celebrated his day swinging in his cobweb hammock, rocking on reggae, smoking a joint, and having his very own Keti Koti abolition celebration.

I had been held up in the Virgin Islands, St. Maarten, and Statia due to stormy weather. My plan was to wait for the perfect conditions before making the big crossing, straight south, to Trinidad and Tobago, past the

Windward Islands, Martinique, St. Lucia, St. Vincent and the Grenadines, with Barbados far to the east. Guadeloupe was to be avoided due to a plague of raccoons. The Guadeloupe raccoon is a common raccoon, endemic on the two main islands, Basse-Terre and Grande-Terre, and the focus of great controversy.

In 2003, two biologists, Wilson and Helgen, acquired world fame when they discovered a little raccoon, which they surmised had to be a subspecies of the common raccoon. With their find, the scientists were able to ride the high waves of respected explorers for a while, as researchers from all over the world flocked to the islands. Unfortunately, their find turned out to be a case of insular dwarfism, caused by malnutrition, or the specimen had been a very young animal. Was this a case of fraud by scientists eager to attract funds for their research? Were the new Pirates of the Caribbean cloaked in respectable academic gowns?

It is known, however, that on the island Conzumel near Mexico, a dwarf raccoon lives as an authentic species, loved by the tourists of cruise-ships.

Raccoons pose a serious threat to pleasure boats, and the damage they can cause in a short amount of time is comparable to a mini typhoon. I rather used my waiting time to study the islands and their history in more detail and to prepare for the large trip.

Today's slavery in Africa

"Anansi, history has completely turned on itself. What I am about to tell you is not terribly politically correct and runs against the current climate of revenge and damage claims. Yet, it is part of history and must be told. We are now talking about slavery in this day and age. I see you look bewildered.

Currently, descendants of former Caribbean slaves are crossing the Atlantic again, but this time migrating to Europe, to the countries of their former slave masters; not just a few of them, but hundreds of thousands. You can spot them at the airports every day, where they occupy the lounges waiting for the cheapest possible flights to take off. Packed with as many bags as they can possibly carry and always pulling along a number of little children, they migrate to Europe, officially as tourists, but in reality never to return to their islands.

On average the narcotics police at the airports makes 10-15 arrests for each of those flights, as many try to make a little extra money as drug mules. Baby diapers and wheelchairs seem to be popular hiding places.

At the same time, we still witness a lot of slavery in Africa. Hundreds of thousands of young people and children are sold or kidnapped every year. Ruthless gangsters sell them to work in agriculture, mostly in the West African cacao industry. The younger children are used for herding cattle, goats, and camels in the Sahel.

On one of my trips through the Sudan desert, I came upon a well, where herds of hundreds of animals gulped down water that was hoisted up from the bottom of a narrow shaft. The space down below was so confined that only little children could work there.

In today's world one can buy a child in most of the Sahel for as little at twenty dollars. With a lot of diplomatic pressure, countries may sign abolition agreements, but that means very little in practice. Official signatures are rather efforts to appease rich western nations to pay development funds to corrupt politicians.

The Global Slavery Index, published in November 2014, put the total number of slaves on the African continent at 6.4 million, including 5.6 million in Sub-Saharan Africa. An additional 800,000 are in the northern region, including Morocco, Algeria, Tunisia, Libya, and Egypt.

The abolition of slavery is not as simple as an on-and-off switch. You cannot just give slaves a piece of paper that states that they are free; they cannot even read. They have no education or money to support their families. Manumission takes far more than that. You need to re-educate and re-train these people so that they can take care of themselves. Many children who were sold at an early age suffer from malnutrition and will have physical and mental defects for as long as they live. Their life expectancies are very much reduced."

"I not care!" mumbled Anansi, "Not my problem. Timbuktu problem is African problem. We, African slaves in the Caribbean, and the Americas never got any help from Africa. Africa never protested brutal treatment by plantation overseers. Africa never freed us."

"Yes, you are right. African kings, chiefs, and their cronies took the money, became super rich, and lived in great luxury. That is what they still do. They do not care about slaves or poor people. But Anansi, you cannot say that you are not your brother's keeper. We all signed and supported the Human Rights Act by the United Nations of 1948. Yes, we have to care and take care. The western world has already spent over one trillion US dollars in foreign aid to Africa over the last twenty years. It's got to make a difference."

"I not African brothers' keeper!" insisted Anansi. "No man, too busy with my troubles. My mother in Surinam, my father Essequibo, my brothers in Bijlmermeer, near Amsterdam. Many sisters, all on Caribbean islands. You see, I am a spider in the middle of family web. With many long silk threads at all. They pull, I know they need me."

Anansi's attitude was that of so many in the Caribbean, the US, and also in Africa itself. People do not want to be bothered. The lack of empathy, sympathy, and compassion amongst descendants of former slaves will never seize to amaze me.

"Sorry, Anansi, have you no heart? I cannot watch the suffering of all these desperate people. They get jam-packed into ramshackle boats, trying to get from Libya to Lampedusa, and many, many drown and never make it. People of the Caribbean, many of them descendants of slaves, do not want to know about African slavery; they do not want to discuss it, and they refuse to help. The most amazing fact is that when Surinam became independent in 1975, more than half the population moved to Holland, the country of their slave masters. Nobody went to Africa."

"You silly white man. In Holland, nice welfare, free house, free school, free doctor, hospital nursing. Even free money, every month! In Africa? Nothing! Right, nothing!"

Admiral Abraham Crijnssen

"Let's get on with our historical account. I introduce you now to Admiral Abraham Crijnssen. He was born in 1610 or 1615 in Vlissingen, or Flushings as the Scottish enclave in the harbor town of Veere called it. And in 1665 he became Commander of the Admiralty of Zeeland. Crijnssen tried to rescue whatever possible from the greedy British who eagerly stole Holland's wealth and prosperity.

From 1600 till 1653, the Dutch Republic enjoyed enormous profits, not from the Dutch slave trade, which had hardly started yet, but from salt, sugar, herring, and piracy. But the second part of the 17ᵗʰ century was a complete disaster. In 1672, known as the *Ramp Jaar*, the Disaster Year, the Dutch people were *redeloos*, its government *radeloos*, and the country *reddeloos*: senseless, desperate, and beyond rescue."

Anansi chuckled but did not understand the 'redeloos, radeloos, and reddeloos' part.

"Dear Anansi, the second part of the 17ᵗʰ century was incredibly tough. The fledgling Dutch Republic was about to go under."

"You, silly white man. Golden Age, Amsterdam and London, streets all gold from the slave trade. Everything, every building, every luxury from selling flesh, African black flesh."

"Maybe, but let us be correct with historical facts. Most of the trading companies of the early 17ᵗʰ century went bankrupt. Money was made on piracy, not yet on the slave trade. The Dutch brought 400,000 slaves to Surinam, 16,000 to Essequibo, 15,000 to Berbice, 11,000 to Demerary, 25,000 to Recife, and 100,000 to the Spanish colonies, via Curaçao. The Dutch share in the total of the slave trade to the New World was never more than five percent. No European country suffered bigger financial losses due to the slave trade than the Dutch.

Piracy was the big moneymaker. Look at Heyn's capture of the Spanish treasure fleet, which brought the biggest dividend ever. The accounts of the West India Company are still available for all to see and audit."

My account did not sit well with Anansi. He was used to hearing another scenario, one of filthy profits hand in hand with unspeakable cruelty and sadism - one of hatred, exploitation, and racism.

"Golden Age, not so golden then? Who is lying, man? Do not tell, all white guys lying. Your game also lying, not?"

WIC and its decline

"Anansi, how could the WIC make a profit on trading slaves with the Spanish colonies when a war was going on between those countries until 1648? Yes, in 1662 and again in 1685, the Coyman family and the WIC got temporary Asientos. Not before. The profits came only in the late 17ᵗʰ and 18ᵗʰ century.

After 1627 the WIC of Zeeland tried setting up plantations in Berbice and Essequibo as the colony Nova Zeelandia, and the WIC in Surinam after 1667, but the profits were most questionable. Contracted independent overseers squeezed out every last drop from the slaves, but the shareholders mostly went without dividend.

Indeed, privateers and pirates made tons of money, but the Republic was faced with an economic disaster. There was no tax in the Republic; everything was financed with treasury bonds. The statesman Johan van Oldenbarnevelt had brokered a ceasefire with the Spanish in 1609. At the closing of the Synod of Dordt, the first international meeting of protestant churches in Europe, in 1618, the power-hungry Prince Maurits, eager to become king, had van Oldenbarnevelt arrested, and in 1619 beheaded over some religious dispute. Maurits' *coup d'état* was the starting point for the founding of the WIC in 1621. It also meant that the war with Spain resumed.

The immensely profitable VOC, founded in 1602, had become the largest multinational in the world. Likewise, the profit forecasts for the WIC were astronomical, but its role in maritime war sunk the company. The WIC may have been modeled on the VOC, but its role turned out to be that of an informal navy. The company issued pirate licenses to privateers, who were in it for their share. There were also no ethics in war.

The zenith of WIC power was during 1640-1645. At that time, the company controlled New Netherland in the present US, New Holland, part of Brazil, Curaçao, Aruba, Tobago, and several other islands in the Caribbean. Guyana, Surinam, and Fernando de Noronha, 200 miles off the shore of Brazil, formed the arrival point for transatlantic shipping. For a few months, a Dutch expedition also occupied Valdivia and Chiloé in Chile. Privateering turned out to be the most profitable operation, not necessarily for the WIC but certainly for its privateers. The end of the Eighty Years' War with Spain reduced the number of treasure fleets to target.

The Anglo-Dutch Wars of 1652-1654, 1665-1667 and 1672-1674 were also a substantial drain on WIC resources and trading posts. WIC's efforts of setting up plantations in Dutch Brazil, Berbice, Essequibo and Surinam turned out to be costly operations with large capital investment, which required careful, longtime planning. An all-compassing network of Caribbean islands, fortified and equipped to control the shipping lanes, was mostly lost to the British. The cutthroat competition from other European nations weakened the power of the WIC transatlantic enterprise even further.

The Peace of Münster of 1648 brought great economic disaster for Zeeland because trade on the rivers Schelde, Sas, and Zwin moved to Flemish ports. Zeeland voted against the treaty without success.

Johan Maurits van Nassau-Siegen, the Dutch king of Brazil, was called home and the Portuguese 'moradores' rebelled against WIC rule. In 1654, the Portuguese armada retook Recife and the whole of Dutch Brazil. In 1664, the English occupied New Amsterdam and renamed it New York.

Already in 1648, the WIC was all but officially bankrupt; the wars had exhausted the company. Reorganization for creditors was announced, and refinancing followed. It made little difference: bankruptcy was officially declared in 1674 and again in 1791.

From 1675-1733 the WIC shipped and delivered 170,016 slaves from the coast of African Guynea and Angola, 2,790 per year, not enough to balance the huge expenditure. After 1713 and 1733, when the WIC lost its Asiento to Britain, the company was exclusively engaged in the administration of the remaining African and American overseas territories and fortresses until it was definitively dissolved in 1791.

It was from this mess that Admiral Abraham Crijnssen of Flushing, Zeeland, tried to rescue whatever could be rescued. But as an old Dutch saying goes, it was like mopping up with the tap still running."

Salvage operations: Surinam

"Colonizing Caribbean islands was like playing musical chairs. European nations, pirates, buccaneers, and privateers danced around the archipelago like little boys, all mesmerized by the idea of astronomical rewards. The defense of most of the islands was no more than a few forts with or without heavy guns and only a small garrison of fewer than one hundred men.

The aim was to control the shipping routes. Rumors about British conquest and plunder of Caribbean islands and South American colonies greatly worried Dutch investors. Ordered by the State of

Zeeland and the WIC, Admiral Abraham Crijnssen put together a fleet of seven privateers, including three frigates, to investigate and lend assistance. They left the harbor of Veere in Zeeland on December 30, 1666.

Crijnssen's official orders were to attack and occupy Surinam, liberate Nova Zeelandia (Essequibo and Berbice) from the British, and retake Tobago and St. Eustatius. The French, under Admiral Antoine de la Barre, joined the Dutch against the British. The British half of St. Kitts fell immediately, followed by Antigua and Montserrat. The Dutch re-conquered the island of St. Eustatius, and then captured Surinam. The British had already left Essequibo, Berbice and Tobago.

Then Crijnssen and de la Barre combined forces and organized a Franco-Dutch invasion of Nevis on May 20, 1667. Due to poor communication between the French and Dutch, confusion ruled and the English repelled the joint forces. In the aftermath, the French moved on to Martinique and the Dutch sailed north to attack the Virginia colony.

Good gracious, Anansi, I have bombarded you with so many facts again. Are you still able to take it all in? What? You were sleeping through it all? How can you know how to handle today if you have no idea where it came from?"

The attack on the French ships at Martinique by Willem van de Velde
the Younger, oil on canvas, 1675 © Royal Collection Trust

Martinique

"In early June 1667, a new English fleet, under the command of Rear Admiral Sir John Harman, reached the West Indies and attacked the French. By July 6, Harman had sunk, burnt, or captured the majority of the French ships, twenty-one in total. With the French fleet destroyed, Harman then attacked the French at Cayenne, forcing its garrison to surrender. The English fleet continued on to recapture Surinam by October.

The news of the Peace of Breda, signed on July 31, marking the end of the Anglo-Dutch war, had not reached the fighting forces yet. Horrified by reports of the British conquests, Crijnssen sailed back to the Caribbean to find the French fleet destroyed and the English back in Surinam. Part of the Treaty of Breda stipulated that each side would keep the possessions it held on July 31, so Surinam was returned to the Dutch.

With the infrastructure on most of the islands destroyed, the resurrection of trade demanded fresh capital. Financed by the Dutch states, the Coymans brothers bought the Spanish Asiento in 1662 for six million guilders, the highest price at that time. Two Genoese bankers and merchants, Grillo and Lomelius, with an office in Panama, sold out for cash and then got deeper into the perilous slave transports.

The WIC Coymans were to ship 24,000 *Pièce d'Indie* in seven years, a special name for an African of the Ashanti coast. The profit potential was as much as 300 percent, but the turnover very slow and the risks enormous. In 1672-1674, the WIC filed for bankruptcy. The costs of transport, defense, warfare and piracy were just too high. The game of musical chairs was over, but what remained was a potpourri of people, cultures and ethnicities without a common denominator. The world will forever have to deal with the effects of the transatlantic slave trade."

That evening I spent hours in the galley and made Surinam chicken.

Surinam chicken

Ingredients
1 lb. of chicken thighs or wings
2 large onions
1 leek
1 green or yellow pepper
2 tbsp. ketjap manis
3 tbsp. tomato ketchup

1 tbsp. sambal oelek
Plain flour to coat the chicken

Instructions
Fry the onions, leeks and peppers in a casserole pot.
Once slightly softened, remove from the pot.
Using the same pot, fry the floured chicken until slightly golden on the outside.
Then put the onions, leeks and peppers back into the pot.
Add the ketjap manis, tomato ketchup, and sambal oelek to the pot.
Add water until the chicken is just covered, and stir.
Leave to cook on low heat for 1½ hours.

22 MORE LOCAL CHARACTERS

Make me a planet, each player will build his own planet to provide a beautiful home for the dear animals of The Little Prince – the fox, the sheep, the elephant and the snake – but make sure there aren't too many volcanoes and baobab trees! - *The Little Prince*, Antoine de Saint-Exupéry

"Dear Anansi, the Caribbean Leeward islands look like the Creator tossed a speckle of rocks into the ocean, and, voilà, an archipelago was born. Some of the larger islands are inhabited and many others, not. On the nearly uninhabited islands, I met a king, a prime minister, a businessman, a professor, a thief, a priest, a young couple, and just a man, all archetypes of their particular culture, shaped by centuries of Caribbean life, and living in isolation, frozen in their roles.

The king we already met earlier on, as well the businessman, a priest, and a young couple. This time we will go and visit a prime minister, a professor, a thief, and just a man, all surrounded by invisible creepy creatures.

Allow me, dear Anansi, to start my stories as if they were fairy tales.

After all, that was what they were in many ways, and - by the way - so are you."

A prime minister

"On a little island in the Caribbean lived a prime minister all by himself, and I decided to pay him a visit. Anchoring my boat was a bit complicated since this little island did not have any protected bays and hardly any shallow grounds. With a few extra lines to shore, I was hopeful that the boat would be stable, at least for a few hours. Thus, I rowed my dinghy ashore.

The prime minister's office was right on the little beach where I landed. His Excellency was sitting behind a large desk, neatly decorated with his island flag and my flag - according to protocol.

I stood to attention and crossed my heart when his and my national anthem blasted from crackling loudspeakers placed along the beach.

'Your Excellency, thank you for being so kind to receive me. You must be very busy with your island.'

'Yes,' he said enthusiastically, as if he had not spoken to a living soul for quite a while. 'I am also lucky that there are no people on my island. You know, people are not like plants; they have no roots. Today, they are here, and tomorrow they are gone. For hundreds of years, these rocks welcomed pirates one day, and wealthy traders the next. One never knew in advance, like one never knew if that very day would be your last one. We can never count on people, but the ocean is always here.'

'My island is a rock in the ocean. And where land meets water, an enormous amount of problems need to be taken care of. I, as prime minister, have prepared contingency plans for hurricanes, mudslides, floods, tidal waves, and all other natural disasters. We are even ready for mosquito invasions from the Orinoco and transatlantic sand storms from the Sahara. We have been warned that the ice cap of the North Pole is breaking up and a collision between drifting icebergs and our island is possible.'

The more the prime minister talked about state affairs on his island, the more he became infused with his own importance. There was no smile on his face; to the contrary, his manner was solemn.

'Last week, I spotted a swarm of flamingoes circling the island,' he said with extreme concern as if the world was coming to an end. 'They tried landing here and maybe even nesting. That could have an enormous impact on our flora and fauna. Our evacuation plans are all current and updated.'

Just the thought, moved the prime minister. He showed some real emotion. I saw his lips quivering, and tears filled his eyes. The thought that one day, in a panic, he might have to leave his beloved island was just too much for the brave man.

'The most important measures of all,' said the prime minister, 'concern how to deal with waves of boat refugees from Venezuela, who try to enter without proper visas and work permits.'

'But prime minister, wouldn't you be happy to have more people on your island? They may bring some commerce, help you with natural disasters, and even bring in visiting family members.'

'You know very well that many of these people are criminals,' he replied, suddenly grim and somewhat nervous. 'They steal and rob whatever they can. They are gangsters, drug dealers, rapists, and drug traffickers, and come to launder their dirty money.'

After a little pause, he added, 'Yes, some may be good people, but they can easily go through the proper diplomatic channels and apply for the required permits.'

Then the prime minister rose and with a resonant voice swore a solemn oath, 'I hereby pledge that I will do everything in my power and all the powers invested in me and my office to protect my island.'

Bravo,' I said and kindly applauded. So, how are you going to protect your beaches and landings, prime minister?'

'Well, most of that is classified, and I cannot divulge state secrets to you or any other person. But just look, we have surveillance cameras all around the island, and our allies cover the area with airborne radar systems. We know every boat on the ocean, every take-off and landing of planes, and even submarines do not escape our attention. We will get them, no matter how they come.'

'Prime minister, I heard that your little island is a hub for a vast drug trafficking and distribution network. Why, if you are so well-informed, are you not taking any measures to block those activities?'

The prime minister was getting irritated. 'Yes, there is some activity, but that is part of a bigger scheme. You could call it a larger sting operation. It is classified, and I cannot talk about it.'

With such nonsense, I was ready to land the heaviest bomb on his head. 'But prime minister, it is also rumored that you received, or still receive, large amounts of money for allowing this hub to exist.'

'You should not listen to fake news and false rumors. Our banking system is confidential and offshore, so nobody knows anything about my finances but me. I would even build a wall all around my island if that were necessary. I pledged to keep out all evil.'

With an ice-cold voice he barked, 'You better leave now since it looks like your boat is dragging anchor.'

And that was the end of my audience with the prime minister.

Yes, Anansi, many ministers and prime ministers have become part of organized crime related to drugs, the cancer that grew in the Caribbean in the last generation, and that is eating out its heart.

Before I move on Anansi, I have to acquaint you with the invisibles of the Caribbean. They are all over, sometimes in large concentration, and, no matter how strange it sounds, they determine reality. Let me tell you how I became aware of them."

Enanitos Verdes

"The total solar eclipse of February 26, 1998, brought a load of scientists and amateur cosmographers to the islands of the Lesser Antilles, to Curaçao and Bonaire, from where, supposedly, the event could be observed without any interference. Full of expectations, the most prestigious of guests and celebrated scientists set up camps at Westpunt, Curaçao, and in other deserted, pitch-dark areas. But on February 26, the clouds were so thick that little or nothing could be seen.

Scientists being scientists, they turned their wandering eyes to the soil under their feet. Large circles of petrified fish bones pockmarked the entire area. One thing was immediately evident to them; these circles could not be natural phenomena. Archeological researchers took samples, and carbon dating put the date of origin at 1,500-2,000 years earlier. Speculations about who the archaic campers might have been ran wild. After twenty years of theses and antitheses, the most interesting scenario I learned was the one in relation to you, my Ashanti ghost of the transatlantic migration and sailing companion.

One day I met a local woman, maybe a witch, with a great knowledge of folklore, herbs and local medicine. It really did not matter much to me what people called her. After a while we became friends and she was so kind to share with me the following story.

'Enanitos Verdes,' she said, 'were little green dwarfs, descendants of the Toko oshe of the Zulu in Zimbabwe. Their migration is a long story, but long before Columbus discovered the Americas, the continent had been discovered by many other civilizations, and among those, the Tokoloshe of the Kingdom of Stone, the Zim Bab-we. Many more Tokoloshe followed the first settlers on the transatlantic crossings, mostly from Luango, or Luongo in today's Angola, where the WIC had set up a trading post to ship slaves.

Others will tell you that Tokoloshes resemble zombies, poltergeists or gremlins. *Tokoloshe* means 'bag carrier' in Zulu, which refers to their big scrotums. Tokoloshes were, or still are, the Priapus of the Zulu, the ultimate demigod of eternal fertility.

Their Caribbean descendants, the Enanitos Verdes, are similar; they are malevolent, horned dwarfs, half-man, half-spirit. Many locals believe they still hang out in the caves that reach from the ocean far inland; at night they roam around residential buildings. As a precaution, parents put the beds of their little daughters on piles of bricks, too high for any Enanito to crawl into their beds.'

After some research, I was able to add to the enchantress' story some of my own South African experiences. Theodore Petrus, a famous anthropology researcher and lecturer at Nelson Mandela Metropolitan University wrote that the Tokoloshe was believed to be a dwarf-like male creature with pronounced sexual characteristics. That Tokoloshe still play a substantial role in the lives of many Zulus becomes apparent from a court case dated 04/14/2009, when a Tokoloshe case was brought to the magistrates. The Hwange Newspaper reported the following:

Tokoloshe brought to court. Solani Sibanda from nearby Binga was heard, after female members of the same family stated that they always woke up 'tired and wet in nether regions'. One morning, the victim testified that Solani, their grandfather, had sent a dwarf-gremlin-like creature, with horns curving downwards, into their bedrooms. In court, they pointed to their grandfather as the owner of the Tokoloshe.

"Well, there you have it. Grandfathers rape their granddaughters using a Tokoloshe, and similar traits can also be expected from the Enanito Verdes on the Caribbean islands.

If, Anansi, the local island courts would ever handle such cases in the Caribbean, there is little doubt that scores of witnesses would come forward with similar testimonies. This story is revealing, and it makes many stories of incest on the islands very understandable.

May I recommend putting empty birds' nests, as an evil eye, over the door? It will ward off all Enanitos and is better than any surveillance camera.

By the way, Anansi, this morning I met with the prime minister of a very small island. He got upset when I asked him about narco trafficking and the dirty money he receives from that trade. Do you think it is possible that the prime minister is an Enanito Verde in disguise?"

"Oh yes," said Anansi. "Europeans, bad people, big mistake. All Afro-Caribbean family, innocent of narco-trafficking. Press not true. False, fake news. Tokoloshes and Enanitos Verdes, they all do narco. All narco boys, Tokoloshe, Enanito Verdes, not my children."

"Hm, Anansi, I do not know, but I promise you that I will visit a famous professor, a thief and just a man, and ask their opinions and advice."

A professor

So, on yet another little island lived a professor. He was also all alone, and since I had promised Anansi, I decided to visit him right away. When I entered his library, a spacious room that doubled as debate chambers, a grossly obese man, balancing *pince-nez* reading glasses on the tip of his nose, was sitting behind a very large desk.

Books piled up on top of the desk, and on either side of it formed a wall with crenellations and rectangular gaps. It sheltered the esteemed professor from any possible attack. After all, being a professor on a small island must be a very dangerous job.

The learned man was dressed in a blue and red academic gown and wore a square cap on his bulging purplish head. He was ready to defend any thesis, but I did not say anything as not to upset him too early in our chat.

"I am the provost, and also the dean of all faculties, and chief of staff of academic affairs, and I welcome you as a visitor in the conquest of knowledge," he said ceremonially. "We thrive on strife, dissension, quarreling, and controversy, my dear confrère, but all in good taste and with humor."

"Professor, when you are compounding all there is to know about your island, who goes out to check the facts?"

I thought that he would appreciate my concerns.

"My scouts used to leave no stone unturned on this island, but now I am alone. The last scout left so long ago that I cannot remember, but the precise date and hour are registered in the Grand Register of All Migrations. I have to guard all the knowledge collected in these books so that no one can come in and compromise the truth and nothing but the truth."

"But professor, who would come when you are alone on the island, and who would want to falsify your data?"

Who would be interested in these data anyway, I thought, but did not say anything; it was better to keep quiet.

"You are right, the chance that someone will come is a contingent liability, but nevertheless a liability. We have to shield ourselves against recklessness, especially when it comes to security and do so with thoroughness. I pledge that I will stay here behind my desk till my last breath, and defend my data with my life if necessary."

I noticed that there was no room for debate with the professor, but still I dared to ask a question. "But if you are unable to verify your data, how do you know that they are the truth and nothing but the truth?"

The professor and his huge body rose from his chair and towered above his parapet. With a thundering voice he proclaimed, "When the Day of

Reckoning arrives, right after the end of time following the Armageddon, all will be explained. And the academic truth will always remain the truth, the one and only truth."

"So, professor, I came here to ask you about the role of the Enanito Verdes in the drug trafficking that is plaguing the Caribbean. Are they to blame, is it maybe also the fault of some of the locals, or is all culpability on the side of the Europeans? The Day of Reckoning may be a bit too long for me to wait. I am sure you have a clear opinion and maybe even a clear theory. Could you share your hypothesis with me?"

"Hmm," sighed the professor. "Crime is a product of the criminal mind. Therefore, you have to identify those with such a mind. Yes, they could be Tokoloshe or Enanito Verde. I recommend you start your research by visiting a criminal mind. On the next island, there lives a thief. Please go and visit him, and maybe you will be able to formulate a hypothesis worthy of testing."

On yet another little island in the Caribbean, there lived a thief. It appeared that he was also the only person on his island. The poor man was very depressed since he was starting to doubt his status as a thief.

When I visited him, he was overjoyed and immediately poured his heart out, "You see, my childhood was stolen from me by a thief. I was the victim. And after a thorough and very lengthy investigation, the conclusion by the court was that I was the only suspected thief. They reasoned that only I could have stolen my youth, and no one else. Since I realized the importance of the course of justice, I accepted my fate and became a thief for life."

"But you are the only person on this island, there is no one else, so it must have been you who stole your childhood," I said, expecting him to be relieved. "You cannot steal something that already belongs to you. Therefore you are not a thief. You should be happy, my friend."

"You are stupid. I am the only person on this island, as you said, except for you, a visitor today. If I am not a thief, then what am I? In all the languages of the world, you can look up the meaning of the word 'thief' in a dictionary. And my whole life I have been a thief. It may not be the best reputation, but I have learned to live with it. And now, after all these years, I will no longer be a thief - I will be a nothing."

The thief broke down in tears and started sobbing uncontrollably. Hoping to console him, I said, "But you are still a suspect, and that is something nobody can take away from you. Once a suspect always a suspect."

He looked at me with deep suspicion through his tears, "You are only saying that to make me feel better. You see, in our family we have a long history of being thieves. It goes back many, many generations. At first we were not aware of it, but then European settlers arrived and they knew immediately that we had criminal minds. Severe punishments were doled out, even executions, and some were tortured to death. So, after a while we all knew that we were thieves and had to be treated as such. We were happy to keep up the skills of thievery from generation to generation. Unique skills, like an artistic craft, were passed on from father to son as the most valuable family heirloom."

"Yes," I said. "I perfectly understand. You were branded thieves at the convenience of the conquistadores and got used to it to the point that you are now even proud of it. Initially, it may have taken away your dignity, but then it returned. You gained global recognition, and with it even more dignity."

"Yes," the thief said. "And now they will strip me of my dignity again, since I can no longer be a thief."

"I know you are not going to tell me, but one more thing. Could it be that you do not have a criminal mind but it was all the doing of the Tokoloshe and the Enanito Verdes who arrived in your wake? You see, I could even try to find you other Tokoloshe or Enanito Verdes, so your pure mind will become criminal again, and you could keep your proud reputation as a clan of thieves."

I was not sure if he liked my suggestion and realized that there was too much sadness on this island. I left without saying goodbye. It was all right - one does not have to be polite to thieves.

Just a man

Rowing back to my sailboat in my little dinghy, I spotted another man, waving to me from a far-away white beach. It could have been a man in trouble, so I made a detour.

The man was just a man. The sun had burnt his skin and bleached his bushy cropped hair grey-blond. With the sun setting, a halo surrounded his head. Gnarled callous hands with long fingers pulled in the sheet of my dinghy. He made some noises but his voice was raspy and I could not make out what language he spoke. It did not matter. In silence, we ate a fruit and drank some coconut juice.

The man did not know about a king, prime minister, businessman, professor, or thief. He was just a man on an island.

Yes, I had met them all, a king who was all set and ready to dole out decorations to his subjects in grand ceremonies, but ultimately lacked such subjects; he was all alone. How much longer would he have to sit on his throne, dressed in a heavy ermine mantle, with all his regalia, wasting time and history?

Then there was a businessman who issued deeds of ownership, even for the things that were not owned by anybody. All alone on his island, he was miserable and played at being a businessman to keep up pretenses.

The professor was too afraid to leave his desk to do field research and become a real scientist. He had become a man torn between bureaucratic duty and academic zeal.

Then there was the thief, who was very depressed because he was alone on his island and there was nothing to steal so that he could keep his status as a thief. He feared that even his clan's heritage of thievery would be taken away from him, and thus, he became a victim in anticipation.

The priest was absorbed in his worship of God in the church he built with cocaine money. The young couple refused to accept the realities of life, even when it came to a new life of the next generation. In their minds, they all relied on tricky Tokoloshes and mean Enanito Verdes to make up for their shortcomings.

Their Enanito Verdes always seemed to be up in arms to defend their masters, no matter what.

Killings were never far away. But all my new island friends were going through hard times. They were alone, and all values and denominations paled against the reality of their isolation, a phenomenon so typical for the Caribbean that I wondered what I could do to help them out of their misery.

At first, I considered proposing they all move to just one island and work together. Unfortunately, they were so attached to their mother soil that such an option was ruled out immediately. Therefore, I proposed a federation of islands, with free traffic and trade, the Caribbean Economic Union, or CEU.

Imagine... The thief could steal from the businessman. The businessman could buy and sell to the professor, the thief, and the king. The king would expand his territory and rule over four islands. The prime minister would have a king to serve, the priest would bless them all, and the couple would start a new generation, with many godparents. The professor could expand his library four times, especially if he got the thief, the king, and the businessman to become his scouts. And they would all send their Enanito Verdes on errands and to talk to one other.

This would bring a purpose, profit and happiness to all four; they would only gain and lose nothing, I naively thought. But I knew that my suggestion would be met with deep mistrust. And, yes, as it turned out, all four were eager to kill me with a vengeance and then one another. Kill the messenger instead of dealing with the message. The first one to react was the businessman. Afraid of competition, he immediately declared me a *persona non grata*. The king refused to see me, revoked my decorations, and commanded a travel ban, and the professor moved his desk into an ivory tower.

The thief organized armed robberies, which must have made him happy. All four started bad-mouthing me behind my back and ordered their Enanito Verdes to do as much harm as possible. Soon I found senseless destruction wherever I appeared.

The priest accused me of blasphemy and banned me. The prime minister told everybody that I had tried to corrupt him, and the couple became more aggressive than ever before.

I very much regretted ever making any suggestion to alleviate the misery of my so-called island friends. The lesson I learned was that the status quo is the result of a lengthy process of many minute steps that ultimately materialize in an equilibrium that is not to be disturbed. People can be so very comfortable in their misery, that any effort to change it, even for improvement, should be abandoned.

"Dear Anansi, none of them got to use their body bags to ship my remains back to the US or Europe, as they so publicly had announced they were eager to do. I remember the man, whom I could not understand. Like brothers, we ate his fruit and drank his juice. He made me happy, and maybe, I did the same to him."

After so much history, ghosts, and haunted islands, cruising south was a joy. And visiting some of the many little Leeward Islands, a dream came true. Crystal-clear ocean water displayed the sea bottom and its pallet of colorful life. Water closed around my body like a warm blanket. And then, there were the night skies, speckled with countless numbers of stars, sparkling larger than teacup saucers. Balmy nights and low-key reggae; nothing could be more enchanting. The embracing fragrance of night flowers was everywhere. Powder Puff may make you sneeze. You will never find a larger variety of rosemary - in all colors and shapes. Botanists from around the globe search every inch for new species, and hundreds are discovered here each year.

The Windward Islands in the south are larger, more complicated, and far more dangerous. They all come with a most complex package of history.

I hummed an Enanitos Verdes song about love as I drank another local rum.

Gotas de mar
Son tus ojos,
tu mirada
Cocktail de amor
Derramándose en mi cama.

Tears of sea
Are your eyes
Your look
Cocktail of love
Spilling on my bed.

23 WINDWARD ISLANDS, TRINIDAD AND TOBAGO

The Spaniards were all dismissed, cold-bloodedly slaughtered, except for Berrio himself and his Portuguese companion Alvaro Jorge, both of whom he brought back to his ship. San José was burnt down. - *Accounts of Sir Walter Raleigh, Explorer* (circa 1552-1618)

"Dear Anansi, a lot of blood flowed in Trinidad, wasted blood of all races and creeds. Trinidad is very confusing, to say the least. It was a Spanish island, with a French or Patois-speaking population, under the British flag, with a racial mix from around the world; Amerindians and Europeans and later, Hindus, Chinese, Lebanese, and Africans. Blood flowed every time the island changed flags.

You may get confused, so the location is as follows. The Windward Islands lie south of the Leeward Islands and are the southern, generally larger islands of the Lesser Antilles within the West Indies. Their position on the map is approximately between latitudes 12° and 16° N and longitudes 60° and 62° W.

You, Anansi, you and your ancestors must have made it through Trinidad, one way or another, either migrated voluntarily, or sold as merchandise. Trinidad became the playground of Spanish conquistadores, British people in search of El Dorado, French settlers and plantation holders, and the homeland of the mighty Caciques."

Caciques and Caribs

"A native chief of Trinidad, with the impressive title and name Cacique Wannawanare, meaning the Laughing Gull, granted the Spanish an area for settlement in 1592 which stretched from the St. Joseph region to Domingo de Vera e Ibarguen. By that action, Cacique Wannawanare lost the battle to foreign invaders.

Before we move on, let me explain a few things about the so-called Amerindians and Caciques. A Cacique is a leader of an indigenous group of Amerindians. The name comes from the Taíno word *kasike,* or *kassiquan,* meaning 'to keep house', and was used for pre-Columbian tribal chiefs in the Bahamas, the Greater Antilles, and the northern Lesser Antilles. In the colonial era, Spaniards extended Cacique as a title for the leaders of any indigenous groups. The Cacique system, or *Caciquismo,* is totalitarian with an absolute ruler. All and everything belongs to the Cacique. Without his consent, nothing can happen, no matter how little and silly, but the extent of the Cacique's power depends on the size and structure of his clan. In Taíno culture, the Cacique rank was established democratically through a vote of many clan elders.

Today, the organization of drug-trafficking gangs in Colombia and the Caribbean mimics the Caciquismo structure.

Yes, there were people in the Caribbean and South America long before Columbus ever reached the New World or Africans landed involuntarily in the 17th and 18th centuries. And these people did have elaborate cultures, institutions, and governmental structures. According to historians, between 1492 and 1510, an estimated 10-20 million Amerindians perished from disease and brutal treatment. Some ethnic Carib communities remain on the American mainland in countries like Venezuela, Colombia, Brazil, French Guiana, Guyana and Surinam in South America, and Belize in Central America. The size of these communities varies widely. Those who survived fought bitterly for years to keep foreign invaders out, but ultimately had to give in to the new arrivals.

The Amerindians of the Caribbean were Ciboney, Taino or Arawak, and Caribs or Kalinago. Many died from measles and flu after initial contact with the Europeans, diseases for which they had not developed immunity. Somehow, the Kalinago on the island of Dominica managed to stay alive. Dominica is a mountainous Caribbean island nation with tropical rainforests.

'Famiglia Indiana Caraiba' print, published by Giambattista
Sonzogno, 1818

The Kalinago maintained their independence for many years by taking advantage of the island's rugged terrain. Eventually, in 1903, the British granted the island's east coast, known as the Carib Territory, to these indigenous people. This entire area was wiped out by the hurricanes of September 2017 (Irma and Maria). The last of the Caribs, the Kalinago, do now have to live integrated with migrant, western and African cultures instead of on a remote reservation. They could easily be absorbed and become extinct within one generation.

The storms were devastating. Thousands of trees snapped like match sticks and washed up on the shore. There, they piled up into large barricades, blocking the main roads of the island. According to Prime Minister Roosevelt Skerrit, not a single street island-wide was spared the fury of Maria's 280 km/h (175mph) winds, which islanders described as the sound of a 'demented animal'.

Indiscriminate in its destruction, the storm tore apart homes, ravaged businesses, and wiped out infrastructure and agriculture; the 'nature isle' was demolished by nature itself. Dominica's famously lush mountainsides are today an irreverent brown, as if Maria has sucked the color and life out of the place. Felled trees line the beaches.

Marie Lewis, a local woman, says her four-year-old daughter now sticks her fingers in her ears every time it rains. 'I am still in shock,' she says, gazing at the ruined remains of the gas station and community center. The livelihood of the last Caribs is gone.

The big question after the recent hurricanes was: to rebuild or not to rebuild? It will be up to the international community, since the island lacks sufficient funds. We could be witnessing the last of the Kalinago disappear and become extinct, a process that commenced some 500 years ago.

Hundreds of years of ethnic cleansing by British and French settlers affected Dominica and Trinidad especially severely. In recent history, English settlers rededicated the River Massacre on Dominica, between the small town of Massacre and Mahaut, to commemorate and pay homage to the murdered native villagers. In addition to ethnic cleansing and natural disasters, the narco industry has emerged as a new killer. The drug trafficking rapidly gained in popularity also on Dominica as a way to make quick money, but at the cost of ever-increasing waves of brutal violence.

Only 3,000 Caribs remain, most living in poverty and among increasing social unrest. It is not surprising that after a 550-year assault, most of the original population of the Caribbean is nearly extinct. Only several hundred ethnic Carib descendants live in Puerto Rico, the US Virgin Islands, St. Kitts and Nevis, Antigua and Barbuda, Guadeloupe, Martinique, St. Lucia, Grenada, Trinidad, and St. Vincent. Black Caribs, descendants of African slaves and Amerindians, live on all islands and specifically on St. Vincent."

"You tell horrible stories, silly white man, stories I never heard before. Anansi listen as always. You think I sleep? Anansi hear everything. Always, always and always."

Sir Walter Raleigh

"As I already mentioned, Wannawanare's surrender in Trinidad attracted a large number of settlers, especially from the neighboring islands of Martinique, St. Lucia, Grenada, Guadeloupe and Dominica. Almost overnight, they migrated with their slaves, freed coloreds and mulattos to the new lands, and developed tobacco, cocoa, and, later, sugar industries. Soon the island became very rich and a great attraction for pirates and privateers, amongst them the infamous Sir Walter Raleigh.

Sir Walter Raleigh, by monogrammist H, oil on panel, circa 1588 ©
National Portrait Gallery, London

In 1595, Sir Walter Raleigh raided these new Spanish settlements on Trinidad and the capital of San José. Thus, Trinidad's first encounter with the British was bloody, very bloody. Raleigh, as a rule, took no hostages. He murdered without blinking an eye, but this time he captured the Spanish governor, Antonio de Berrío, the founder of the town San José, and another native chief, the 100-year-old Cacique Topiawara. The official account states:

The Spaniards were all dismissed, cold-bloodedly slaughtered, and San José was burnt down.

The 100-year-old Cacique Topiawari was kept alive because Raleigh reportedly 'marveled to find a man of that gravity and judgment, and of so good discourse'. Raleigh offered Topiawari the support of the Queen of England against the tyranny of the Spaniards. That was the official strategy of the British, who looked for partners to break the Spanish monopoly in South America and the Caribbean. But behind all the political and military pretension loomed the lust for gold.

Queen Elizabeth's pirates squeezed all prisoners they encountered on expeditions for information about El Dorado, a long-rumored City of Gold, and supposedly located somewhere in South America. Raleigh left empty-handed, and shortly after, the Spanish restored their control over the island. Sir Walter Raleigh never found the golden city of El Dorado. He did come across glittery rocks with mica in riverbeds that he mistook for gold, and filled his ships with these worthless stones. Lacking the heavy equipment and staff needed to organize expeditions, he tried to convince the natives to deal with the British long-term instead of the Spanish.

Raleigh is credited for bringing back to England and Ireland the first potatoes, though Hawkins and Drake also claim that as their achievement. 'Roots of round form, some as big as walnuts, some even greater', soon became the staple of the masses in England and Ireland.

Raleigh also brought back tobacco plants, or *Uppowoc*. Raleigh was certainly responsible for making tobacco smoking fashionable in England. The Spanish word *tobacco* stuck, not *Uppowoc*.

Raleigh, the major tobacco city in North Carolina, still carries Sir Walter's name. The city was established in 1587, in a venture sponsored by Sir Walter Raleigh, John White, and a group of colonists on Roanoke Island at the site of a former Indian settlement. These early entrepreneurs founded the 'Cittie of Raleigh', about 190 miles from present-day Raleigh, oblivious of the devastating effects of tobacco smoking that have only become obvious over the last fifty years. With the millions who have died from lung cancer, it is not certain that the citizens should be proud of their founders."

The French on Trinidad

"The French attempted to take control of Trinidad several times, but ultimately, in 1797, a British force under Sir Ralph Abercromby invaded the island. Port of Spain, the new capital, became a melting pot of Spaniards, Africans, French Republican soldiers, retired pirates, French nobility and British colonial rulers. After the abolition of slavery, the British brought in indentured labor from Tamil and Chinese areas, and that completed the racial mix one can witness today.

Anansi, you claim to be the spirit of the Akan and specifically the Ashanti of Ghana, but I am not so sure any longer. The mixture of races is so extensive and it happened over so many generations that it looks like you are a composite of all races in the world."

"Yes, who?" cried Anansi. "I am stranger in world. No home, nowhere!"

I am not sure Anansi liked his new identity; it came with so many more strings attached.

Jakob von Kettler, oil on panel, 17th century © Rundāle Palace Museum, Latvia

Duke Jakob von Kettler and Kunta Kinteh

"Dear Anansi, let me tell you about another silk thread in your web that connects you to family members in Gambia, Tobago and Latvia. It may sound like a fairy tale, but it is real history. There was an ambitious German duke, Jakob von Kettler (1610-1682), Duke of the Duchy of Courland and Semigallia, a vassal state of the Polish-Lithuanian commonwealth, nowadays known as Latvia.

Jakob built one of the largest merchant fleets in Europe, with its main harbors in Windau and Libau. He traded with all the big European powers of those days and quickly learned that big profits were to be made in the transatlantic triangular trade.

So Jakob set out to colonize shipping stations on either side of the Atlantic Passage, in Gambia (Africa) and Tobago (the Caribbean).

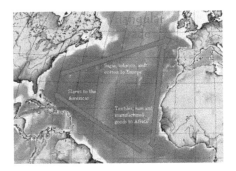

Map showing the transatlantic triangular trade

In 1651, the duchy established a colony in Africa on St. Andrew's Island in the Gambia River. There Duke Jakob built a fort on the remains of a Portuguese settlement. Jakob's fort on St Andrew's Island in the Gambia River, from where he shipped thousands of slaves, became world famous as Kunta Kinteh Island (renamed in 2011).

Kunta Kinteh was a fictional character in Alex Haley's novel and TV series *Roots* from 1976. Supposedly Kunta Kinteh, or a similar historic figure, was one of ninety-eight slaves in 1767 on the slave ship *Lord Ligonier*, brought to Annapolis, Maryland.

The TV mini-series added a failed slave uprising during the voyage. The cruelty displayed set off enormous reactions amongst millions of viewers around the world. That show has shaped the general public's view of the transatlantic slave trade for generations, though there were many historical inaccuracies and elements of sensationalism.

In the minds of millions, the transatlantic slave trade became a Fanonian epic of race struggle between black and white.

Only today, we witness how history has proven Frantz Fanon wrong. Africans today trade more slaves than ever before; Africans sell other Africans without any qualms. Fanon was a Martinique-born Afro-Caribbean psychiatrist, philosopher, and revolutionary (1925-1961) who was a big influence during the North African independent wars. It was not a class struggle, as Karl Marx had suggested, but a race struggle that would become the end of history, according to Fanon.

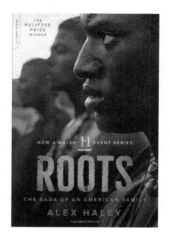

Book cover of Roots: The Saga of an American Family, by Alex Haley

Duke Jakob also set up a trading post on Tobago in 1637. Courlanders established a real working colony there in 1652, growing pepper and tobacco. The duchy abandoned Tobago in 1666, and the WIC of Zeeland took over both that and St. Andrew's Island in Africa.

I do not know what to think of those thousands of tourists, mostly Afro-Americans, who go to visit Jakob's fort on Kunta Kinteh Island and pay their respects to a fictional figure, whereas today slavery is thriving all around them, all over the west coast of Africa, the Sahel and Sahara, and last but not least in Gambia, the very home of the Kunta Kinteh monument commemorating historic slavery.

This, Anansi, shows how carelessly people deal with history, not only in the West but also in Africa. Often they prefer fiction to fact. It saddens me."

Lebanese

"In this story about the people of the Lesser Islands, last but not least I need to mention the Lebanese of Trinidad.

Trinidad's thriving economy and political stability was the ideal location where they could establish their new lives. They brought with them a healthy business acumen. While they were more or less penniless upon arrival in Trinidad, they managed to get economically successful due to hard work and sacrifice.

I love to hear these type of uplifting accounts. No matter how displaced they are, people can make it if they want to."

Anansi squeaked in protest, "Silly white man, not always. Not uplifting. Many suffer. You only talk about the winners!"

I will prepare hummus tonight, a Syrian dish in honor of that courageous and wonderful people. Hummus may seem exotic, but it is one of the simplest dishes to put together. There's no cooking involved, it can be done in less than five minutes, and you can play around with the flavors you like. My hummus has a slight kick with a subtle smoky undertone and offers a great excuse to put 'Caribbean Sunshine' (Scotch bonnet peppers) to use.

Five-minute hummus

Ingredients
2 cans of 15 5 oz. chickpeas
2 cloves garlic
2 tbsp. tahini
1/8 tsp. black pepper
¼ tsp. salt
3 tbs. olive oil
Juice of 1 ½ lemon
1 scotch bonnet pepper (optional)
2 tbsp. water

For presentation
Chopped parsley
A few whole chickpeas
Paprika
A drizzle of olive oil
Drain and rinse the chickpeas with cool water
then place the ingredients in your food processor.

24 LEEWARD ANTILLES

The Queen (Isabella II of Spain) is large in stature, but rather what might be called bulky than stately. There is no dignity either in her face or figure, and the graces of majesty are altogether wanting, as was described by a British contemporary. - From Wikipedia, the free encyclopedia

---

When we sailed westward from Tobago, we ran into Margarita Island, Las Roques, and Aves Archipelago before we reached the Dutch Antilles: Bonaire, Curaçao, and Aruba. Margarita caters to massive tourism and offshore gambling, whereas Las Roques and the Aves archipelago are a paradise for birds and sea life.

Was Count Jean d'Estrées cursed?

What is in a name? Do you not wonder sometimes how it is possible that people's name becomes their destiny? A Rocky becomes a fighter, a Sweetheart a pacifist, and a Little Princess a pedantic prima donna.

That is what surprised me about the French commander, Count Jean II d'Estrées. His name, d'Estrées, and the word "disaster" are so very close;

at least in how they sound they are next of kin. One wonders, was that name his curse?

With a bit of Caribbean superstition it is a sure thing that Count Jean's family name and the confusion over Isla de Aves and Archipelago Las Aves were the ruin of half the French fleet in 1678 and the death of twenty sailors.

The Isla de Aves is a tiny island just south of Statia and Saba, west of the Windward Islands. Mind you, the name is confusing and similar to the Archipelago de Aves just east of Bonaire and west of Los Roques. The island and the archipelago are hundreds of miles apart, but obviously not in the mind of Count Jean.

Count Jean's catastrophe took place during a major campaign in the Franco-Dutch war of 1672-1678. In 1678, France sent a fleet of thirty ships from St. Kitts under the command of d'Estrées to burn down Curaçao - once and for all. But at the Las Aves Archipelago the drunk d'Estrées' crew, thinking that they were at Aves Island, made serious navigational errors and nine ships ran aground or struck reefs and sank; twenty men drowned. The French maritime charts may have confused the Las Aves Archipelago with the Island. With the loss of half his fleet, d'Estrées returned to France in disgrace. Was it a disastrous curse that was hidden in Count Jean d'Estrées name? At the time, many were convinced.

The disaster for the count and France became a blessing for the Dutch. For the next hundred years, Curaçao celebrated the lucky date with a special holiday of Thanksgiving. Curaçoa won that battle but lost the war.

Aguirre, Redlegs Greaves, and Margarita Island

Many pirates, buccaneers, and privateers seem to have been without ethics but, surprisingly, others showed some humanity.

Anansi, set to ridicule everything, lectured me for a change, "All beings situational ethics! What right and what wrong? You spinning stories!"

"Me?! I give lessons in history. That is not spinning stories!"

"Anansi just spin long silk threads, so very long, forget where I started. Some of your stories have such long threads."

"Yes, you may be right sometimes, but allow me to tell this story of right and wrong. In search of gold, pearls, and ultimately the city of El Dorado, Lope de Aguirre, a very violent and rebellious conquistador, conquered Margarita Island in 1561. Isla de Margarita, part of Venezuela, lies in the Caribbean Sea, about 40 kilometers north of the mainland.

Margarita Island, Venezuela

Margarita Island was famous for its abundance of pearls, and the Guaiqueríes divers who knew where to find and harvest the precious teardrops. Aguirre, nicknamed El Loco, styled himself the Wrath of God, the Prince of Freedom or the King of Tierra Firme depending on his mood and the circumstances. His cruelty was to be understood as divine retribution in the name of freedom and the King of Spain.

El Loco put a minimum quota on pearl fishermen, and those who did not meet it were soon dead. Blood flowed like wine and the lives of the Guaiqueríes quickly lost their luster. Soon, there were no divers left to get the pearls. El Loco had killed them all."

Pearl divers, Margarita Island, artist unknown, work on paper, circa 1600

Red Legs Greaves

"About one hundred years after El Loco, there was a real change of heart. Around 1675, the behavior of Red Legs Greaves, another pirate, demonstrated an attitude and behavior in stark contrast to the bloodiness of El Loco. Greaves' nickname *Red Legs* referred to his family background of poor white Irish and colonials of Barbados where he was born. The Irish settled in Barbados with the English from the 1620s, a few as merchants but most as indentured servants. In addition, thousands of Irish convicts and military prisoners arrived in the 1650s. Nevertheless, the majority of Irish people in Barbados entered into indenture contracts - officially voluntarily.

As an orphaned child, Red Legs Greaves was sold into servitude. He tried to escape his miserable existence as a domestic slave and became a stowaway on board a ship, which he thought was a cargo vessel. When discovered, it turned out to be a pirate ship, and, immediately, he was drafted into the services of privateer-buccaneer Captain Hawkins (not the privateer we met earlier with the same name).

Captain Hawkins was a successful man and - like so many in those days - had a reputation for exceptional cruelty, especially towards prisoners. Red Legs Greaves soon grew to hate Captain Hawkins and, as the legend goes, the two eventually fought a duel over the torture of a prisoner. Red Legs ended up killing Hawkins.

The story goes that Red Legs Greaves rejected the needless torture of prisoners. As the new captain, he rewrote the ship's articles, prohibiting mistreatment of prisoners and allowing the surrender with honor of merchant captains during battle.

But pirates have to pirate to make money, so Red Legs moved on to the island of Margarita and found his riches. The inhabitants expected the usual bloodbath to follow, but Red Legs was different. Once he and his men had captured Margarita, he became known for his humanity and morality. After the conquest of Margarita, Red Legs had made enough money and retired as a gentleman farmer, living under an alias in Port Royal, the famed haven for pirates and buccaneers on Jamaica. What made Red Legs immortal was not his ethics but his narrow escape from Port Royal prison during an earthquake on June 7, 1692.

Port Royal prison cell, Jamaica

While living in Port Royal, he was recognized and outed by a former crew member who eagerly collected the ransom that had been put on his head. The British governor had issued a new anti-piracy law to clean up the pirating economy of Port Royal and replace it with slave-trade profits. So Red Legs was arrested and found guilty of piracy in a court of law. He was sentenced to hanging in chains till death would follow, a cruel verdict that wasn't abolished in England and its colonies until 1834.

In 1692, while imprisoned in the dungeon of Port Royal, awaiting his execution, the town was hit by an earthquake. Red Legs was one of the few survivors, and was picked up by a whaling ship. His miraculous rescue made him repent and he spent the rest of his life as an advocate and champion for the rights of crew members. He also became a protector of whalers by fighting pirates who targeted them.

Isn't that a wonderful tale, Anansi? How evil can turn into good; maybe there is justice after all."

Anansi hung in his web, juggling twenty pearls with ten legs. I had clearly lost him after the pearl divers. He was humming what seemed to be his most popular song these days.

> *In the heart of the blue Caribbean,*
> *where ships trade in silver and gold.*
> *There's a sail on the distant horizon,*
> *a sight that will turn your blood cold.*

The flag of the old skull and crossbones
is engraved on our gold bandolier,
It's a symbol of death and destruction
– a touch of the bold buccaneer.

Isla de Aves and the Dutch poop wars

"Anansi, I know you rather blow with the wind. Let me tell you another story, about how greed, oversight and inaccuracies nearly caused war and mislabeled an entire island. I call this story *Isla de Aves and the Dutch poop wars.*"

Map showing Isla de Aves

"Go ahead, you tell stories like I spin threads of silk, no matter where," Anansi mumbled as he was threading together a string of genuine Margarita pearls.

And Anansi sang again,

What goes up must come down
The spinnin' wheel got to go 'round.

Undeterred, like an Empedocles, I spoke into the wind and recounted the following story about bird poop wars, "Gunpowder was the lifeblood of all traders, privateers, pirates and buccaneers. Each WIC ship that departed Holland or Curaçao carried up to 10,000 pounds of gunpowder. Saltpeter was the primary source but experiments with *guano*, bird poop, as an alternative drove demand sky high. The excrement was believed to be rich in nitrate, a much sought-after ingredient in agricultural fertilizer, and perhaps useable for the production of gunpowder.

In fact, guano from birds at sea does not have high concentrations of nitrates, and never became important for the production of explosives; however, bat and cave-bird deposits have a much higher nitrate content and are used for gunpowder production.

The Dutch obtained intelligence that Americans were prospecting guano on Isla de Aves. American prospectors stealing Dutch bird poop was just too much. In 1854, the Dutch government sent a warship to Isla de Aves to intercept the theft of their resource.

The captain of the Dutch warship informed the American prospectors on the island that the Dutch considered Aves as part of the territories of the Republic. Even though Aves was never permanently settled by the Dutch, the inhabitants of Statia and Saba had made use of the island longer than anyone can remember, which constitutes proof of possession. At gunpoint, the prospectors had no choice but to leave.

Many years later, in 1857, three Boston entrepreneurs, Shelton, Samson, and Tappan, tried again, and annexed the island of Aves, which they had discovered in an abandoned condition, based on the Guano Islands Act of 1856 that legalized annexing of abandoned islands. The US government unilaterally passed the Act, allowing any unclaimed or unoccupied islands containing guano to be annexed.

At the same time, the governor of Curaçao received a request to mine guano on Aves from a group of businessmen on Dutch St. Maarten who had assured themselves that Aves was recognized as a Dutch possession by the Dutch government.

With two prospector groups already in the race, nobody welcomed a third. But communications were slow and poor in those days, so, independently, in 1858 and 1859, the administrator of St. Eustatius also granted concessions to collect guano on Aves. He issued a provisionary concession license and requested confirmation by the Dutch colonial governor on Curaçao.

Battleships were too expensive to chase bird poop prospectors, so the Dutch authorities on Curaçao, in charge of St. Eustatius and Saba, decided to conduct diplomatic negotiations over the ownership of Aves, which the Venezuelans also claimed, probably confusing it with Archipelago Aves, just off the Venezuelan coast.

After many years, the quarreling parties agreed to arbitration by the Queen of Spain, and in 1865 Isabella II ruled on the issue. The choice of Isabella as arbiter was not strange since the queen was very popular in Europe as well as in the New World, in spite, or because, of her terrible constitutional malady.

Francisco de Asís de Borbón (1822-1902)

The malady was the effeminate Francisco de Asís de Borbón, her cousin and brand-new spouse, who she had had to marry for constitutional reasons. She was not the kind of woman to maintain a facade. Francisco had to move out of the queen's quarters one day after the wedding and make place for her lover, General Serrano. It was a story that was recounted endlessly in those days in every tavern and pub in the Caribbean. Isabella's judgment acknowledged the rights of the inhabitants of St. Eustatius, Saba, and St. Maarten to fish in the waters around Aves but allocated sovereignty to Venezuela. The Dutch accepted the ruling since their interest was only in the profits of bird poop.

Later, the Dutch officially argued that Isabella had mixed up Isla de Aves with Las Aves Archipelago. Therefore, the ruling had to be considered an administrative error. In less formal circles, sailors and traders were convinced that Spanish, or maybe American, bird poop prospectors had paid off the queen. The laughter about the queen, her husband and bird poop roared for decades. The official records were never changed. Since the guano mines on Aves were exhausted by about 1900, nobody cared any longer and the island was abandoned again."

And Anansi sang from the musical *Hamilton*, while he roared with laughter.

The room where it happened
No one else was in
The room where it happened.

Spanish ragu, or French ragout of seabird

Catching seabirds is not all that easy, but after a few tries and the strategic placing of netting in combination with enticing bait, I managed to get three large seagulls. There is little meat on their air-filled bones, except for the breast piece.
Before putting the seagull breast into the stew, let it simmer in butter or olive oil for about 45 minutes on low temperature. Then add to the stew.

Ingredients
2 tbsp. extra virgin olive oil
1 Spanish onion, chopped
8 oz. chorizo sausage, chopped
2 short-cut bacon rashers, chopped
14 oz. canned chickpeas, drained
14 oz. canned crushed tomatoes
2 tbsp. tomato paste
1 pinch of ground cumin
1 pinch of salt to taste
1 pinch of pepper to taste

Instructions
Heat olive oil in a large saucepan.
Add the Spanish onion and cook for 5 minutes until softened.
Add the chorizo and bacon, and cook for 2 minutes.
Add the tomatoes, tomato paste, ground cumin, and drained chickpeas.
Bring to a simmer and cook for 12-15 minutes, stirring regularly.
Season to taste with salt and ground pepper.

25 CURAÇAO, THE END OF A LONG SEA VOYAGE

Once a new technology rolls over you, if you're not part of the steamroller, you're part of the road. - Stewart Brand

---

Oil refinery and GreenTown

"Dear Anansi, after all these horrific stories of cruelty, suffering and disaster, we are now moving to a glimmer of hope, GreenTown, the city of the future on the unlikely island of Curaçao.

Today, Curaçao accommodates the odd traveler in search of sun, sea, sand, and sex. Somewhat out of tune with the tropical paradise fantasy is a huge, black-smoke-billowing oil refinery. It deters tourists but attracts industry, trade, shipping, and finance. A tug-of-war is going on between old industrialists and the new hospitality industry.

The first energy revolution started around World War I, with oil as fuel, requiring massive exploration, exploitation and refinery. Oil exploration and exploitation in nearby Venezuela at the beginning of the 20th century made Curaçao, a Dutch colony, a major refinery hub. The Dutch oil company Shell took advantage of the proximity of the island to Venezuela's rich oil fields and built the Isla oil refinery there during

World War I. Curaçao boasted the perfect deep-water harbor for transatlantic tankers and smaller ones from Maracaibo.

Twenty years later, a second global conflict shook the world: World War II. It became a unique business opportunity for the Shell refinery. Soon, all Allied troops depended on Curaçao fuel. The war was far away and gasoline production on Curaçao could take place unhindered by enemy threats. Occasionally, a German submarine was spotted off the island's coast, but the enemy never managed to cause severe damage.

Shell remained on the island for decades thereafter, and became a major employer, especially in the 1950s and 1960s when the number of jobs at the refinery topped 10,000. The plant excelled in the production of a large variety of oil-related products. Once Shell lost its upstream profits of Venezuelan wells, due to nationalization, the refinery became a liability. Oil refining had always been a part of the expense, not of the income. Shell left in 1985 and Petróleos de Venezuela, S.A., Pdvsa, took over as a tenant.

Today, environmentalists want the refinery to close down. Oil is no longer popular since fossil fuel is not sustainable, they claim. Venezuela boosts the largest oil reserves in the world, but that does not make much difference for the environmentally faithful. Many are convinced that gasoline cars will become obsolete within a few years. By 2020, electric cars are supposed to be the thing in the automotive market.

Environmentalism has become a faith, and its faithful are no less fanatical than those of any religious extremist conviction. The pollution from the refinery does not agree with their romantic image of the island. A proposal entails the closure of the oil plant and a new, environmentally-friendly industrial city. The economic concerns of such an action have only been addressed through fantastical projections of potential employment; so far, they've not been substantiated. GreenTown is the proposed solution.

In order to close down the refinery for good, another economic pillar would have to replace the 8 to 9 percent of the GDP that the refinery now contributes, admitted Mr. Leito, one of the GreenTown promoters, in an interview.

Plan of GreenTown, Curaçao

With GreenTown, Curaçao is promising to become a leader of innovation in the Caribbean, if not the entire world. The energetic words of GreenTown advocate Andres Casimiri speak for themselves:

GreenTown presents a once-in-a-lifetime opportunity for economic and community development with the potential to make Curaçao the leader in sustainability in the Caribbean."

"Ai, no!" yelled Anansi. "I am tired, months on the ocean. Only screaming seabirds. Ghosts of pirates, slaves, enanito. No more! Please!"

Anansi's web was no longer in the top of the mainmast. Lazy and fat, he had moved down and set up his web in the galley where food was abundant.

"But Anansi, please listen to this booming speech from Casimiri:

GreenTown wants to replace the heavily polluting oil refinery on Curaçao with a lively, green and vibrant city district around the harbor, generating more than 16,000 new jobs, and a significant increase in government revenues and be powered solely with sustainable energy.

With thundering rhetoric, he continued his sermon:

Where our grandfathers were traded, we will build a city that will gleam in greatness, shine in durability, and sparkle as a witness of our perseverance and technology.

These guys have guts, wouldn't you think so? They propose a gleaming city in the middle of the ocean, which will cost billions to construct. After more than ten years, not a single investor has showed up, nor any financing or seriously interested parties. The reality is that the crime rate on the island is twenty times that in the US or Europe. Local gangs fight turf battles through machine-gun drive-by shootings without any respect for the lives of innocent bystanders. That is not unique for Curaçao but has become the standard on most Caribbean islands.

Extensive corruption paralyzes efforts by law enforcement to clean up the island. Politically, there is very little support to attack the narco industry. Interviews with school kids showed that the ideal of many is to become successful drug dealers, not engineers or software designers. A lack of trained staff has already crippled the hospitality economy. There is not much enthusiasm for working hard and changing your future.

You will not believe it, but after a hundred years of oil refining on the island, the local university does not have a course, class, or faculty to train these oil engineers. Every year, a brain drain takes place; entire shipments of youths go to Holland, supposedly to study, but never to return to the island other than on vacation and the occasional family visit. Years of migration of the brightest and the best has depleted the growth potential of the economy. Isolationism and protectionism have bred populism and nationalism. The result is the stagnation of the economy and a shrinking society next to a shadow economy fueled by drugs.

At times, even I lose hope, but that is only human."

Space expedition Curaçao

"And, dear Anansi, that is not all. On Curaçao is also a guy with a company, taking people to outer space on commercial flights. Now, that is something exciting and never heard of before. You better start knitting your space suit. Listen to this press communiqué from Willemstad:

The acquisition signals XCOR's commitment to being 'the most active space flight company in the world' through a marked increase in integrated sales activities and multiple wet lease operations."

"Ai man," touted Anansi. "Those guys bust already, closed up shop. Stock market scam. Flying pigs in the sky!"

I looked for news online. Perhaps Anansi was right. Maybe it was fake news, or a fake company with a lot of noise, a stock-market scam like so many others we have seen.

XCOR Space Expeditions - William Murphy, 2014

Well, my friend, there could just be a little setback. It really does not matter. There will be another one.

"Anansi, you were right! I found it. They are belly up!"

Deep-sea water cooling

"Okay, but there is more, much more on Curaçao. A number of companies are using deep-sea water for cooling their buildings. Now that is a really cool idea.

Here is another press release:

A number of companies in the Hato airport area want to join in the seawater-cooling project, which is being developed between Curaçao Airport Holding and International Ecopower. The project is part of the master plan to develop the airport.

And, Anansi, then there is also a great development in using salt water for golf-course irrigation. The Barbary Beach Golf Resort has a factory growing special grass.

With more and more golf courses using reclaimed water for irrigation, salinity is becoming a bigger issue. Here is how you can effectively manage it.

Let me tell you about Utopia."

Utopia

"Sir Thomas More must have had Curaçao in mind when he wrote his book *Utopia*, although at that time the island wasn't known yet in England. With prophets, though, you can never be sure. In More's 1516 book, a vision described an island society in the South Atlantic ocean, off the coast of South America. Maybe More had studied Hieronymus Bosch's *The Garden of Earthly Delights*, the artist's Utopia.

The word *utopia*, from the Greek *eutopia*, means 'good place' or even 'no place', and is - strictly speaking - the correct term to describe a wonderful, perfect place. In English, eutopia and utopia sound alike.

More and Bosch were not the first guys to dream of a perfect world. Plato wrote his *Republic*. In about 380 BCE the philosopher outlined his ideal state in which the wisdom of rulers will supposedly eliminate poverty and deprivation through fairly distributed resources, though the details on how to do this are unclear.

On More's island, there are socialist, capitalist, royalist, democratic, anarchist, ecological, feminist, patriarchal, egalitarian, hierarchical, racist, left-wing, right-wing, reformist, free-love, nuclear-family, extended-family, gay, lesbian and many more utopias.

Many societies tried to realize such dreams. In the United Arab Emirates is the dream city of Masdar. GreenTown and Masdar look very

277

similar on paper. Maybe that was the role model for Casimiri's dream of GreenTown on Curaçao, the only difference being that the UEA has the money to build it and Curaçao does not. Does that make GreenTown a disaster bound to happen?

Masdar City under construction in January 2012. Abu Dhabi, United Arab Emirates - Jan Seifert

Never mind, Anansi. Isn't all that exciting, all these people with fantasy lands and space travel ideas?"

A sound bite from Casimiri echoed in the background:

Dismantling the nearly century-old refinery will propel Curaçao again into the Caribbean's limelight and make it once more one of the wealthiest countries in the Caribbean.

"No man!" Anansi cried. "Casimiri, space cake clown! Too much work, too much money, and no people on this island. Tomorrow, Captain Decken and I go to the bottom of the ocean. Treasure hunting at the bottom of the sea."

Captain Hendrick van der Decken's passing

That night, I summoned Captain Hendrick van der Decken to the front deck.

"Captain, you have not told me all there is to know about you, your crew, and the ship. We have come to our final destination. I demand your final confession. It is now the time to come clear, make a clean slate, tell me the whole account and then you may die in peace. Your game is over; you have haunted the world long enough. We learned your side of the

VOC truth. Your message of never giving up was heard and understood. But now is the time to disappear and allow something new to take place; a new adventure awaits the world."

The confrontation shocked the captain for a while, but then peace set upon him. After all, he had known for a long time that one day he would have to go.

Hoarsely, the captain made his final confession. "As I told you before, a sudden and terrible gale sprung up when we tried to round the Cape. My first officer said that the storm would capsize the ship and drown all aboard. The sailors urged me to turn around but I refused. Squalls tore at the sails and water spilled down into the hull. Yet I held my course, pressed on, challenging the wrath of God Almighty. In panic my crew mutinied. Without any thought, I killed the rebel leader and threw his body into the boiling seas.

The moment the rebel's body hit the water, my vessel was lifted out of the water and became airborne. We had become a mirage, a fairy tale. All we stood for, all we believed in, all we fought for, nothing really mattered any more. I could not accept it and held my course, no matter what. Now after all this time, now I know that nothing really matters."

"It really does not matter", above the door of the author's home in Amsterdam

"Yes, my friend, it really does not matter."

And that was the eulogy I delivered over the corpse of my ghost captain as he disappeared into thin air and was never seen again. May he finally rest in peace. I pledged that his epitaph would be written over my door forever.

Submarine

And on the island of Curaçao, the island of fast fantasies, there is also one of the world's most advanced research submarines. Yes, we could go to the sea bottom and do underwater archeology, as suggested.

As I was ready to go for a dive, I searched in my galley for Anansi, but he was gone. Then I looked for him on the main mast and the mizzen. There were spiders but none of them talked like Anansi. Anansi had vanished. Maybe he had become a spider like all spiders. I never met a talking spider again.

My friend with the submarine took me treasure hunting in the cemetery of shipwrecks, the Registry at the Bottom of the Ocean.

We did not find much. Whatever we had imagined, it all existed in our minds. Reality is a concoction of so many things in just a fleeting moment. History is a conceptual illusion; many get lost in delusions and need guidance. The world needs an illusionist.

With GreenTown, space travel, and submarines behind me, with months of sea travel and cathartic living, it was time to celebrate my home harbor with real friends, no talking spiders or simmering midnight ghosts, no Enanitos Verdes, no Duppies.

The time for space cake was over. So that evening, we, my real flesh-and-blood friends and I dined on *keshi yena*, filled cheese shell.

Frugality was the keynote of island living in earlier times when provisions had to last from the visit of one sailing ship to the call of another. In this classic recipe the shell of a scooped Edam (the thin rind remaining after a family had consumed the four pounds of cheese) is filled with spiced meat, then baked in the oven or steamed in the top of a double boiler.

For these methods of preparation the red wax must be removed from the empty shell after it has been soaked in hot water. In a more dramatic version, the filled Edam, with the red wax intact, is tied in cheese cloth and suspended in boiling water for 20 minutes. The wax melts away in the hot water, leaving a delicate pink blush on the cheese.

Here is the recipe:

Keshi Yena

Ingredients
1 lb. chicken breasts
1 lb. chicken thighs
Salt and pepper
Poultry seasoning
Minced onion
4 quarts water
2 tbsp. salt
12 peppercorns
1 or 2 onions
1 celery stalk with leaves
Bay leaves, bruised
3 tomatoes, peeled and chopped
4 onions, sliced
1 large green pepper, chopped
1 tbsp. parsley, chopped, or a few drops of Tabasco
2 tbsp. ketchup
¼ cup pimento olives, sliced
1 tbsp. capers
¼ cup raisins
2 tbsp. piccalilli
3 eggs, reserving about 6 tbsp.
1 or 2 hard-boiled eggs

Instructions

Use chicken or beef for the filling.
For the chicken filling, rub with the juice of several limes:
1 lb. chicken breasts
1 lb. chicken thigh

Season the breasts and thighs with:
Salt and pepper
Poultry seasoning
Minced onion

Let them stand for several hours.
Arrange the pieces in a shallow baking dish.
After browning the chicken under the broiler,
bake it for one hour at 350 degrees, deboning it when cool enough to
handle, or choose this more frugal method of preparation.
Brown the chicken in three tablespoons butter,
then place it in a heavy kettle with:
4 quarts water
2 tsp. salt
12 peppercorns
1 or 2 onions
1 celery stalk with leaves
Bay leaves, bruised

Bring to a boil, reduce the heat, and simmer for 20 minutes, or just until
the chicken is tender.
Strain and reserve the broth, discarding the vegetables.
Debone the chicken and set aside.
After the chicken has been prepared by one of the above methods, sauté
two tablespoons butter with:

3 tomatoes, peeled and chopped
4 onions, sliced
1 large green pepper, chopped
1 tbs. parsley, chopped, or a few drops of Tabasco
Salt and pepper

Add in and stir in well:

2 tbsp. ketchup
¼ cup pimento olives, sliced
1 tbsp. capers
¼ cup raisins
2 tbsp. piccalilli
The chicken, or 1 lb ground beef, lightly browned, if beef is to be
substituted for the chicken.
Simmer until the tomatoes are reduced, about 20 or 30 minutes.
Remove from the heat and let the mixture cool. If the keshi yena is to
be baked,
preheat the oven to 350 degrees.
If it is to be steamed, begin heating water in the bottom of a double boiler.
Beat and add to the meat mixture:
3 eggs, reserving about 6 tbsp.
Generously butter a casserole or the top of a double boiler.
Before placing the cheese shell in it, spoon 3 tablespoons of the reserved
beaten egg into the bottom of the container.
Half fill with the meat mixture and add:
1 or 2 hard-cooked eggs
Fill the shell to the top with the remaining meat and cover with the
original cap of the Edam from which the wax has been removed or a few
slices of cheese.
A word of caution! Never use soft young cheese for keshi yena.
Drip the remaining 3 tablespoons of beaten egg over the top of the cheese
as a sealer.
(Place the lid on the double boiler.)
Set the casserole in a pan of hot water, or the double boiler top over the
simmering water.
Cook for one hour fifteen minutes.
Reverse the keshi yena on a heated platter and keep warm, for the cheese
becomes hard and unappetizing if permitted to cool.
In place of the cheese shell, two pounds of Edam or Gouda slices may be
used to line the cooking container. The slices should overlap and create
the same effect as the shell.
Add the filling, cover with additional slices and follow directions for
baking or steaming the shell.

The traditionalist with a great deal of time and patience may scoop out a
4-pound Edam or Gouda, taking care not to pierce the shell.

EPILOGUE

Hurricanes Irma and Maria of 2017 posed a tough question for the Caribbean islands: to rebuild or not to rebuild? And a far more intriguing dilemma: Can Caribbean mini and micro states continue to exist independently?

The devastation on Puerto Rico, St. Martin, Barbuda, and Dominica was so extensive that it may take ten years or more, and hundreds of billions of dollars, to rebuild. Tens of thousands of Caribbean island dwellers decided that it was better to leave the destroyed isles and rebuild their lives elsewhere; they voted with their feet.

In Puerto Rico at least 300,000 left the ravages of 250,000 wrecked houses, with a US $90 billion rebuilding price tag. This exodus came on top of the recession of 2007, leaving a public debt of US $74 billion. Since then, and before the hurricane, 450,000 Spanish Puerto Ricans left the bankrupt island for greener pastures. Whether the Republicans liked it or not, the US had to welcome waves of Puerto Rican immigrants, who all carry US passports. Soon, a *West Side Story II* can be written about the tribulations of the 750,000 newcomers.

Hurricane Irma approaching the Leeward Islands on September 5, 2017 - Wikimedia

The people of St. Martin could almost do the same as the Puerto Ricans, but with the Kingdom of the Netherlands and the Republic of France as financiers and migration destinations. Thousands used their Dutch and French passports to migrate to Europe, and island administrators were eager to present their rebuilding invoices to the Kingdom and the Republic.

Barbuda's 1,638 residents were all evacuated before the storm hit. Since 98 percent of all buildings on the island were destroyed, they have nothing to return to. The island, a sovereign nation in a Commonwealth with Antigua since 1981, cannot turn to a big brother, like the UK, for reconstruction funds and a new home.

The Republic of Dominica was also left out in the cold after nearly total destruction. Its 75,000 people not only lost their homes, but also their livelihoods, with the rainforest uprooted and gone, once a major attraction to visiting tourists. For them there is nothing but charity or humanitarian aid.

The hurricanes deflated decennia of discussions, rebellion, bloodshed, and uproar by populists and nationalists who propagated the formation of sovereign micro and mini states in the Caribbean. Micro and mini states are not sustainable as we have all witnessed; even larger entities like Haïti and Cuba are suffering. The effect is a new mass migration to Europe and the US.

The Caribbean, once united as Spanish territory, and strictly organized into the viceroyalties of New Spain and Peru, disintegrated into more than forty countries, territories, and autonomous regions. These entities are all competing with one another for the same markets: tourism, transfer traffic and trade, and financial services. Ten oil refineries promised to change the equation, and for about a hundred years they did.

Large revenue streams from refining millions of barrels per day, and an extensive ex-pat community, contributed substantially to the prosperity of Caribbean economies. But with the construction of the largest refineries in the world in Venezuela, part of those revenues evaporated. Now, many consider oil refineries a liability that is threatening the idyllic, tropical tourist environment.

Ultimately, people will vote with their feet. Decades of migration of the brightest and the best have left behind nothing but crippled societies and economies.

If change does not come from within, it will certainly come from the outside. The disastrous developments in Venezuela have already had enormous negative effects on most of the smaller islands. The ruinous narco industry in the wake of Colombia's civil war caused enormous bloodshed in most of the Caribbean, as well as a health crisis, with socio-economic destruction for generations. Catastrophic storms wiped out entire island communities.

The hurricanes in 2017 made it clear; none of these islands can survive economically as the entities they are today. They need to form larger units, with economies of scale, capital, and flexible, skilled labor markets. The staggering import duty barriers of tariffs and goods specification, work permits and visiting visas have to disappear. Populist and nationalist politicians have been the stumbling block. Their slogans of national identity and pride have produced nothing but poverty and non-functional, crime-ridden societies; yes, under a proud colorful national flag.

It is not likely that an international messiah, a political trailblazer, will stand up and lead the urgently needed charge. So, change will take its own course, mostly by attrition.

Dear Reader

I hope you enjoyed reading about this journey in the Caribbean and would appreciate it if you could possibly take a few moments to leave a short review online.

Thanks a lot in advance!

———

Never give up!
Even if you have to keep trying till Doomsday!

Jacob Gelt Dekker

The author embarking on a deep-sea dive.

ABOUT THE AUTHOR

Dutch author, dentist by trade, businessman, multi-millionaire, serial entrepreneur, world traveler, philanthropist, visionary, independent mind, gifted narrator, source of inspiration, *uomo universale*, cancer survivor, ecologist, optimist, charismatic, eternal student, disciplined, fearless, a man with a mission. - Note by the Publisher

Lightning Source UK Ltd.
Milton Keynes UK
UKHW02f0408280418
321738UK00005B/187/P